BOLLYWOOD ODYSSEY

THE SINGING TAXMAN'S JOURNEY INTO FILM MUSIC

AJAY MANKOTIA

Readomania

Readomania
An imprint of Kurious Kind Media Private Limited
readomania.com
Email: contact@readomania.com
Facebook: facebook.com/iamreadomania
Twitter: twitter.com/iamreadomania
Instagram: iamreadomania

First Published in 2023 by Readomania

This is a work of creative nonfiction. The views, opinions, and experiences expressed in this book are entirely the author's own and from his own knowledge, research, interactions, and memories. We regret omissions or errors, if any. The publisher will not be liable in any manner to any person by reason of any mistake or omission in this publication.

Edited by Indrani Ganguly (Managing Editor, Readomania)

ISBN: 978-93-91800-47-5

Typeset in Palatino Linotype by Shine Graphics
Printed in Delhi

Comments on the Book and the Articles

Zindagi ka hassil yehi hai ke jo kaam karna hai usko dilli lagan se kijiye aur mukammal kijiye. Bas iss se kaamyaabi hai.

—**Farida Khanum**, *'Mallika-e-Ghazal', Legendary singer*

Ajay... *Gungunana insaan ki fitrat hai. Main bhi Sahnewal ki galiyon mein gungunaya karta tha. Aur gungunate ek shauq paida ho jata hai gaana gaane ka. Aapko bhi shauq paida ho gaya hoga. Aur jab shauq mein shiddat aa jaye toh phir mehfilon ki talaash hoti hai, aur apne apne hunar ke jaam uchhale jaate hai...*

—**Dharmendra**, *Legendary Actor, quote to the music group Luttf, of which the author is a member*

A true behind the scenes look at the Hindi film music industry. A fresh viewpoint on music composers and singers...a must for lovers of Bollywood music.

—**Ehsaan Noorani**, *Music Composer, part of trio Shankar-Ehsaan-Loy*

It was an absolute pleasure for us, our families, and our friends in the film world to read the wonderful tribute to our late father. The respect and adulation our father commanded has been painted with vivid colours, care, sensitivity, and love.

—**Anita Raaj**, *Actress;* **Bobby Raaj**, *Film Producer; Children of Jagdish Raaj*

Terrific reading for all. Of special interest to me is the article on judges referring to music to make prosaic judgments readable and interesting. This book is also a magical mystery tour of the music world with engrossing perspectives on musical legends and captivating aspects of Hindi film music.

— **Justice Madan B. Lokur**, *Former Judge of Supreme Court of India, presently Judge of Supreme Court of Fiji*

The well-researched in-depth articles written by Ajay Mankotia on Bollywood Music/Singers, are not just a collection of a number of stories. It has the details of songs and the musical craftsmanship based on which they were recorded and the circumstances under which they were created. The hard work and dedication are evident in the writings unlike some of the others which have more show than substance.

My good wishes for the book.

—**Dinesh K Prabhakar**, *Violinist, Vocalist, Composer, Son of Husn Lal (of Husnlal-Bhagatram, music director duo)*

Heartiest congratulations and best wishes to Ajay Mankotia on the article written on my father. A very interestingly written article with a fresh approach to his music. The facts are well known but how they are presented makes all the difference.

—**Sangeeta Gupta**, *Daughter of Madan Mohan*

Ajay Mankotia impresses me as a magician of words, who creates brilliant imagery of the great legends of Bollywood, with strokes of vivid colours and sparks of intelligence very few writers possess. I wish him good luck in all ventures.

—**Subhashini Swar Jalalabadi**, *Daughter of Qamar Jalalabadi*

This is one of the best pieces of writing on beloved Papa in a long long time...God bless him.

—**Nitin Mukesh**, *Singer, Son of Mukesh*

Ajay Mankotia's passion for Hindi film music is apparent. His writing and analysis are refreshingly fresh. Bollywood music lovers will find this book very engaging.

—**Javed Badayuni**, *Son of Shakeel Badayuni*

I wanted to thank Ajay Mankotia for writing such a beautiful article about my father and his work. My family and I truly loved it and enjoyed reading it. I personally have read such a well-written piece about my father after a very long time. Thank you so much for remembering him.

—**Chhaya Ojha**, *Daughter of Ravi*

Thank you for writing that lovely article on my grandfather—Ravi—Music Director. Truly appreciate it.

—**Neha Khanoria**, *Grand-daughter of Ravi*

This is a very well-written and well-covered commentary on the maestro's (Ravi's) work...also enumerating some not-so-well-known songs of his which were simplistic but heart-touching compositions. Well done, Ajay Mankotia. Keep them coming.

—**Shikha Vohra**, *Daughter of Anil Biswas*

It's a lovely article (Ravi), I must say.

—**Rajesh Duggal**, *Son of Rajendra Krishan*

The article is a brief glimpse of what Noor Jehan and her legacy stood for and is beautifully written by Ajay Mankotia. There is so much more to her that people didn't get to see or hear especially her personal life which only her loved ones got to witness. Still this article does bring back lots of memories for us.

—**Ahmad Ali Butt**, *Actor, TV host, Singer, Songwriter, Noor Jehan's grandson*

To Amma

Who also gave me Music…

Contents

Preface

I grew up hearing my parents sing in Air Force parties at our house. We siblings weren't allowed in the drawing room except to wish the guests, after which we had to leave. The sound of singing would waft to our room in spite of the closed door, and we would cringe with embarrassment. The loud clapping and requests for more, because they were indeed good singers, especially my mother, would prolong our uneasiness. But I suppose, that's the way with children.

My mother could have, if she had so chosen, become a top professional singer of the country. In the 1950s, she was with All India Radio, Delhi—trained in classical music (as well as dance) and a very popular singer. She had sung (and danced) before foreign dignitaries when they came visiting India. She sang on Independence Day at Red Fort in 1948. But after her love affair, and subsequent marriage with my father, an Air Force officer, himself a good singer, she decided to give up her professional career. Instead, she sang with my father at parties, gave birth to three kids, raised them, and after a while, started teaching Hindi and Music. She finally retired at 85, much beyond the official retirement age. The school wouldn't let her go; all the students wanted her. Even after retirement she was requested to conduct mammoth music programs involving hundreds of children. She is 90 as I write and still does her *riyaaz*, listens to music, admonishes me for my mental block against contemporary music, and offers an honest critique on my singing. And she reads my music articles thoroughly, with relish sometimes, and tells me how to improve next time.

My maternal uncle, Satish Bhatia's music has been an abiding part of our lives since the very beginning. He was in

All India Radio his entire life and retired as Chief Producer (Light Music). He composed prolifically for operas, ballets, theatre, ensembles, orchestras, and dance drama. He composed music for V Shantaram's *Boond Jo Ban Gayi Moti* with hit songs such as *'Yeh Kaun Chitrakar Hai'*. His contribution to music, and the respect and adulation he earned cannot be fully described here. We were blessed to have met Lata, Usha, Hridayanath, Jaidev, Bhupendra, Madan Mohan, Jagjit Singh, and so many others in his house.

So, music was all around me since the cradle. Film music also made its presence via radio and a turntable. From the age of four, Hindi film music became a constant companion. I was completely hooked to the music of the '60s and strove to know the details of the music directors/lyricists, the compositional style, the instruments used, the prelude and interlude music. This passion and quest for knowledge has remained to date.

When my father was posted in Chandigarh in the late '60s, I was exposed to Pakistani film music. Mehdi Hassan, Ghulam Ali, Iqbal Bano, Farida Khanum, and others became my listening pleasure much before others in the country became familiar with them.

My mother and uncle formally tried to teach me music, without success. I finally took lessons for a few months at the age of 35, when I was posted in Mumbai. The musical training thereafter became intermittent, and except for short durations at various points of life, where music teachers would come weekly, there has been no sustained formal training for me till date.

In Mumbai, I was fortunate to have met and befriended OP Nayyar, whom I would meet regularly. I met other music directors and singers too.

But the singing bug had bitten. I would do *riyaaz* regularly on the harmonium. This plodding has enabled me to sing in public as an amateur. I have sung in several shows. My wife and I have produced, directed, scripted, and co-hosted music theatre at various venues. We have also been involved in music shows produced by others.

A very interesting incident bears mention. My mother sang five songs for the film *Maldar* in 1951, whose music was composed by my maternal uncle. Sadly, she lost the 78 RPM discs. A search with HMV also yielded nothing. My mother reconciled to never listening to her songs again. Until, one day about ten years ago, I saw a YouTube posting of her song. I immediately got in touch with the person who had uploaded it—an old-disc collector based in Jodhpur. Lo and behold! He had all her songs on discs which he converted into MP3 and sent to me. You can imagine how ecstatic and moved my mother (and the family) became listening to her lost songs after more than 60 years. Later, I bought all the discs from an old-disc collector of Indore. My mother's songs are a pleasure to hear, and the pride that I had in her talent got further strengthened.

I have been writing articles on music for various publications for a long time now. These articles on music directors, singers and Hindi film music are essentially based on my personal knowledge—stemming from either my meetings with them, or through the association of my mother/uncle with them, my analysis of their music and their songs. It's a 360-degree tour with a personal element thrown in, wherever possible.

This book is a compendium of such articles. They cover Hindi film music. There are pieces on Pakistani singers too. Articles range from biographies to music analysis; from the various facets of Hindi film music, to the making of an iconic song; from Gandhi's contribution to music, to how and why songs are referred to in legal judgements.

I am equally passionate, if not more, of English music. I have attended concerts all over the world of many classic rock bands and have met many of them. I write on that music too. But that collection will hopefully see the light of day later.

In the meanwhile, I hope this book is found to be entertaining, educative, and motivates the reader to discover, or re-discover, the allure of a Rafi, the charm of a Roshan, the spell of a Noor Jahan, the magnetism of a Sahir; indeed, the magic of the Golden Period of Hindi film music.

Ajay Mankotia
New Delhi, 2023

1

The Disrupter

OP Nayyar

I was struck by the aristocratic aura surrounding the man. Despite his advanced age, his bearing was erect, eyes piercingly sharp, mind alert and skin had a pearly glow.

Attired in a white buttoned-up shirt, white trousers, white shoes, and a quaintly incongruous black hat, he was barking an order to the hotel waiter. Sitting on an easy chair, a glass of whisky stood by his side.

Introductions over, he politely asked me to take a seat. Millions of questions swirled in my mind as I stood before my childhood idol. Instead, I just sat tongue-tied the whole evening, imbibing every word he uttered. It was 16th January 1998—his 72nd birthday.

I was posted in Mumbai in the 1990s. I would meet him frequently, and over time, befriend him. Our friendship lasted several years, till the day he died.

I grew up listening to OP Nayyar. His music had a robustness and a rhythm which set him apart from the other composers. His songs were bewitching, easy on the ears but difficult to reproduce. The songs were playful and naughty, seductive and sensuous. He brought the folk and the modern together in perfect harmony. Of course, when one is young, everything appears larger than life. But his music has stood the test of time and continues to fascinate me and millions of his fanatic followers.

Each time I hear his songs, I discover something new—a subtlety here, a finesse there. The *murkis,* the *harkats,* the *khatkas,* the *taans* which embellished his tunes take on a new meaning.

The use of the accordion, clarinet, cello, piano, sarangi, dholak, and santoor imparted a wide and innovative spectrum to his orchestration.

The poor sarangi! Hindi film music had accorded it a rather limiting role—either in the *kothas* or as mournful accompaniment to melancholic songs. No music director had violated the rule. Till 'The Disruptor' came along and changed all rules of Hindi film songs. Not in small measure, but wholesale.

OP Nayyar took the sarangi out of the confines of the *kotha* and let it soar into the sky; from being an adjunct to a dirge, he transformed it into an upbeat musical instrument. He gave it a feel-good melody, a fast pace. He gave it respect. You could hear it sing joyfully, to be released from typecasting. Hear *'Yeh Kya Kar Dala Tune'* (*Howrah Bridge,* 1958), and *'Aankhon Hi Aankhon Mein Ishara Ho Gaya'* (*CID,* 1956).

Take the santoor. The beat allotted to it by music composers was gentle. It was elevator music. OP Nayyar used it as a fast-flowing brook—still soft but now more insistent—in the prelude to *'Jaayiye Aap Kahaan Jaayenge'* (*Mere Sanam,* 1965). Never was the santoor used like this.

The foremost contribution of OP Nayyar to Hindi film songs was rhythm. His innovations in the percussion section were so revolutionary, and catchy, that they became his trademark. It was a delight to hear OP Nayyar explain the intricacies and nuances of his extraordinary 'off-beat' offering to the Hindi film song.

First the tonga beat. He popularized it so much that it is now indelibly linked to him.

Think tonga, and OP Nayyar's name invariably comes to mind. Take for example—*'Banda Parwar Thaam Lo Jigar'*

(*Phir Wohi Dil Laya Hoon*, 1963), *'Zara Haule Haule Chalo More Saajna'* (*Saawan Ki Ghata*, 1966), *'Yun Toh Humne Lakh Haseen Dekhe Hain'* (*Tumsa Nahin Dekha*, 1957), *'Piya Piya Mera Jeeya Pukare'* (*Baap Re Baap*, 1955), and many others.

Castanets are a Spanish percussion instrument consisting of two round pieces of wood or shell which are held by the fingers and clicked together in rhythm to music and dance. OP Nayyar used it extensively in his songs, and how! The song's complexion changed. Just hear *'Aayiye Meherbaan'* (*Howrah Bridge*, 1958) when Asha croons *"Ishq ke imtihan"*. The song would have been flat without it. Or during *"Kaise pehchanun ki naam nahin janun"* from *'Lakhon Hain Nigah Mein'* (*Phir Wohi Dil Laya Hoon*, 1963). It adds zest and frothiness to the hero's romantic quest.

Almost all Hindi film songs have beat patterns which are straight and regular. But OP Nayyar had other ideas.

Take *'Yeh Haseen Dard De Do'* (*Humsaya*, 1968). You give the song to a tabla player. He will provide the beat pattern which would be simple and linear. But in the hands of OP Nayyar, the beat pattern went through an earthquake. So, while the beat remained the same, its complexion radically changed, as did the song's. The beat patterns are complex yet riveting. Hear *'Aaj Koi Pyaar Se'* (*Saawan Ki Ghata*, 1966) and *'Mohabbat Cheez Hai Kya'* (*Yeh Raat Phir Na Aayegi*, 1966) and see if the beat patterns do not shake you up.

But the revolution OP Nayyar wrought was bringing on board both the Western and Indian beats to songs. His songs are replete with this fusion. He would have the western beat, usually the drums in the *mukhra*. In the *antara*, the dholak would take over. It wasn't contrived, it didn't look forced. Dholak was the most natural choice for the composition that he imparted to the *antara*. Then back to the drums in the following *mukhra*. This dual usage gave the song a hitherto unknown texture. One example—*'Balma Khuli Hawa Mein'* (*Kashmir Ki Kali*, 1964).

OP Nayyar was referred to as a rebel composer, a maverick. All India Radio found OP Nayyar too trendy and banned most of his songs. Radio Ceylon was the only source.

This iconoclastic trait of his was invariably one of the topics of discussion that OP Nayyar and I used to have. He had retired from the film industry and was living as a paying guest in Thane, near Mumbai. OP Nayyar's family had severed ties with him for his 'wayward' behaviour and he had left all his possessions with them. OP Nayyar was not bitter about it because, as he told me, he deserved what he got. His primary source of income was music royalty. His new passion was homeopathy and astrology.

I would drive down very often to Thane—with a bottle of Black Label—and spend the evening with him. Just the two of us in his small room. He would serve boiled eggs for snacks. Late in the night, he would serve dinner of mutton which he had bought personally earlier in the day and cooked over slow fire. The family he lived with was very tolerant and allowed him these liberties.

Though he would be initially reluctant, after a few pegs, and my persistence, he would talk about his music. He would patiently unfold his musical journey that began in the early '50s with *Aasman* (1952) and took off with *Aar Paar* (1954).

There was no music system in his room. Just a carton of diaries, letters, and photographs. He would show them to me. Some of the letters, written by known names of the playback industry, were explosive stuff. He showed me a postcard with the handwritten *mukhra* of his famous song *'Pyaar Par Bas Toh Nahin Hai Mera'* (*Sone Ki Chidiya*, 1958).

It was signed but he kept his palm over the name. "Guess who has written it?" he asked, smilingly.

"Talat Mahmood, of course?" I replied.

He shook his head in disbelief. "And here I thought you knew all my songs." Of course, I knew the answer but wanted him to confirm, which he did.

OP Nayyar was a master in adorning words with notes. Equally commendable was his superb selection of singers. He understood their strengths and limitations and was able to bring out the best in them.

Geeta Dutt was not a trained singer, yet under OP Nayyar's baton her renditions were masterful. She used to sing sad songs and bhajans. OP Nayyar transformed her into a singer who could now sing all songs—happy, sad, sultry, romantic.

The magical combination of OP Nayyar and Asha Bhosle is one of the abiding milestones in the history of film music. It was OP Nayyar who was responsible for shaping and styling her vocal line. Asha Bhosle was not only heavily influenced by Geeta Dutt but also suffered from Lata Mangeshkar complex. What OP Nayyar did was to give her confidence and help her come out of that complex. OP Nayyar was very proud that more than anybody else, it was he who had really moulded her voice. His bitterness about Asha Bhosle would surface now and then. How she only gave credit to RD Burman, and not to him, in making her what she finally became

In the early 1970s, when OP Nayyar was no longer the top music director, his personal relationship with Asha was on the rocks as well. The two finally split in 1972. Prior to that, they had recorded '*Chain Se Humko Kabhi Aapne Jeene Na Diya*' (*Pran Jaye Per Vachan Na Jaye*, 1974). This was the last song of Asha under OP Nayyar and won her a Filmfare Award.

Mohammed Rafi held a very special place in OP Nayyar's heart and vice versa. Their combination yielded timeless classics straddling every mood—from the rumbustious to the romantic. OP Nayyar had immense respect and fondness for the singer. Rafi had penned a variant of the '*Tumsa Nahin Dekha*' title song for OP Nayyar—'*Yun Toh Humne Lakh Sangeet Kaar Dekhe Hain, Par Nayyar Jaisa Nahin Dekha.*' Yet, Rafi was at the receiving end of OP Nayyar's strict discipline when he was thrown out of the studio when he reported late for a recording and was kept out for many years. OP Nayyar had to then use Mahendra Kapoor perforce—a singer he detested because of his tendency to go off-key. He would contemptuously refer to him as 'Charandas'—a person given to touching the feet of all and sundry.

Mohammed Rafi's loss was Mahendra Kapoor's gain. Just imagine all the songs that he sang were meant for Mohammed Rafi! How would the songs have sounded? '*Badal Jaaye Agar Mali*' (*Baharein Phir Bhi Aayengi*, 1966) in Mohammed Rafi's voice!

After three years, Mohammed Rafi landed up at OP's house and sought forgiveness. They both embraced each other and cried. "Rafi was a much better man than I," OP Nayyar conceded to me. But by then, OP Nayyar's career was going downhill which even Mohammed Rafi could not salvage.

The walk down the melody lane never failed to enthral me. OP Nayyar was the only composer who did not record a single song of Lata Mangeshkar. I raised this issue with him. Contrary to public perception, he stated that he did not have any problems with her at all. In fact, he admired her greatly. "But can you think of any of my songs that she could have done justice to?" he used to ask. "Her voice would not have suited any of my songs. Can you think of any?" I let it pass.

OP Nayyar told me that no singer could achieve more than 80 percent of his vision of the song.

Sometimes, whenever he was in a generous mood, OP Nayyar used to command me to sing. Though initially I considered singing before the maestro to be sacrilegious, I became more and more comfortable over the years with OP Nayyar's constant encouragement.

Two incidents shall forever be etched in my memory. OP Nayyar had come to our house for dinner in Mumbai. Towards the end of the evening, with everyone in good spirits, he asked for my harmonium. I was stunned since all along our friendship he had steadfastly shunned the instrument. He then asked me to sing.

There I was attempting his *'Aapke Haseen Rukh'* (*Baharein Phir Bhi Aayengi*, 1966) while OP Nayyar was polite not to wince in public and throw me out of my drawing room. What a magical evening it turned out to be with his evergreen masterpieces with OP Nayyar indulgently shepherding the proceedings on the harmonium!

Self-respect (or ego) never left OP Nayyar till his last days. His voice, though frail, was still commanding, his bearing still erect, his passion for homeopathy and astrology as strong as his earlier passion for music. He could not stand fools in his heydays; he couldn't stand them till the end. He could sift the real from the frauds. Yet, he had a mellow side which I saw in the second incident.

After a typical evening, he asked me to sing the Iqbal Bano song *'Ulfat Ki Mayi Manzil Ko Chala'*, which I barely managed.

"Sing it again."

Embarrassed, I gave it another go.

"Once again."

Completely mortified, I gave it my all. His eyes had already started welling up during my third attempt and he was in full cry as I finished. He asked that I dial my mother (Usha Bhatia, who had been a singer on AIR, Delhi before her marriage and whom OP Nayyar had heard and admired).

Expecting a severe dressing down from both, I was shocked when he told her that the song had transported him back in time and he had been overcome with emotion.

On 28th January 2007, the Emperor of Melody breathed his last. In a style so typical of him, the King of Rhythm clipped-clopped his way to join his Maker—leaving behind a legion of fans and a treasure trove of immortal melodies.

Composers like OP Nayyar do not die. He will continue to give us unadulterated joy through his songs. *Tareef karoon ka uski jisne OP Nayyar ko banaya.*

2

The Maestro Who Democratized Ghazals

Jagjit Singh

I saw his work ethic up close. My maternal uncle, Late Satish Bhatia, retired Chief Producer (Light Music), All India Radio, Delhi, and music director, had composed the music of a TV serial called *Apna Apna Aasmaan,* which was to air on Doordarshan in 1992. The singer, who was to record the title song, flew in from Mumbai and reached the recording studio in Daryaganj, Delhi at 11 am. The track was ready.

He needed to learn the melody and record. It would not have taken much time for a professional like him. But no! He had not done his daily *riyaaz* because of the early morning flight and would first need to do that. No question of singing or even listening to the composition before that. So, there he sat—inside the studio with the studio harmonium—and began. For three hours he practised, eyes closed, completely focused, oblivious to the people outside whom he could have seen through the glass partition had he wanted to. It was a spiritual experience to see and hear him. I wish the whole session had been recorded.

Riyaaz was over by 2:30 pm. "Lunch?" he was asked. "After the recording," he said. He listened to the tune, read the lyrics, and began practising. He was ready by 3:30 pm. The recording began. There were some retakes—some at my uncle's bidding, some on the singer's insistence even though my uncle felt the part was fine. And by 5 pm, the title song in different variants was ready. The producer was ecstatic, my uncle was highly satisfied, and the singer was very happy with the final product. "Let us have that lunch now," he declared. Mughlai food from Jama Masjid was served. And then the producer dropped him off to the airport in his car. My transfer orders to Mumbai had just been issued a few days earlier. He said he looked forward to meeting me during my stint there.

If you miss one day's *riyaaz,* only the singer can notice the difference, not the public. But this was no ordinary singer.

You cannot become Jagjit Singh just like that.

The ghazal in India remained cloistered in the rarefied closed confines of the cognoscenti. It remained beyond the reach of the people. Its language, its *gayaki,* its intellectual content, its classical moorings, its very persona made it unattainable to the non-members of the exclusive club. Hindi film music, especially the ghazals of Madan Mohan, exposed the common listener to this fascinating world. But these were few and far between, whetting the appetite of a burgeoning educated middle class wringing their hands in despair at their difficulty in negotiating a Begum Akhtar. The landscape was ripe when Jagjit Singh released *The Unforgettables* in 1977.

The ghazals and the nazms were easy to understand, the style of singing was simple, the instrumentation (including a guitar—"Blasphemous," cried the puritans!) gave a modern feel, the length was equivalent to the average attention span, the voice was rich and pure, and there were duets too (in ghazals? Really!) with his wife Chitra whose skill levels and voice quality were different, making the pairing incredible. The sequestration was over, the rigidity was unshackled, the genre could finally come out to gulp fresh air. The record was a colossal hit. You and I know every song in it.

In terms of literature, Jagjit Singh had condensed a Stephen King story in the *Reader's Digest*. Made it accessible to the public without compromising its integrity or thematic basis. Yet, he ensured that he did not pedestrianize it and turn it into pulp fiction. That would be left to other ghazal singers who would follow him. So, while he sang *'Thukraao Ki Ab Pyar Karo, Main Nashe Mein Hoon, Jo Chahe Mere Yaar Karo, Main Nashe Mein Hun'*, he took care not to cross the line.

From the High Road, he brought the genre to the Middle Road, avoiding any drift further down. The Middle Road had various shades—romantic, introspective, philosophical, agony, ecstasy, joyful and tearful. Lyrics were in everyday words. Tunes that you and I could hum and never forget. And best of all, one could play and sing them in get-togethers, breaking the hold of Hindi film music on our musical entertainment. This transformation did not turn the ghazal into flippant music. Instead, it democratized it. So, while Begum Akhtar and her ilk still had a fan following, these were mere islands in the ocean that Jagjit Singh began ruling over.

Jagjit Singh's songs made a place in the listeners' hearts. His endearingly familiar honeyed voice intertwining so beautifully in their lives, a seamless part of their joys and sorrows. He laid a lot of emphasis on simplicity and clarity. Whether it was a bhajan, a folk song, a ghazal or a film song, Jagjit Singh cast a hypnotic spell because he sang from the heart. Simple tunes with no gimmickry. His charismatic voice would be a balm over wounded sensibilities.

Not only was Jagjit Singh a great artiste, he was also known for his kindness and generosity to the poets whose songs he sang. He would acknowledge their contribution in concerts and share his success with them.

At the pinnacle of his life and success, Jagjit Singh lost his only son Vivek in a tragic road accident. Shattered beyond measure, he did not sing for six months after that. He then turned to his tanpura for solace. Music became an instrument to heal and to come to terms with the tragedy.

He began to exhibit his spiritual and philosophical side and mellowed his already sobering voice and began venturing into bhajans.

Though he did sing the most memorable songs in films, they were limited in number. And rightly so. The musicality of his voice, the pain and depth embedded in it would not have lent itself to a hero running around trees. Playback singing at a commercial level would have destroyed Jagjit Singh as we knew him. We are glad he stayed this side of the fence and went across only occasionally when the script demanded it and enriched films such as *Saath Saath* (1982) and *Arth* (1982).

There was a difference between Jagjit Singh the recording artist, and Jagjit Singh the performer. The song on the disc has its constraints. It is limited by time, it is straight and narrow, it is tight in its structure and presentation, it is formal and wears a tie. But on stage, the song becomes something else. The innovations, the embellishments, the spontaneity, the flexibility, the connect to the audience—feeding into and feeding off the adulation—moving into the unexplored musical territory and finding the way back, the uninhibited rendition make the experience like no other. Jagjit Singh was a master performer. His audience never felt let down. Sometimes he would even change the melody, say of an *antara* which the commercial considerations of the disc may not have permitted. I heard his live recording of '*Sadma Toh Hai Mujhe Bhi*' at a concert in Hong Kong. The song was sung at a leisurely pace and the *antara* was changed. The effect on the audience was electric. His extended exposition of it was something one experiences but rarely. Unfortunately, most recordings of his live shows were done privately. Once in a while, when one hears them, one marvels at the way he experimented with songs while retaining its essential melody already seared into our hearts and minds.

Of course, Jagjit Singh as not alone. His wife Chitra played a vital role in the success of the duo. Audiences doted on their contrasting characteristics—his heavy bass voice in contrast to her trill tone, his gregarious personality versus her quiet demeanour, his Punjabi charm complementing her classic Bengali beauty. After the death of their son, she stopped singing altogether.

I have attended numerous Jagjit Singh concerts. Of those, two stand out. One was in Mumbai where he sang while MF Hussain painted alongside. The song was an extended ghazal, and Jagjit Singh, unperturbed by the goings on alongside him, sang in the only way he could—soulful, melodious, embellishments at the right places, no musical jugglery, straight from the heart. MF Hussain began interpreting the ghazal on a huge rectangular whiteboard with a blue marker. This was not a collision of two art forms, but a collusion of masters in depicting the feelings of the poet by way of song and painting. The painting was auctioned after the program to the highest bidder from the audience.

The other was his *Ghazal Symphony* held at Leisure Valley Park (open-air) in Gurgaon in 2011. Besides his core musicians, a symphony orchestra of 30 musicians backed him. This was a novel concept. And yes, the twain did meet, and how! There was a richness and depth added to the performance and added a hitherto unknown dimension to ghazal rendition.

All his albums are outstanding. One album that stands out for me is *Shiv Kumar Batalvi—Birha Da Sultan*. It is an extraordinarily soft and heartfelt collection of Batalvi's poems. Some poems can only be conveyed by singers chosen by God. These poems only reach their fullness through the vocal chords of such chosen singers. If you have not heard the album, I urge you to listen to it. It is in Punjabi but that does not matter. It goes beyond music—it is divinity.

Till his untimely death, Jagjit Singh remained a perfectionist. He firmly believed that every morning was a new beginning, every album was a new album, and every concert was a new test. Everything could be done better, so try it.

Born Jagmohan Singh Dhiman in Rajasthan's Ganganagar to a Sikh family, Jagjit Singh who was a Grade-B artist in AIR, Jalandhar (he would do live concerts for them six times a year), would have scarcely known that one day every radio station, every recording company and every music lover would rate him beyond grades, above superlatives and that his legacy will live on forever.

Jagjit Singh, *aapki khushboo se saara ghar, saari zameen, saara shahar hamesha mehkega.*

3

Twins in a Film

You would recall the masterpiece from *Ek Saal* (1957)—'*Sub Kuchh Luta Ke Hosh Mein Aaye Toh Kya Kiya*'. Who was the singer? Talat Mahmood, of course, you would say. The quivering silken voice could only belong to him, you would add. This was Ravi's first outing with Talat and what a wonderful job he did.

You have all heard '*Jaayen Toh Jaayen Kahaan*' from *Taxi Driver* (1954). Whose voice do you remember? The soulful Talat's, of course. This song became so popular that it fetched SD Burman the Filmfare Award for Best Music Director (those days the award was for songs, not movies). It is said that one day SD Burman lost his way while on a walk and that gave birth to this song.

Wait, I haven't finished yet. Some of you may recall the romantic song of Dev Anand in *Roop Ki Rani Choron Ka Raja* (1961)—'*Tum Toh Dil Ke Taar Chhed Kar*'. Again, whose voice comes to mind? Talat, surely? One of the few playful songs he has done.

And the list continues—'*Ai Mere Dil Kahin Aur Chal*' (*Daag*, 1952), '*Dil Matwala Lakh Sambhala*' (*Bewafa*, 1952), '*Mera Qaraar Le Ja*' (*Ashiana*, 1952).

Let me tell you why I am belabouring this point. Many would be shocked to know that Lata Mangeshkar has also sung these songs. So why is only the Talat version of these songs (called twin songs or tandem songs) fresh in public memory? What is the mystery?

Before we do that, consider this fact: the supreme quality of Talat's voice made all singers nervous. Lata, in particular, dreaded singing duets with Talat because she felt that his rich and smooth voice would render hers dull in comparison.

But here's another shocker. Many feel that Lata comes out poorly in comparison to the other male singers as well in twin songs. Let's begin with Rafi. Remember the romance imbued *'Ehsaan Tera Hoga Mujh Par' (Junglee,* 1961)? Lata also sang it, but her version remains consigned to the archives, not the airwaves. And the ultimate emotion-packed accusatory *'Dil Jo Na Keh Saka'* (*Bheegi Raat*, 1965)? You immediately think of Rafi and how well he sings the upper notes in the *antara*, made even more breathtaking by the echo effect. And Lata's version? Did she even have one? Yes, she did but it didn't make it to the charts. And there are many more—*'Zindagi Bhar Nahi Bhoolegi Woh Barsaat Ki Raat'* (*Barsaat Ki Raat*, 1960), *'Taqdeer Ka Fasana' (Sehra,* 1963), *'Mere Mehboob Tujhe'* (*Mere Mehboob*, 1963), *'Aaj Kal Mein Dhal Gaya'* (*Beti Bete*, 1964), *'Dil Beqaraar Sa Hai' (Ishara,* 1964), *'Pardesiyon Se Na Akhiyan Milana'* (*Jab Jab Phool Khile*, 1965), *'O Mere Shah e Khubaan'* (*Love in Tokyo*, 1966), *'Jab Jab Bahaar Aayee' (Taqdeer,* 1967), *'Teri Aankhon Ke Siwa' (Chirag,* 1969), *'Tum Mujhe Yun Bhula Na Paoge'* (*Pagla Kahin Ka*, 1970). The list is not exhaustive.

Not so fast, many would say. You have conveniently missed two popular songs where Lata bested Rafi. And no one would hold a contrary opinion—*'Rahe Na Rahe Hum' (Mamta,* 1966). Does anyone even know that Rafi-Suman Kalyanpur sang it too? And *'Aji Rooth Kar Ab Kahaan Jaiyega'* (*Arzoo*, 1965). Rafi stood no chance.

These are, however, along with some other songs, exceptions in an otherwise skewed list in favour of Rafi.

Why only Rafi? Consider Mukesh. Mukesh? But he was a not a trained singer; his range was limited. How could he even compete with Bharat Ratna Lata—the complete singer, the perfect nightingale? Decide for yourselves. Take *'Aa Laut Ke Aja Mere Meet'* (*Rani Rupmati*, 1957). Can you imagine any other singer doing justice to this song, Lata included? What Mukesh lacked in musical training, he made up with his pathos-filled voice. Forget Lata, no male singer could compete with him, as we shall see momentarily. '*Mujhko Is Raat Ki Tanhai Mein*' (*Dil Bhi Tera Hum Bhi Tere*, 1960)—Mukesh won with a massive mandate. There are other songs too—'*Humne Tujhko Pyar Kiya Hai Jitna*' (*Dulha Dulhan*, 1964), '*Jyot Se Jyot Jagate Chalo*' (*Sant Gyaneshwar*, 1964), '*Jis Dil Mein Basa Tha Pyar Tera*' (*Saheli*, 1965), and so on.

However, the honours were even in these two songs—'*Raat Aur Din Diya Jale*' (*Raat Aur Din*, 1967) and '*Chandan Sa Badan*' (*Saraswatichandra*, 1968). There are no absolutes in film music, as in life.

And now, Kishore Kumar. '*Jeevan Ke Safar Mein Rahi*' (*Munimji*, 1955) straightaway invokes Kishore, not Lata. Yet, she has a version too. It just came and went without the slightest impact on public memory. '*Chhoti Se Yeh Duniya*' (*Rangoli*, 1962)—Shailendra's taunt to Shankar-Jaikishan—was Kishore all the way. Lata was not on the radar. Same with some other songs—'*Ajnabi Tum Jane Pehchane Se Lagte Ho*' (*Hum Sab Ustad Hain*, 1965), '*Khilte Hain Gul Yahaan*' (*Sharmilee*, 1971).

Why pick on only Lata? Asha came out poorly compared to Talat in '*Ai Gham e Dil Kya Karun*' (*Thokar*, 1953); likewise, Geeta Dutt in '*Preetam Aan Milo*' (*Mr and Mrs 55*, 1955)—how could anyone compete with CH Atma? Suman Kalyanpur compared to Rafi in '*Chaleja Chaleja Chaleja Jahan Pyar Mile*' (*Jahan Pyar Mile*, 1970) though some may insist the honours were even with Hemant Kumar in '*Na Tum Hamein Jano*' (*Baat Ek Raat Ki*, 1962).

The conclusion is that female singers fare badly when compared to their male counterparts in twin songs. There are, of course, exceptions but these are too few and far between. Some people may like a female version and that's their personal choice—nothing wrong with that; but they don't constitute public memory as reflected in popularity of songs. Why does this happen?

Historically, Hindi films generally have had strong male-oriented story lines. Not only were the male actors paid more but they appeared first in the credits. The scripts were written around the hero; the film was sold in the name of the hero. Even the villains and comedians were men. It was natural that the songs were composed keeping the hero in mind as was the picturization of the song and its placement in the film. The publicity and airtime were similarly done. No wonder then that the distaff end of the twin songs got a short shrift!

The other reason is that when the song is composed for a male, its tuning, texture, nuances, embellishments, and range are structured in a style suited to a male voice. Any female singing it will fail. Just consider Lata's *Shraddhanjali*—her ode to male singers of yesteryears. She is technically perfect, she is dulcet, but these aren't the only qualities required to make a song memorable. The idiom of the song, if favouring a male, cannot accept a female; and vice versa. That's why Lata excels in '*Rahe Na Rahe Hum*' and '*Aji Rooth Kar*', which were composed for a female; even Rafi stood no chance.

How about duets? This is a big challenge. If the composer can find the middle ground suiting both genders, then the honours are shared equally. But that doesn't always happen, and the dominant singer stands out.

Sometimes the full-throated power of the singer tilts the scales when one sings from the pit of one's stomach without wavering in sweetness and emotion. And a prime example of that is Noor Jehan. Listen to her sing in all pomp and splendour '*Kuchh Log Rooth Kar*' (*Andaleeb*, 1969) and '*Hamari Sanson Mein*' (*Mere Hazoor*, 1977), which were composed with Ahmed Rushdi and Mehdi Hassan in mind. But she let them have it.

Now let's see how the male singers stack up against each other in twin songs. Consider *'Tum Bin Jaoon Kahan'* (*Pyar Ka Mausam*, 1969). No song has divided listeners, music aficionados, even families, as much as this one. Who was better—Rafi or Kishore? Many consider this song to be the tipping point when Kishore moved ahead of Rafi. *Aradhana* (1969) came just after that. The reason was that the original Bengali version *'Ek Din Pakhi Ure'* was sung by Kishore; also, the fact that Kishore's version got more airtime (radio was the primary source of songs; not many people had gramophones and records) to balance out Rafi, who was ruling the roost till then. Also, Kishore's version came right at the beginning of the movie and set the mood for the three other versions that followed. His masterly yodelling certainly helped.

Even Kishore's sad version sounded wistful and soulful. Rafi only got to sing after the two Kishore versions. Even though his rendition was top drawer, it was not enough.

But like I stated earlier, by way of a disclaimer, your personal choice may be Rafi. And that needs to be acknowledged and respected.

Similarly, *'Zindagi Ek Safar Hai Suhana'* (*Andaz*, 1971). Kishore's zest and youthfulness, and incomparable yodelling, snatched the song from under Rafi's nose.

Let's see how Rafi fares before Mukesh. Just one song needs to be mentioned—*'Saranga Teri Yaad Mein'* (*Saranga*, 1961). The composition of the song was such that only the King of Pathos could do justice to it. No other male singer, including Rafi in this case, could even come close. Many even don't know that Rafi also rendered this song, but his version sunk into the deep dark ocean with nary a trace.

Even Manna Dey could not trump Mukesh's heart-touching rendition of *'Zindagi Khwaab Hai'* (*Jaagte Raho*, 1956). Mukesh invested the song with emotion with consummate ease but Manna, otherwise technically the best Hindi film singer, seemed to be trying. Alas, what matters is what appeals to the heart, not mind. Manna's version wasn't used in the film.

This brings me to a rather interesting feature existing in Hindi film music those days.

During the '50s, HMV used to have version recordings of popular Hindi songs on their discs, which were not necessarily part of films. This was a concept imported from the West where popular songs used to be recorded by various singers. So, a Rafi would sing a Mukesh, a Hemant would do a Talat, and so on. But the singers, after some time, when unfair comparisons started being made, got together, and forced HMV to scrap this concept. But even after abandoning the idea, one song that fell through the cracks was Talat's rendition of '*Chal Ud Ja Re Panchhi*', which Rafi had sung for the film *Bhabhi* (1957). Talat's version (not used in the film) was already in the market, releasing as 'Version Recording FT21027 Twin/Black Label 78 RPM'. This song clearly belonged to Rafi; Talat could not win every time.

So why was there a need to have twin songs in films and engender comparisons and attendant controversies? One purpose could be for the song to serve as a reminder, as a jog to the memory of childhood days—'*Bachpan Ke Din Bhula Na Dena*' (*Deedar*, 1951) sung by Lata/Shamshad Begum in one version, and later by Rafi in the second; and '*Phoolon Ka Taaron Ka*' (*Hare Ram Hare Krishna*, 1971) sung by Lata, and later by Kishore. Or could serve as a taunt to infidelity and unkept promise—Meena Kumari's earlier version pledging troth was later used by Pradeep Kumar to point out her betrayal in '*Dil Jo Na Keh Saka*' (*Bheegi Raat*, 1965). Or it could be the parents and children singing their respective versions of a family song—'*Yaadon Ki Baaraat*' (*Yaadon Ki Baaraat*, 1973), or '*Tum Bin Jaaon Kahaan*' (*Pyar Ka Mausam*, 1969), for example. But I suppose the main reason was expediency—when you have a good product, why not have more than one singer sing it.

The institution of twin songs began to lose its lustre from the '80s onwards. But a marked change was taking place even with these few songs. With films developing a conscience and heroines getting meatier roles, more and more songs were being composed for women characters. The earlier imbalance in twin songs began to get redressed.

With '*Tujhse Naraaz Nahin Zindagi*' (*Masoom*, 1983), Lata edged ahead of Anup Ghoshal; *Rudaali* (1993) had one twin song—'*Dil Hoom Hoom Kare*' sung by Lata and Bhupen Hazarika (also the music director). Both did a commendable job. The movie also had a triplet song—'*Samay O Dheere Chalo*' sung by Lata, Asha, and Bhupen. Asha was top class. *Maya Memsaab* (1993) had '*Ek Haseen Nigaah Ka*' by Kumar Sanu and Lata. Lata was far ahead.

Kumar Sanu, however, just about came ahead of Lata in '*Kuchh Na Kaho*' (*1942-A Love Story*, 1994); '*Jadoo Hai Nasha Hai* (*Jism*, 2003)—Shreya Ghoshal beat Shaan; '*Iktara*' (*Wake Up Sid*, 2009), the female version sung by Kavita Seth became more popular than the male version sung by Tochi Raina and others. It fetched her the Filmfare Award for best female playback. '*Bahara*' (*I Hate Luv Storys*, 2010)—the female version of Shreya Ghoshal and Sona Mohapatra became more popular than the beautifully rendered male version of Rahat Fateh Ali Khan.

These days the concept of twin songs has got a complete makeover in the form of remakes/remixes. My children, who had never heard '*Zaroorat Hai Zaroorat Hai*' by Kishore Kumar (*Man-Mauji*, 1962), '*Main Chali Main Chali*' (*Padosan*, 1968) and '*Chhod Do Anchal*' (*Paying Guest*, 1957) heard it the first time from the Bombay Vikings (1999) in the form of '*Kya Soorat Hai*', '*Woh Chali*' and '*Chhod Do Anchal*'. Similarly, '*Khoya Khoya Chand*' (*Kala Bazar*, 1960) in *Shaitan* (2011) and

'*Jata Kahan Hai Deewane*' (*CID*, 1956) in *Bombay Velvet* (2015), both sung by Suman Sridhar.

While the remakes/remixes cater to the new generation and do not lend themselves to comparison with the original songs, they go a long way in fostering interest in the classics, and keeping them alive in the present generation, albeit in a new avatar.

4

The Unheralded Tunesmith

Ravi

Chances are, if you ask any middle-aged music lover to state (not rate) the names of seven Hindi music directors of the 1960s, very few would come up with Ravi. Which is a real mystery!

Let me explain why I am mystified. When I first met Ravi in the mid-90s, he very proudly (justifiably) told me that no Indian wedding used to be complete without at least two of his songs—*'Babul Ki Duyaen Leti Ja'* (*Neel Kamal*, 1968) and *'Aaj Mere Yaar Ki Shaadi Hai'* (*Aadmi Sadak Ka*, 1977). How true that was.

Add to the mix the optional *'Mera Yaar Banha Hai Dulha'* (*Chaudhvin Ka Chand*, 1960) and *'Doli Chadh Ke Dulhan Sasural Chali'* (*Doli*, 1969). Round it off with *'Ai Meri Zohra Jabeen'* (*Waqt*, 1965) in the pre-wedding mehndi ceremony, and you had Ravi ruling the nuptial musical landscape. No self-respecting wedding band could do without Ravi in its repertoire.

Now think of beggars singing on the streets, or traffic intersections, or on local trains during the 1960s. Two songs stood out—*'Amma Ek Roti De'* (*Samaj Ko Badal Dalo*, 1970) and *'Gareebon Ki Suno'* (*Dus Lakh*, 1966). Both Ravi.

Let's consider lullabies. Two of the most popular ones had not only been composed by Ravi but had been penned by him as well—*'Chanda Mama Door Ke'* (*Vachan*, 1955) and *'Tim Tim Karte Taare'* (*Chirag Kahan Roshni Kahan*, 1959). In fact, Ravi wrote lyrics for many more songs.

So, with all these songs being an integral part of the aural scenery of middle-aged Indians since their childhood, Ravi not being on the recall list is an enigma. He was certainly under-rated despite composing memorable music in 112 films.

Just consider his oeuvre in his two-decade stint in the Hindi film industry—songs ranging from romantic '*Chaudhvin Ka Chand Ho*' (*Chaudhvin Ka Chand*, 1960), to peppy '*Baar Baar Dekho*' (*China Town*, 1962), to madcap '*CAT Cat Maane Billee*' (*Dilli Ka Thug*, 1958), to seductive '*Shishe Se Pee*' (*Phool Aur Patthar*, 1966), to pathos-filled '*Sab Kuchh Luta Ke Hosh*' (*Ek Saal*, 1957), to heart-rending '*Chalo Ek Baar Phir Se*' (*Gumrah*, 1963), to rumbustious '*Dil Karta Oh Yaara Dildara*' (*Aadmi Aur Insaan*, 1969), to devotional '*Badi Der Bhai Nandlala*' (*Khandan*, 1965). He was truly a colossus.

He has recognition to prove it. Two Filmfare Awards for *Gharana* (1962) and *Khandan* (1966). Rafi was eternally grateful to him for his first Filmfare Award for best singer for '*Chaudhvin Ka Chand Ho*' (*Chaudhvin Ka Chand*) in 1960.

Lata won the 1965 Filmfare for Ravi's '*Tumhee Mere Mandir*' (*Khandan*). Mahendra Kapoor won it for Ravi's '*Chalo Ek Baar*' (*Gumrah*) in 1964, and '*Neele Ganga Ke Tale*' (*Humraaz*) in 1968. Asha won it for Ravi's '*Garibon Ki Suno*' (*Dus Lakh*) in 1968. Salma Agha won in 1983 for Ravi's '*Dil Ke Armaan*' (*Nikaah*). A formidable achievement!

In the 1980s and '90s, Ravi worked successfully in Malayalam films as Bombay Ravi. He won his only National Film Award for best music direction in 1994 for *Parinayam* and *Sukhrutham*, and two Filmfare Awards (Malayalam)—*Sargam* (1992) and *Parinayam* (1994).

Ravi (Ravi Shankar Sharma), born in 1936, came to Mumbai aged 24, to become a singer. He sang in choruses—under SD Burman in *Naujawan* (1951) and Hemant Kumar in *Anand Math* (1952). After working for a few years as Hemant

Kumar's assistant, he branched off (at Hemant's insistence) as an independent composer, his debut film being Devendra Goel's *Vachan* (1955).

Goel and Ravi would have a life-long collaboration of several successful films. Similarly, with BR Chopra. Ravi also worked a lot with South Indian film makers such as SS Vasan, AV Meyappan, Vasu Menon, and Sivaji Ganesan.

Ravi was a minimalist. His orchestra was spare, barring exceptions. His music never overwhelmed the singer. Its effect was always tender and soft. The singer always remained centre-stage, giving the artiste full carte blanche to exhibit his/her vocal mastery.

His interludes were gentle and non-obtrusive. Even in a song such as '*Zohra Jabeen*' (*Waqt*, 1965), with its inherent Punjabi boisterousness, the dholaks and clapping did not overpower the singing and the effect was endearing, not brash. He managed to mould his music to suit the mood brilliantly. This was craftsmanship of the highest order.

The Rafi-Ravi combination yielded outstanding songs. They did 235 songs in 79 films. Some of the mesmerizing ones are— '*Chaudhvin ka Chand Ho*' (*Chaudhvin Ka Chand*, 1960), '*Mujhe Pyar Ki Zindagi Denewale*' (*Pyar Ka Saagar*, 1961), '*Baar Baar Dekho*' (*China Town*, 1962), '*Na Jhatko Zulf Se Paani*' (*Shehnai*, 1964), '*Chhoo Lene Do Nazuk Hoton Ko*', '*Yeh Zulf Agar Khulke*' (both *Kaajal*, 1965), '*Tujhko Pukare Mera Pyar*' (*Neel Kamal*, 1968), '*Yeh Wadiyan Yeh Fizayen*' (*Aaj Aur Kal*, 1963), '*Zindagi Ke Safar Mein*' (*Nartaki*, 1963). And the list goes on.

Asha was Ravi's main female singer—385 songs in all. Songs are too many to enumerate but have a look at some—'*Hey Rom Rom Mein Basne Wale*' (*Neel Kamal*, 1968), '*Sheeshe Se Pee*' (*Phool Aur Pathar*, 1966), '*Aaj Yeh Meri Zindagi*' (*Yeh Raaste Hain Pyar Ke*,1963), '*Mujhe Gale Se Laga Lo*' (*Aaj Aur Kal*,1963), '*Uljhan Suljhe Na*' (*Dhund*, 1973), '*Tora Man Darpan*

Kehlaye' (*Kaajal*, 1965), *'Aage Bhi Jaane Na Tu'* (*Waqt*, 1965), *'Jab Chali Thandi Hawa'* (*Do Badan*, 1966), *'Zindagi Ittefaq Hai'* (*Aadmi Aur Insaan*, 1969).

Though she did a few songs, Lata was at her dulcet best with Ravi—*'Woh Dil Kahaan Se Laoon'* (*Bharosa*, 1963), *'Ae Mere Dil-e-Naadan Tu Gham Se Na Ghabrana'* (*Tower House*, 1962), *'Laage Na Mora Jiya'* (*Ghunghat*, 1960), *'Lo Aa Gayi Unki Yaad'* (*Do Badan*, 1966), *'Aapki Inayatein Aapke Karam'* (*Vandana*, 1975), *'Gairon Pe Karam'* (*Aankhen*, 1968).

The Sahir-Ravi pairing resulted in the most outstanding music in the BR Chopra films. Mahendra Kapoor was the main male singer and Ravi brought out the best from him, more than any other composer. Mahendra Kapoor was masterfully controlled by Ravi to bring out softness and sublimity. Songs such as *'Chalo Ek Baar'*, *'Aap Aaye'*, *'In Hawaon Mein'*, *'Aa Bhi Ja'* (all from *Gumrah*, 1963), *'Neele Gagan Ke Tale'*, *'Kissi Pathar Ki Moorat'*, *'Na Moonh Chhupa Ke Jiyo'* (all from *Humraaz*, 1967), and from *Waqt* (1965), *Aadmi Aur Insaan* (1969) and *Dhund* (1973) form an indelible part of the nation's musical memory.

I met Ravi a few years before his death at his house, appropriately called *Vachan* (his first film). Frail of health, he was still mentally alert and dexterous on the keyboards. We spent a glorious afternoon together talking about his life and music. He told me that the room we were sitting in was the same where Rafi had broken down during rehearsals of *'Babul Ki Duyaen'* (*Neel Kamal*, 1968).

Ravi asked Rafi's brother-in-law Zaheer Bari, his secretary and manager, about it. He was told that Rafi's daughter had recently got married and Rafi had gotten emotional. The paternal emotion came out clearly and so endearingly in the recording.

Another incident that was narrated was regarding the song *'Yeh Zulf Agar Khulke'* (*Kaajal*, 1965). The word "*acchha*" is repeated several times and the challenge was to sing it differently each time. Rafi suggested he be given the chance to try, which he did with such superlative effect.

I was fortunate to have heard Ravi sing his best-known songs for me. He also played for me a tape of a song he had composed and sung himself as a tribute to Rafi.

I discussed with Ravi the controversy surrounding his bhajan '*Darshan Do Ghanshyam*' (*Narsi Bhagat*, 1957) so evocatively sung by Hemant Kumar, who gave his best to his former protégé. The movie *Slumdog Millionaire* had used the bhajan without Ravi's prior permission. To add insult to injury, the answer shown in the film regarding its lyricist was wrongly mentioned as Surdas.

The lyrics were penned by Gopal Singh Nepali. Ravi told me that he had arraigned the filmmakers. Later, I learnt there had been an out-of-court settlement. Ravi also told me he had no knowledge of classical music and had been asked by the Narsi Bhagat maker to listen to a Raag *Kedar* based bhajan of the forties, based on which Ravi had come up with the tune. This honest self-effacement of a fact not well-known was in line with Ravi's simplicity and modesty—two qualities which endeared him to the film industry.

I was aware of the personal problems Ravi was facing with his son. It showed on his face, on his drooping shoulders. When I left, I couldn't but remember Ravi's own song '*Is Bhari Duniya Mein Koi Bhi Hamara Na Hua*' from his film *Bharosa* (1963).

How Ravi is still remembered in the remotest corners of the country was driven home to me when I was in Upper Assam, three hours from Dibrugarh. The head of production of the urea plant was hosting a dinner for me during my official visit. He was an Assamese and wasn't fluent in Hindi.

He requested me to sing a Rafi song from *Do Badan* (1966). Which one? I was testing him. Any of the three, he replied. Impressed, I asked which I should sing first. '*Bhari Duniya Mein*', he suggested. Ok, let's do it together. He knew every word. We then went on to '*Naseeb Mein Jiske Jo Likha Tha*', finally ending with '*Raha Gardishon Mein*'. By this time, all senior officers had joined in. Who says Ravi had been laid to rest! He was well and alive in Namrup!

Ravi's *pièce de résistance* is from an eminently forgettable film *Ustadon Ke Ustad* (1963):

"Sau Baar Janam Lenge,
Sau Baar Fanna Honge,
Ai Jaan-e-Wafa Phir Bhi,
Hum Tum Na Judaa Honge."

Ravi passed away on 7th March 2012. We doff our hats to this musical genius who can never be *judaa* from our respect and love for his unforgettable melodies!

5

The Colossus

Mohammed Rafi

The Bharat Ratna is the highest civilian award of the Republic of India. Instituted on 2nd January 1954, the award is conferred in recognition of exceptional service/performance of the highest order, without distinction of race, occupation, position, or sex.

Please note the qualifications required—"exceptional service/performance of the highest order". If Mohammed Rafi does not fit the bill, then that is the biggest disservice that the government, not the people, can do to him. If it were left to popular choice, Rafi would already have received it—perhaps even when he was alive. But these awards are the prerogative of the government. Lata Mangeshkar got it, deservedly. Even Bhupen Hazarika got it. But Rafi being kept out of the hallowed list is a riddle wrapped up in an enigma.

Consider what he got—a Padma Shri—the lowest tier of the civilian awards which four to five persons from the film industry annually get in the normal course. Rarely does a Colossus walk the earth who rules the minds and hearts of not one but several generations across a subcontinent with an immeasurable contribution by way of joy and upliftment, of inspiration and hope, of contentment and edification through his inimitable craft. And, this is what his reward is. It is not that the legacy of Rafi suffers—it is the credibility of the official recognition that gets adversely impacted and exhibits a huge disconnect between the governing and the governed. Fifty years later, many of the Bharat Ratna awardees would be forgotten and only find a mention in the textbooks. But Rafi would still be heard in the roadside *dhaba,* or a remixed version of his songs would be playing in a nightclub, or music clubs would still be singing his songs. And on 31st July and 24th December, the media, especially the radio stations, would be all about him. Hundreds of programs dedicated to him would be staged.

Every fan of Rafi knows his history, his songs, the godliness in his voice, his range and technique, his versatility in singing every genre with equal felicity and impact. There is no value addition one can make to the extensive literature already out there. Go to the website dedicated to him and see what active and well-informed discussions and facts are there.

But there are certain obvious things that are staring us in the face that we sometimes lose sight of.

I rate the song '*Kar Chale Hum Fida*' from *Haqeeqat* (1964)—a film on the Indo-China War—as THE ultimate patriotic song ever composed. If ever an official laureate were to give for the greatest all-time patriotic anthem, this should be it. '*Ae Mere Watan Ke Logon*' is outstanding. But '*Kar Chale*' is several notches higher—ask any military person. Madan Mohan's composition, particularly the martial interludes, instil pride and patriotic fervour, the taar-shehnai which brings up the end of the interludes brings pathos, Kaifi Azmi's lyrics aptly bring out the sacrifices of our brave hearts, and Rafi's emotional singing at the high scales brings it all together, moving the nation to acknowledge its debt of gratitude to the soldiers. The song remains relatively underrated and needs to be placed on the top shelf of the pantheon. Whenever there is tension in the Himalayas, the valour shown by our armed forces and the sacrifices made by them makes this song very apt. "*Saans thamti gayi, nabs jamti gayi, phir bhi badhte kadam ko na rukne diya, kat gaye sir humare to kuchh gham nahi, sir Himalaya ka humne na jhukne diya, marte marte raha baankpan sathiyon, ab tumhare hawale watan sathiyon.*"

Post the war, when the morale of the nation was low, Rafi sang two non-film songs—'*Awaaz Do Hum Ek Hain*' and '*Watan Ki Abroo Khatre Mein Hai*'. Mehboob Khan, the well-known film director, filmed these songs on his *Mother India* (1957) actors Raaj Kumar, Rajendra Kumar and Sunil Dutt, and his *Son of India* (1962) actor Kamaljit. The Films Division of India would show these songs as part of its newsreel at all film theatres. Khayyam was the music director and Jan Nissar Akhtar, and Sahir Ludhianvi were the lyricists, respectively.

There were many other songs of Rafi in the patriotic genre.

In one song, Rafi (like Lata in '*Ae Mere Watan Ke Logon*') managed to draw tears from the eyes of Nehru—many years before Lata did. The song was a private song released in 1948, a few months after Gandhi's assassination: '*Suno Suno Ae Duniya Waalon Bapu Ki Ye Amar Kahani.*'

Gandhi's death came as a jolt to the nation as well as the film industry. As a mark of tribute, this song was conceived. It required the composing genius of Husnlal-Bhagatram, the lyrical brilliance of Rajendra Krishan and the soulful appeal of a young Rafi to make people rededicate themselves to Gandhi's ideals. Days leading up to and following Independence had seen horrific violence that killed millions and Gandhi himself. The song underscores the futility of the madness which had convulsed the nation. On Independence Day in 1948, Rafi was invited to sing this song at Nehru's house. The song had such an effect on Nehru that tears rolled down his cheeks! The song reportedly sold a million copies in the first month of its release.

In *Jagriti* (1954), Rafi sang one of the most inspirational songs to a young nation still finding its feet after Independence: '*Hum Laye Hain Toofan Se Kashti Nikal Ke, Is Desh Ko Rakhna Mere Bachon Sambhal Ke*'. Another inspirational song was '*Jahan Daal Daal Pe Sone Ki Chidiya*' from *Sikander-e-Azam* (1965) which never fails to stir pride and love for the nation. Rafi sang for Bhagat Singh in *Shaheed* (1965): *'Ae Watan Ae Watan Humko Teri Kasam'* and *'Sarfaroshi Ki Tammanna'*.

Rafi immortalized the message of Nehru in his *'Meri Awaaz Suno'* from *Naunihal* (1967): *"Meri aawaaz suno, pyaar ke raaz suno, maine ek phool jo seene pe sajaa rakhaa tha, uske parde main tumhein dil se lagaa rakhha tha, tha judaa sabse mere ishq ka andaaz suno."*

If ever the tenets of secularism, tolerance, peaceful co-existence, and respect for all faiths were to be encapsulated in one song, that would be *'Tu Hindu Banega Na Musalman Banega'* from *Dhool Ka Phool* (1959).

For whom hasn't Rafi sung? He has sung for most Mughals. Emperor Babar in *Babar* (1960)—*'Tum Ek Baar Mohabbat Ka Imtihan Toh Lo'*; Emperor Jahangir in *Adl-e-Jahangir* (1956)—*'Apna Hi Ghar Lutane Diwana Ja Raha Hai'*; *Noor Jehan* (1967)—*'Aap Jabse Qareeb Aaye Hain'*; *Mughal-e-Azam* (1960)—*'Ae Mohabbat Zindabad'*; Emperor Shah Jahan in *Taj Mahal* (1963)—*'Jo Wada Kiya Hai'*; Bahadur Shah Zafar in *Lal Quila* (1960)—*'Na Kisi Ki Aankh Ka Noor Hoon'*.

In fact, he didn't restrict himself to the Mughal rule in India but went across to Baghdad which was under Mughal rule and sang for the son of Rustom-e-Baghdad in *Rustom-e-Baghdad* (1963)—*'Chand Jaisa Badan Phool Sa Pairhan'*. He sang a eulogy for Rana Bhim Singh in *Maharani Padmini* (1964)—*'Gir Gaya Sher Babbar'*.

He sang for Tansen in *Sangeet Samrat Tansen* (1962)—*'Deepak Jalao Jyoti Jagao'*, as well as his rival Baiju Bawra in the movie *Baiju Bawra* (1952)—*'Man Tarpat Hari Darshan Ko Aaj'*.

Rafi even sang for a Tatar in *Changez Khan* (1957)—*'Mohabbat Zinda Rehti Hai'*, for a lovelorn subject of Halaku—Changez Khan's grandson—who was Emperor of Iran in *Halaku* (1956)—*'Aaja Ke Intezaar Mein Jaane Ko Hai Bahaar Bhi'*. He sang for Samson in *Samson* (1964)—

'*Ek Baat Hai Kehne Ki Aankhon Se*'. He even sang for Robin Hood in the *Adventures of Robin Hood and Bandits* (1965)—'*Mana Mere Haseen Sanam*'. He sang about the plight of the Jews in *Yahudi* (1958)—'*Ye Duniya Ye Duniya Haye Hamari Ye Duniya*'.

He has sung for every actor, big and small, extra, comedian, character actor, villain. He has sung for Raj Kapoor, whose ghost voice was Mukesh and sometimes Manna De (for example, all songs of *Do Ustad* released in 1959). He has even sung for Kishore Kumar—for example, '*Man Mora Bawra*' in *Raagini* (1958) who was the actor in the film. Yodelling is associated in popular mind with Kishore Kumar. But even Rafi has done it '*Un Se Ripi Tiki Ho Gayi*' in *Agra Road* (1957) and '*Gussa Fuzool Hai*' in *Reporter Raju* (1962). He also sang the first rap song in Hindi films—'*Worli Ka Naka*' in the movie *Do Ustad* (1959).

He has sung for labourers, doctors, soldiers, politicians, farmers, rickshawalas, tongawalas, vegetable sellers, magicians, pickpockets, mithai sellers, toy sellers, insurance agents, sellers of magic potions, beggars, mendicants. He sang for Mehmood suffering from rhotacism in *Chhote Nawab* (1961)—'*Ilahi Tu Sun Le Hamali Dua, Humein Sirf Ik Aasra Hai Tela*'. He has even sung for a barber, a profession from where he started—'*Mera Naam Phataphat, Mera Kaam Phataphat, Sir Mudwalo, Bal Katalo, Katoon Ga Jhatpat*' in *Shehzaada* (1955).

He has sung all genres—nothing was off limits. Romantic, serious, introspective, patriotic, exuberant, bhajans, dance numbers, qawwalis, ghazals and classical songs. The music directors even made him sing songs inspired by foreign songs—'*Ae Dil Hai Mushkil*' in *CID* (1956) based on '*Oh My Darling Clementine*'; '*Sar Jo Tera Chakraye*' from *Pyasa* (1957) based on '*Harry Black and the Tiger*'; '*Dekho Abto Kisko Nahin Hai Khabar*' from *Janwar* (1965) based on '*I Want To Hold Your Hand*'; '*Kaun Hai Jo Sapnon Mein Aaya*' in *Jhuk Gaya Aasman*

(1968) based on *'Marguerita'*. Rafi made them better than the originals.

He sang in all regional languages. He even sang in English—*'Although We Hail from Different Lands'* based on the tune of *'Baharon Phool Barsao'* from the movie *Suraj* (1966) and *'The She I Love'* based on the tune of *'Hum Kale Hain Toh Kya Hua'* from *Gumnaam* (1965). He sang in Creole, Dutch, Sinhalese, Arabic, Persian.

For a singer of such an extraordinary talent, he was remarkably simple. OP Nayyar told me that after his tiff with Rafi because the latter had arrived late (he had been held up in a Shankar-Jaikishan recording), resulting in Rafi being banished from his studios for many years, it was Rafi who landed up at his house to make up though OP Nayyar was clearly to blame for his disproportionately severe action. They both embraced and cried. OP Nayyar told me that Rafi was a much bigger person than he or anybody else for that matter.

A small-time music director Momin Khan, whom I knew in Mumbai, told me that he was present during the recording of *'Jo Wada Kiya'* from *Taj Mahal* (1963). After the recording, Rafi was so happy that he distributed his recording fees to all the musicians and with folded hands asked them to pray ("*dua karo*") for the song's success, which of course it was.

Other music directors also told me about Rafi's simplicity. Ravi told me that Rafi had broken down during rehearsals of *'Babul Ki Duyaen'* in *Neel Kamal* (1968). Ravi asked Rafi's brother-in-law Zaheer, his secretary and manager, about it. He was told that Rafi's daughter had recently got married and Rafi got emotional. The paternal emotion came out clearly and so endearingly in the recording.

Usha Khanna was all praise for Rafi's humility when I met her. At the recording of one of the Asha-Rafi duets she was not fully satisfied with one part of the song but was hesitant about telling him. He sensed it and told her,

"Usha, tumne humse nahin seekhna. Hamein tumse gaana seekhna hai." (Usha, you don't have to learn from us. We have to learn how to sing from you.)

Khayyam told me that Rafi was humility personified and never ceased to be a student of music and was always keen to learn the intricacies of music.

Mubarak Begum told me she may never have sung the evergreen duet with Rafi—'*Mujhko Apne Gale Laga Lo*' from *Humrahi* (1963). She recorded the song as a filler, to be dubbed by Lata Mangeshkar later. Music director Jaikishan waited till the last minute for Lata to show up, but she never did. So, Mubarak was retained. But Rafi also played a part in persuading Jaikishan to retain Mubarak to encourage her.

How many singers have film songs dedicated to them? '*Na Fankar Tujhsa Tere Baad Aaya, Mohammed Rafi Tu Bahut Yaad Aaya*' sung by Mohammed Aziz appeared in the film *Kroadh* (1990) sung onscreen by Amitabh Bachchan.

Rafi's song from the film *Gumnaam* (1965)—'*Jaan Pehechan Ho*'—was used on the soundtrack of *Ghost World* (2001). The song has also been used for Heineken's 2011 *The Date* commercial.

Rafi was way beyond an outstanding singer. He was a good human being. He was always experimenting, pushing boundaries, exploring new frontiers. He was not afraid of failure and had faith and confidence in his own abilities and hard work. He never let his listeners down. His songs will forever be sung till music exists.

Rafi has ticked all the boxes. He has done whatever needed to be done. What more does the government want of Rafi? Rafi does not deserve Bharat Ratna; Bharat Ratna deserves him!

6

Mistakes Made in Film Songs

Sometimes mistakes stare us in the face, but we don't notice—even obvious ones.

I recall, during a weekly 'Zoom' music get-together, I was singing the popular Mohammed Rafi paean to beauty '*Pehle Mile the Sapnon Mein*' (*Zindagi*, 1964) sung on screen by Rajendra Kumar to Vyjayanthimala. It had lilting music by Shankar-Jaikishan and romance-drenched lyrics by Hasrat Jaipuri in which he used his signature style of ending song lines—in this case '*Hai Qurbaan Jaaoon*'.

The first *antara* began: "*Ai saanwali haseena, dil mera tune chheena.*" However, after the third *antara*, he wrote, "*Gore badan par kala aanchal, aur rang le aaya, hai qurbaan jaoon.*"

'*Saanwali Haseena*', '*Gora Badan*'?

A member of the music group pointed it out to me. I have been listening to this song for decades. So have the music lovers. However, this glaring discrepancy has gone unnoticed.

How Hasrat did it is not known. How did it escape the attention of the producer (perhaps, they could be excused—the film was produced by SS Vasan/Gemini Pictures from the South), or, the music directors, and even director Ramanand Sagar?

We will never know. Anyway, it's too late to make amends, so let's keep enjoying and listening to the song.

This song is one among others where 'mistakes' have been committed—whether in lyrics, or, while recording, or, by wrong credits on the gramophone records.

Consider *'Main Pyaar Ka Rahi Hoon'* (*Ek Musafir Ek Haseena,* 1962) composed by OP Nayyar and written by Raja Mehdi Ali Khan.

Joy Mukherji (in the voice of Rafi) serenaded Sadhna: *"Tere bin jee lage na akele."* She (in the voice of Asha Bhosle) responded: *"Ho sake toh mujhe saath le le."*

Joy continued: *"Naazneen tu nahin ja sakegi, chhodkar zindagi ke jhamele"* and awaited her response.

She sang back: *"Jab bhi chhaye ghata, yaad karna zara, saat rangon ki hun main kahani."*

Joy would certainly have been perplexed by her response which had nothing whatsoever to do with what he had sung to her.

However, if Sadhna had responded, *"Na main hun naazneen na main hun mahjabeen, aap hi ki nazar hai deewani",* that would have been appropriate. After all, he called her *naazneen,* she denied it and attributed his addressing her as such to his *nazar* being *deewani.*

But bizarrely, she responded as above, not in the same stanza, but in the next one, which again did not have the remotest connection to what poor Joy had sung to her.

Consider Joy's love-struck rhapsody in the next stanza: *"Pyaar ki bijliyan muskurayen."*

Sadhna responded: *"Dekhiye aap par gir na jayen."*

Joy continued: *"Dil kahe dekhta hi rahoon main, saamne baithh kar yeh adaayen."*

Sadhna then sang: *"Na main hun naazneen, na main hun mahjabeen, aap hi ki nazar hai deewani."*

He was singing about *bijliyan* and her response, given in the first stanza, referring to *ghata,* would have been apposite here.

Asha's stanzas clearly got mixed up and were used wrongly after Rafi's stanzas.

How on earth could this error have taken place?

There was no way the lyricist would have gotten it wrong! He was a much-respected writer who had made a very good name for himself in the Bombay film world, especially while working with Madan Mohan. Even if the stanzas had gotten mixed up while writing them down for the singers, in those days the music director, the lyricist, the filmmaker, and, of course, the recordist, sound engineer and other technicians, besides the entire ensemble of musicians, would be present in the studio.

This glaring error still slipped through the cracks.

Forget the music world. The listening public did not, and still do not, save a few aficionados, know about this slippage. The country has been singing this beautiful song without realizing the mix-up. Incidentally, the song was removed from the film later, not because of the mistake, but to reduce the length of the film.

I raised this issue with OP Nayyar. He denied there was a mix-up. When I persisted and reasoned with him, he relented somewhat but laid the blame on the lyricist. Didn't you have over-riding power over the lyricist, I asked. After all, you had asked Qamar Jalalabadi to amend the lyrics of '*Mohabbat Ka Haath, Jawani Ka Palla*' (*Howrah Bridge*, 1958). That was because a part of the lyrics was not fitting into the meter of the song; it was a minor change for musical reasons, he countered.

OP Nayyar was involved in other such errors too!

The duet of Rafi/Asha '*Chand Zard Zard Hai*' (*Jaali Note*, 1960) was composed by him and written (again) by Raja Mehdi Ali Khan. Strangely, it had two versions (reasons not known even to OP Nayyar)—one for the record, one for the film. The record version, recorded first, began as— "*Raat sard sard hai, chand zard zard hai*".

The film version, however, began—"*Chand zard zard hai, chand zard zard hai*" ("*Raat sard sard hai*" had been removed).

Asha, while recording the film version, apparently still had '*Raat Sard Sard Hai*' implanted in her mind, having recorded the audio version earlier. So, she began singing the film version with '*Raat*' but realized as soon as she uttered '*Ra*' that she had to begin with '*Chand*,' so changed track and sang '*Rhand*'.

Why did you not do a re-take?

OP Nayyar just shrugged his shoulders.

Anyway, he did not believe in re-takes as a rule. The singers would rehearse thoroughly and would give the desired result in the first take itself. Asha managed to buck the trend here.

She did that in another OP Nayyar composition, '*Piya Piya Piya Mora Jiya Pukare*' (*Baap Re Baap*, 1955) in the duet with Kishore Kumar. In the second *antara*, which Kishore was singing, she came in before her turn to end the *antara*, immediately realized her mistake, and stopped. One can hear the short *alaap*. As stated by Asha, Kishore signalled her to continue and complete the song as it was.

After the recording was over, he told everybody that he, being the hero of the movie, would place a hand on his heroine's mouth during that portion. He did that during the shooting. So, no re-take was taken.

OP Nayyar was apoplectic with rage when I mentioned Asha's explanation to him: "I was the master of the studio, how could Kishore dictate the recording?"

It's not that he was a big star who could have his way; in fact, at that time, Kishore Kumar was a minor star. This movie gave a boost to his career, and he went on to act in 68 movies from 1953 to 1968. "But, even if he were a superstar, nothing could happen in the studio without my approval," said OP Nayyar.

So, there you have it—two versions of the incident.

Indeed, we haven't finished with OP Nayyar just yet.

In the film *Heera Moti* (1979), he composed the music and Ahmed Wasi wrote the lyrics. The song '*Sau Saal Jiyo Tum Jaan Meri*' sung by Dilraj Kaur, had a shorter version of only one *antara* in the film, though, in the record, there were two *antaras*. In the record version, the first *antara* was: "*Tum meri maang ki lali ho, mere nainon ka kaajal ho, choodi ki khanak, bindiya ki chamak, tum meri laaj ka aanchal ho.*"

But see how it ended: "*Meri jaan tumhari baahon mein, meri saari umar guzar jaaye.*"

The second *antara* was: "*Tum saath raho toh aankhon mein armanon ki baraat saje, phoolon ki tarah har raat saje, khwabon ki tarah har raat saje.*"

See how it ended: "*Meri maang suhagan kehlaye, jo rang tumhara pad jaaye.*"

Clearly, the end lines had gotten interchanged. The first stanza talked of '*Maang*' as does the ending of the second *antara*. The second *antara* referred to '*Saath Raho*' and the ending of the first *antara* alluded to '*Tumhari Baahon Mein, Meri Saari Umar Guzar Jaaye*'.

I never sought any clarification from OP Nayyar; I didn't want to lose his friendship!

The evergreen super hit song, '*Hawa Hawai*' from *Mr India* (1987), also had a mistake, which would have continued to be unnoticed had not Kavita Krishnamurthy let the cat out of the bag. In one place in the track, she sang '*Jeenu*' instead of '*Jaanu*'. Composers Laxmikant-Pyarelal were aware of it but retained the take. The freshness and 'oomph' might have gotten diluted in the next take, so they played it safe.

Laxmikant-Pyarelal played it safe once more in the famous duet of Lata and Nitin Mukesh, '*Zindagi Ki Na Toote Ladi*' (*Kranti*, 1981) when Lata missed singing '*Ki*' after '*Zindagi*' and instead sang '*Zindagi Na*'. But so adroitly was it done, with the beat intact, and with the remaining words following seamlessly, that to date it remains unnoticed!

When the overall product is a masterpiece, why tinker with it—so it remained. Who would notice anyway?

Laxmikant-Pyarelal were again involved in a minor error in the song, '*Mere Bachpan Tu Ja*' (*Kuchhe Dhaage*, 1973). In the first *antara*, Lata sang: "*Beriyan nu ber lag gaye ve tauba, phulon se jhuk gayi daliyan.*" However, when she repeated the line, she sang '*Bairiyan*' instead of '*Beriyan*'. A subtle pronunciation slip-up, but the meaning changed. How Anand Bakshi, the lyricist who introduced many such Punjabi lines in songs, did not notice this, remains a mystery.

In the song '*Yeh Jab Se Hui Jiya Ki Chori*' sung by Lata in the film *Us Paar* (1974), under the baton of SD Burman, she accidently sang '*chhori*' rather than '*chori*' at the end of the song. The mistake went unnoticed.

Bappi Lahiri recorded a song, '*Phool Ka Shabaab Kya*' by Rafi for the film *Hari Bhari* (1980). The words of the *mukhra* were—"*Phool ka shabaab kya, husn mahtaab kya, aap toh bas aap hain, aapka jawaab kya*". However, during the recording, Rafi mistakenly sang '*Aapka Jawaab Ka*' instead of '*Aap Ka Jawaab Kya*'.

The mistake was noticed by Bappi Lahiri after Rafi had left the studio. Rafi promised to record the song again, but, alas, he died soon thereafter. The film was shelved but Bappi Lahiri eventually used the song—with the mistake—in *Farz Ki Jung* released in 1989. Besides, there are mistakes recording companies make in giving wrong credits or missing out on giving credits.

The birthday song, '*Tum Jiyo Hazaaron Saal*' from *Sujata* (1959) was first recorded in Geeta Dutt's voice. Later, the same song was recorded in Asha Bhosle's voice. This was the version which was used in the movie. The song sung by Asha was credited to Geeta Dutt. It continued to be wrongly credited to Geeta Dutt till Asha and R D Burman convinced HMV and got the credits corrected.

Remember '*Lara Lappa Lara Lappa Layee Rakhda*' (*Ek Thi Ladki*, 1949) which took the entire nation by storm? The song was composed by Vinod. It was sung by Lata, Rafi, and Satish Batra. HMV, by mistake, printed the name of the singer as GM Durrani on the record. This mistake was later rectified at the initiative of a noted film historian who had checked it with GM Durrani himself. Later, HMV printed the name of Batra in place of Durrani.

Here are some more such instances.

In *Aaraam* (1951), the song '*Rootha Hua Chand Hai, Roothi Hui Chandni*' has lyrics by Prem Dhawan, though the 78 RPM record mentions Rajinder Krishan.

In *Ek Tha Ladka* (1951), the song '*Ek Din Tumne Kaha Tha*' only credits Shamshad Begum; GM Durrani is missing.

In *Chham Chhamaa Chham* (1952), the song '*Bandalpur Se Munshi Munakka Ne*' has been credited to Asha Bhosle and Munshi Munakka in the record, whereas its Asha and Kishore. The song '*Taraste Hain, Tadapte Hain*' shows Asha/ Kishore, whereas it is Shamshad Begum/Kishore. The music was composed by OP Nayyar, but, in all fairness, he can't be blamed for this lapse!

In *Shiv Shakti* (1952), the song '*Neelgagan Ke Raja Aaja*' is credited to Asha/Batuk Vyas, whereas it is Asha/Batuk Desai. Similarly, in the song '*Ghia Jaaye Re Ghatmaal,*' the mistake is repeated.

In *Veer Arjun* (1952), in the song '*More Ghungroo Baajen Jhan Jhanan*', only Asha is mentioned, whereas it is both Asha and GM Durrani.

In *Neelampari* (1952), in the song '*Chham Chham, Rahein Dono Saath Hardam*', only Geeta Dutt is credited, not Asha. In the song '*Ek Tum Dooji Main,*' Asha is also mentioned besides Geeta, but Asha did not sing.

In *Jalpari* (1952), the song '*Jo Tamanna Dil Mein Thi*' was sung by only Lata though the record mentions Rafi too. Most songs of this film don't have the names of the lyricists—Bharat Vyas, Ramesh Gupta, Noor Lakhnavi, Kumar Jalalabadi.

In *Aagosh* (1953), the song '*Ho Dheere Dheere Chadd Gaya Nadi Mein Paani*' credits only Lata, and Hemant Kumar is missing.

In *Gunaah* (1953), the song '*Mere Khayalon Mein Aake Galey Laga Ja Mujhe*' has been composed by Roshan though the record mentions Snehal Bhatkar.

The mistakes, especially the ones that take place in the recording studios, humanize that perfect studio sound that one expects in the recording. Hearing this human dimension on the other side of the recording is just as golden as hearing a great song performed with absolute perfection. If the end product is great, these minor hiccups do not matter. Surely, with the advent of technology, such errors are unlikely to occur now. These 'mistakes' thus are a precious memory of the past and constitute a delicious slice of film music of that era.

7

The Unsung Genius

Khayyam

What is it about the Indian Army that it produces musical gems for the Mumbai film industry such as Madan Mohan and Anand Bakshi—both weaving their musical and lyrical magic in heaven now? And Khayyam, who joined them later on August 19th, 2019.

Khayyam joined the Army during World War II and worked there for three years. He was a member of the army cultural troupe (headed by Faiz Ahmad Faiz) performing plays and songs to persuade people to join the force. But that's not his claim to fame!

I first heard of Khayyam not because of his musical genius but because of his wife Jagjit Kaur, a singer of memorable masterpieces. She along with her wealthy zamindar family used to be a neighbour of my grandfather's in Civil Lines, Hoshiarpur.

Both families knew each other well. During our vacations to Hoshiarpur every summer in the '60s, her family's name would invariably turn up in conversations. By that time, Jagjit had already married Khayyam. Khayyam, born Mohammed Zahur 'Khayyam' Hashmi, a Muslim, was from the nearby town of Rahon.

He was from a humble background. Khayyam had attended a music concert where he spotted Jagjit Kaur singing and approached her for *Shola Aur Shabnam* (1961). She sang solos for the movie, including a duet with Rafi.

I have been fascinated by Khayyam's music since childhood, and completely bowled over by Jagjit Kaur's renditions—her ability to switch from a rustic voice to render folk tunes, such as *'Ladi Re Ladi'* from *Shola Aur Shabnam* (1961) to a soft and melodious voice as in *'Tum Apna Ranj-o-Gham'* from *Shagoon* (1964).

I finally met them in their apartment in a Juhu housing colony some years before his death. The flat was modestly appointed. Jagjit Kaur met me very warmly and enquired about my larger family. Khayyam was initially reserved but opened up gradually. While discussing his music, he got emotional, his fingers painting figures in the air and his feet prancing about. It was a fabulous afternoon.

Who would have ever thought that Fyodor Dostoevsky's *Crime and Punishment* would provide the impetus to Khayyam's career? Although Khayyam's *'Sham-e-Gham Ki Kasam'*, sung by Talat Mehmood for *Footpath* (1953), gained immense popularity, it was only with *Phir Subah Hogi* (1958) that Khayyam's genius was recognized.

Director Ramesh Saigal offered Sahir Ludhianvi the opportunity to write the lyrics for *Phir Subah Hogi,* which was based on *Crime and Punishment*. Since Raj Kapoor was the hero of the film it was natural that Shankar-Jaikishan would give the music, but Sahir suggested that he wanted someone who had read and understood the book. And that was Khayyam. Such are the twists and turns of fate with which our film industry is replete!

Khayyam had read Sahir's anthology of poetry, *Talkhiyaan,* and had composed songs for the poems. Sahir by this time was an accomplished songwriter in films. He was very impressed when he heard one such composition. This is how the two developed a mutual admiration for each other. Their association is an abiding milestone in the Hindi film industry.

Every song in the film was a polished gem— *'Woh Subah Kabhi Toh Aayegi'*, *'Cheen-o-Arab Humaara'* and *'Aasmaan Pe*

Hai Khuda Aur Zameen Pe Hum'. Khayyam built on *Phir Subah Hogi*'s success and in later years, cemented his reputation by composing evergreen music for films such as *Shola Aur Shabnam* (1961), *Shagoon* (1964), *Kabhi Kabhie* (1976), *Noorie* (1979), *Umrao Jaan* (1981), and *Razia Sultan* (1983).

It was Khayyam's dream to become a singer-actor like KL Saigal whose movies he used to watch very often. Because of his family's opposition, he went to his uncle in Delhi. There he learnt music from Pandit Amarnath. Then he went to Lahore and became an assistant to the then top music composer Baba Chisti. The Army followed.

After the war, Khayyam returned to his first love, films. Having learnt from Pandit Amarnath it was natural for him to meet his brothers in the industry—Husnlal and Bhagatram. They helped him make his debut as Sharmaji of the Sharmaji-Varmaji composer duo. *Heer Ranjha* (1948) was the first movie he gave music in. After his partner, Rahman Varma, moved away post-Partition, he began working solo.

Khayyam emphasized to me that he never compromised on perfection. For the song *'Jaane Kya Dhoondti Rehti Hain'* (*Shola Aur Shabnam*, 1961), Rafi had to give 21 takes before Khayyam approved it.

I asked him the secret of Asha Bhosle sounding so different in *Umrao Jaan* (1981). That's because I made her sing in a lower octave than her usual scale, he explained. She asked for a week to prepare. On the day of the recording, she got cold feet and asked if she could sing in her own scale. They agreed that they would record in both scales, and she could then select.

Later, when she heard the recording in the lower octave, she was ecstatic and said she didn't know she could sing like that. The songs were a rage and fetched Khayyam his second Filmfare Award (the first being for *Kabhi Kabhie* in

1977) and the National Film Award for best music director. Asha also got her first National Film Award for best female singer.

For Kamal Amrohi's *Razia Sultan* (1983, though the film had begun several years earlier), Khayyam went through the research made by the filmmaker for eight months before starting music composition, of which '*Ae Dil-e-Nadaan*' sung by Lata Mangeshkar captured the mood and feel of the character beautifully. Khayyam decided to give this track more than one pause, each running over five seconds, to dramatize the lyrics. This song, unknown to Khayyam, was to change his life once again.

Till this time, shockingly, he was out of the film world for a long period. From *Kabhi Kabhie* (1976), he staged a miraculous comeback. Khayyam narrated an interesting incident. A day after the recording of '*Ae Dil-e-Nadaan*', when Khayyam was asleep at home, the bell rang at two in the morning. Khayyam was shocked to see Jaya Bachchan and filmmaker Sultan Ahmed at the door.

Apologizing for coming so late, Jaya requested for the tape of the song, saying that Amitabh Bachchan had sent her to fetch it. It wasn't with Khayyam and Kamal Amrohi had it dropped to her house the next day. Then Yash Chopra and Sahir Ludhianvi came to Khayyam's home and offered him *Kabhi Kabhie*.

Khayyam said he always preferred to work with the poets rather the regular film lyricists. That is the reason one finds poetry playing an equal role in Khayyam's compositions as the music. His music brings to life the poetry and does not overpower it. He had very high regard for Kaifi Azmi, Ali Sardar Jafri, Majrooh Sultanpuri, Sahir Ludhianvi, Naqsh Lyalpuri, Nida Fazli, Jaan Nisaar Akhtar, and Ahmed Wasi.

Pakeezah (1972) also owes its completion to Khayyam and Jagjit Kaur. Khayyam told me that when he was working on *Shankar Hussain,* he asked Kamal Amrohi to screen what he'd shot for *Pakeezah.* At the screening, Jagjit Kaur insisted the film was a classic which should be completed. Amrohi regretfully declined stating that Meena Kumari would not agree. It was Jagjit Kaur who persuaded the actress to agree, and *Pakeezah* took off.

During his inexplicably long pauses, Khayyam also provided music for ghazals, devotional songs, Sufi songs and bhajans. The most notable among this is actress Meena Kumari's poems *I Write, I Recite,* for which Khayyam gave music and the nazms were recited by the poetess herself.

With Rafi, he recoded *Shauq Har Rang.* He collaborated with Asha as well. He even composed for Begum Akhtar. That speaks volumes about his range as a composer. He has also composed a few patriotic songs and 45 songs for TV shows. He got his wife to render ghazals by Meer. In all, he composed 194 non-film ghazals and songs.

Let's tabulate his balance sheet.

In 70 years, he composed only 327 songs for 54 films. That's such a shame! Music directors who are not a patch on him have done much more. He did receive recognition though—three Filmfare Awards for best music in 1977 for *Kabhi Kabhie* and 1982 for *Umrao Jaan* and a Lifetime Achievement Award in 2010. He was awarded the National Film Award for best music director for *Umrao Jaan* in 1982 and the Sangeet Natak Akademi Award in creative music in 2008. He was awarded the third-highest civilian honour, Padma Bhushan, by the Government of India in 2011.

Even though the couple are no more, such a classy music director and his melodious wife will never fade away. The discerning music lovers shall always cherish their contribution. This "*pyaar ka bandhan, janam ka bandhan, kabhi nahin toote ga*"!

8

Shahenshah of Ghazals

Mehdi Hassan

He was to the manor born! Sitting majestically cross-legged on the dais, with a receding hairline, an obligatory mullet, and a pencil-line moustache, he surveyed the audience, which had packed the hall to the rafters. Placing his fingers on the harmonium in front, he sang his first note. It was low, deep, pitch-perfect, dripping with honey, the most dulcet song of a bird, impossibly beautiful. It was surreal!

The year was 1977. On the occasion of the centenary celebrations of Muhammad Iqbal, the Pakistan High Commission had organized a music concert at FICCI Auditorium, New Delhi. And who better to musically convey Allama's vision than Mehdi Hassan himself! This was his first visit to India, but there would be countless visits thereafter with sold-out concerts.

I grew up listening to Mehdi on Radio Pakistan in the late '60s and early '70s. Living in a border state, the radio reception was crystal clear. He was the reigning monarch of the Pakistani film playback industry, and his film songs held me in thrall. Of course, there were other playback singers as well—Ahmed Rushdi, Masood Rana, Mujib Alam—but Mehdi was leagues ahead.

Many songs that he later sang in concerts in India and elsewhere were film songs which he elaborated on or 'ghazalized'—slowing the tempo, introducing classical touches and embellishments, adding more stanzas—songs such as '*Duniya Kisi Ke Pyaar Mein*', '*Mujhe Tum Nazar Se*',

'*Rafta Rafta*', '*Ranjish Hi Sahi*' (which I recall coming first for several weeks in the famous count-down show *Shezan Hit Parade*). In the song '*Ab Ke Hum Bichhde*', he changed the tune!

Apart from the film songs, he also created many ghazals in his own music and it was through these ghazals that Mehdi Hassan became hugely famous outside Pakistan. He had a repertoire of hundreds of ghazals and countless songs in many languages.

I attended several concerts of his and met him many times. I was amazed at the sheer excellence at which he continued to sing decade after decade. The out-of-this-world musical chastity and the ability to emotionally overwhelm the listeners continued unabated throughout his singing years, earning him a fanatic fan following and respect of peers.

What made Mehdi unique? What made him a musical species in his own right?

Even though Mehdi was a great classical singer with the ability to render any classical raga with all its emotions and nuances, he chose the lighter version, the ghazal, as his signature form of music. He effortlessly expressed the many dimensions of classical music through the ghazal. No other ghazal singer could match the soft touch, the nuances, the poetic flourish, the bubbling emotions, the magical silences that Mehdi delineated in his renderings. His rendering was totally innocent of pyrotechnics or exaggerated emotions or artificial pretensions. He was simply a total ghazal singer. Mehdi raised ghazal singing, once looked down upon as the art of high-class courtesans, to the level of khayal and dhrupad singing and won for it popular respect and appreciation. He widened the horizons of ghazal *gayaki* immeasurably, augmented its ambit and enriched its landscape.

What imparted timeless appeal to Mehdi's ghazals was that he based his renditions on different ragas which were selected in accordance with the moods of the verse. Thus, Mehdi the composer worked in tandem with Mehdi the singer. What was no less remarkable was that two songs based on the same raga invariably sounded different. He brought a new sensitivity to vocal music, to the utterance of the language.

In a concert I attended at the residence of the Pakistani High Commissioner, Mehdi went out of his way to explain the *nazaakat* of the ghazals he was singing. His velvety, mellow baritone redolent of pathos coupled with his relaxed and poised style of rendition under a full moon created an indescribable magical evening for the listeners. That's what made Mehdi, the *Shahenshah of Ghazals*.

He wasn't always going to be king of this poetic form. Born in 1927 to a clan of minstrels in village Luna in Rajasthan, Mehdi was initially expected to become, like his father and uncle, a singer of dhrupad—the form of singing that grew out of devotional chants in the temples. His forefathers had been court musicians for 12 generations. Mehdi began to perform as a vocalist at the age of eight. In 1947, when Hassan was 20, the family migrated to Pakistan. Mehdi worked as an assistant in a cycle repair shop to support his family. Later, he found work as an assistant in a workshop repairing cars and tractors. But even in such dire times, he did not give up his *riyaaz*. Later he left for Lahore, to Radio Pakistan, looking for opportunities but none came his way. In Karachi, the centre of Urdu films, he was able to secure a few singing assignments. The first song was '*Nazar Milte Hi Dil Ki Baat Ka Labon Par Charcha Na Ho Jaye*' in the film *Shikar* (1956). Initially, he found it tough competing with great playback singers of those days. However, after the song '*Jis Ne Mere Dil Ko Dard Diya*' in the film *Sasural* in 1962, there was no stopping Mehdi, and he ruled the air waves for two decades. Towards the end of 1990s, chest and lung problems caused Mehdi to retire from performing live. Playback singing, he had given up much earlier.

Despite his health problems, Mehdi composed and sang a song with Lata, fulfilling her long-time wish! Lata had been quoted as saying that God spoke through Mehdi's throat. He sang and recorded his portion of the song in Pakistan and sent the tape to Lata. The song '*Tera Milna Bahut Achha Lage Hai*' was released in 2011 in the album *Sarhadein.*

Mehdi—the *kesariya balam*—left for his new home on 13th June 2012. Soft voices, when music dies, continue to vibrate in memory. Hassan's voice is so immortal that it will continue to hypnotize the collective consciousness of the connoisseurs and the masses forever.

In 1957, he had sung '*Teri Har Ek Ghazal Qaabil-e-Daad Hai/Par Meri Aawaaz Mein Bhi Kuchh Baat Hai*'. Mehdi sang it prophetically, knowing that one day his voice would rule over the hearts of the listeners.

9

When Ghalib and Kabir Come to the Aid of a Song

With Taj Mahal as a backdrop, Shailesh Kumar, in Rafi's golden voice, began to recite:

"Tere Teer-e-Neem Kash Ko, Koi Mere Dil Se Poochhe
Yeh Khalish Kahaan Se Hoti, Jo Jigar Ke Paar Hota."

The tourists, at least some of them, would have been excused for thinking that Ghalib's ghazal was coming their way even though the order of the first line had been changed; they must have also wondered why the singer had not started the ghazal with its first couplet—*'Yeh Na Thi Hamari Qismat'*—and had leapt straight to this third couplet on the half-drawn arrow striking the heart, giving perpetual unease, rather than passing through it completely, bringing about instant death. When the couplet ended and the song *'Phir Woh Bhooli Si Yaad'* (*Begaana*, 1963) commenced, it must have dawned on them that the couplet was being used as a song opener. Thereafter, lyricist Shailendra went on to expound on the same theme in the main song.

Shailendra had done it several times.

"Rangi Ko Narangi Kahe, Bane Doodh Ko Khoya
Chalti Ko Gaadi Kahe, Dekh Kabira Roya."

This *doha* of Kabir on the interplay of mind, reality and consciousness, was a song opener, sung by Mukesh, in *'Zindagi Khwab Hai'* (*Jagte Raho*, 1956). Shailendra built up on Kabir's theme beautifully in simple language which was his forte. For good measure, the filmmaker even threw in a poster of Kabir fixed on a lamp post which Motilal addressed while singing the first *antara*. Interestingly, this *doha* inspired the names of two films—*Chalti Ka Naam Gaadi* (1958) and *Dekh Kabira Roya* (1957).

In *Chhote Nawab* (1961), Lata Mangeshkar's *'Chura Ke Dil Ban Rahe Ho Bhole'*, again written by Shailendra, was introduced by Ghalib's well-known couplet:

"Woh Aaye Ghar Mein Hamare, Khuda Ki Qudrat Hai
Kabhi Hum Unko, Kabhi Apne Ghar Ko Dekhte Hain."

Shailendra struck once again. The title song of *Main Nashe Mein Hoon* (1959) began with a couplet that is attributed to Ghalib. Its provenance is unclear, but it ranks high in popularity stakes:

"Zahid Sharaab Peene De Masjid Mein Baith Kar
Ya Woh Jagah Bataa De Jahan Par Khuda Na Ho."

Shailendra then built on it.

But the couplet that wins hands down, having been used in at least three songs, was not written by any legendary poet. Reportedly one Mahtab Rai Taban read the couplet during Sufi poet Khwaja Mir Dard's *mushaira* when he was only 12 years. Mirza Mohammad Rafi 'Sauda'—the Urdu poet based in Delhi, was present at the *mushaira*. Sauda, overcome by the beauty of poetry, praised the boy and made him read the couplet repeatedly.

The couplet:

"Dil Ke Phaphole Jal Utthe Seene Ke Daag Se
Is Ghar Ko Aag Lag Gai Ghar Ke Chirag Se."

At least three songs used it as their introduction. One was a song by Lata Mangeshkar from *Parichay* (1954). Shailendra (yet again) continued with the theme beginning with the *mukhra*—*"Jal Ke Dil Khaak Hua, Aankh Se Roya Na Gaya, Zakhm Ye Aise Jale, Phoolon Pe Soya Na Gaya"*. The second song (where the couplet was sung by Rafi) was *"Taqdeer Ne Hans Hans Ke Mere Dil Ko Rulaya, Fariyad Khudaya, Fariyad Khudaya"* for *Jallad* (1956) sung by Asha Bhosle. The third song was the iconic KL Saigal's *"Andhe Ki Lathi Tu Hi Hai, Tu Hi Jeewan Ujiyaaraa Ha"'* from *Dhoop Chhaon* (1935).

The phenomenon is not limited to black and white films. The film *Main Tulsi Tere Angan Ki* (1978) had Lata-Asha duet *'Chhaap Tilak Sab Chhini Re'* whose curtain raiser was Amir Khusrau's *"Apni Chhab Banaikay, Jo Main Pi Kay Paas Gayi/ Chhab Dekhi Jab Piyu Ki, So Apni Bhool Gayi."* Lyricist Anand Bakshi then expanded on the theme.

The list goes on and on.

Why do we have the couplets at the start of the song? These are well-known couplets known to most music listeners. Their theme is already known. The discerning is aware of the meaning—both literal and metaphorical. They serve as a preamble to a song written on the same concept. The public knows what to expect. They add heft and substance to the song that follows. It is a double-edged sword though, and not easy for the lyricist. The curtain-raiser gives a snapshot of the motif to come. If the lyrics that follow do full justice to the concept, the song is a success. If not, then the introduction looks contrived and its purpose unnecessary.

In Urdu poetry, there is nothing untoward regarding this phenomenon. It is part of the Urdu tradition. You may use it 'as is' or modify it somewhat without losing its essence. There is a longstanding tradition of treating a great master's work as the starting point from where the poet can push off on his own lyrical voyage. Since one borrows from an already known poet, there is no need for any formal acknowledgement. The cognoscenti already knows.

However, for Hindi film songs, listened to by the masses who may not be aware of the poet concerned, the issue is whether the original poet needs to be acknowledged. This is particularly the case when the couplets are not in the introduction. But sharing of credit is not part of the

Hindi film writing convention. Moreover, much of popular Bollywood music anyway borrows heavily from folk songs without as much as a doff of the hat.

Many times, a couplet, or a line thereof, is inserted inside the song where it becomes a part of the lyrics and the neat differentiation between the introductory couplet and the song that follows, discussed above, gives way to the song absorbing it.

Agha Mohammad Taqi Khan Taraqqi wrote:

"Duniya Ke Jo Maze Hain, Hargiz Woh Kam Na Honge
Charche Yuheen Rahenge, Afsos Hum Na Honge."

It underwent a subtle change to *"Yeh Zindagi Ke Mele, Duniya Mein Kam Na Honge, Afasos Hum Na Honge"* in *Mela* (1948) in the Shakeel Badayuni written and Naushad composed song sung by Rafi. To that extent, this is not Shakeel's creation. And since the *mukhra* repeats itself in the song, it constitutes a considerable value addition by the poet without receiving any acknowledgement.

Legendary poet Faiz Ahmed Faiz's *nazm 'Mujhe Se Pehli Si Mohabbat Mere Mehboob Na Maang'* appeared as a song in the film *Qaidi* (1962). It contained the following lines: *"Teri aankhon ke siva duniya mein rakkha kya hai."* Seven years later, this *nazm* would inspire Majrooh Sultanpuri's *'Teri Aankhon Ke Siwa Duniya Mein Rakkha Kya Hai'* in the film *Chirag* (1969). Even here, these lines are repeated throughout the song making Faiz a co-lyricist. But his name does not figure anywhere.

Gulzar did it in *Mausam* (1975), using Ghalib's couplet: *"Ji Dhoondhta Hai Phir Wahi Fursat Ke Raat Din/Baithe Rahe Tasavvur-e-Jaanan Kiye Hue"* as the first line of the song sung by Bhupinder and Lata Mangeshkar. Gulzar simply changed the first word from *'ji'* (heart) to *'dil'* (heart), retaining the rest of the couplet. In the book *In the Company of a Poet,* based on a series of conversations with author Nasreen Munni

Kabir, Gulzar recounted how he wrote it and expanded the thought into a poetic account of the lover's feelings.

This was not the only time Gulzar was inspired by Ghalib. He went a step further in the song *'Satrangi Re'* (*Dil Se*, 1998), in which he wove Ghalib's couplet into his lyrics:

> *"Ishq Par Zor Nahi, Hai Yeh Woh Aatish Ghalib*
> *Ki Lagaye Na Lagey, Aur Bujhaye Na Bane."*

He did not do any favour to Ghalib by mentioning him—his name already appears in the couplet, which is the *maqta* (last stanza) where the poet's name appears.

However, Anand Bakshi credited the poet in the title song *'Ek Duje Ke Liye'* (*Ek Duje Ke Liye*, 1981) when Lata sang: *"Ishq par zor nahin, Ghalib ne kaha hai isiliye..."*

Gulzar courted controversy when he modified the first two lines of a poem by the Hindi poet Sarveshwar Dayal Saxena, who died in 1983. Gulzar changed *"Ibn-e-Batuta/ Pehen Ke Joota"* to *"Ibn-e-Batuta Ta Ta/Bagal Mein Joota Ta Ta"* for the film *Ishqiya* (2010).

Momin Khan 'Momin' wrote: *"Tum Mere Paas Hote Ho Goya, Koi Doosra Nahin Hota."* Hasrat Jaipur, in the love song, *'O Mere Shah-e-Khubaan' (Love in Tokyo,* 1966) changed the line slightly and used it in the song. Incidentally, another couplet from this same ghazal: *"Haal-e-Dil Yaar Ko Likhoon Kyunkar, Haath Dil Se Judaa Nahin Hota"* was used as part of the qawwali *'Phir Tumhari Yaad Aayi Ae Sanam'* from *Rustom Sohrab* (1963). *"Saare Jahaan Se Achcha, Hindostan Hamaara"* of Iqbal was used in the beginning of the song by Raja Mehdi Ali Khan in *Bhai Bahen* (1959). He then tweaked the rest of the lines and added some of his own but retained the patriotic flavour of the original poem. Iqbal was however parodied by Sahir Ludhianvi in his hard-hitting and cynical *'Cheen-o-Arab Hamaara'* (*Phir Subah Hogi*, 1958).

Meer Taqi Meer's *"Patta-Patta Boota-Boota, Haal Humara Jaane Hai/Jaane Na Jaane Gul Hi Na Jaane, Baagh Toh Sara Jaane Hai"* was used in *Ek Nazar* (1972) as the *mukhra*. Majrooh penned the lyrics for the rest of the song.

The song *'Dillagi Ne Di Hawa, Thoda Sa Dhuaan Utha'* in the film *Dostana* (1980) included a line *"Ankhon ka tha qusoor chhuri dil pe chal gayi"*, which is from a ghazal by Jaleel Manikpuri, sung by Mehdi Hassan. Even Sahir could not resist the temptation. In the film *Laila Majnu* (1976), one song drew inspiration from the 18th century Sufi saint Sheikh Turab Kakorvi. His *"Shahr Mein Apne Ye Laila Ne Munadi Kar Di/Koi Pathar Se Na Maare Mere Deewane Ko"* was converted to *"Husn Haazir Hai Mohabbat Ki Saza Paane Ko/Koi Patthar Se Na Maare Mere Diwaane Ko"*.

In the song *'O Yaar Zulfon Waale'* (*Ek Musaafir Ek Haseena*, 1962), Amir Khusrau's *"Zabaan-e-Yaar-e-Man Turki, O Man Turki Na Mee Daaanam"* was used by lyricist Shevan Rizvi.

Khusrau's poetry has been used in other songs as well. His *"Zehaal-e-Miskeen Makun Taghaaful (Persian)/Varaaye Nainaa Banaae Batiyan (Khadi Boli)"*, was used in *Ghulami* (1985) as:

> *"Zehaal-e-Miskeen Makun Ba-Ranjish*
> *Ba-Haal-e-Hijraan Bechaara Dil Hai*
> *Sunnaaee Detee Hai Jiskee Dhadkan*
> *Tumhaara Dil Yaa Hamaaraa Dil Hai."*

Amir Khusrau had penned this very passionate expression of the grief of a girl, in his poem *'Kaahe Ko Byaahi Bides'*. As the original lines go—*"Khwaja Ji, Sun Li Hamre Jiyara Ki Peerh/Ankhiyaan Se Bahe Hai Neer, Kaahe Ko Byahe Bides"*.

It was used in a song from *Suhaag Raat* (1948) and also sung in *Umrao Jaan* (1981). *'Ab Ke Baras Bhejo Bhaiyya' (Sujata,* 1959) also drew its inspiration from it. Like Khusrau, Kabir has also been a contributor to the Hindi film lyrics.

His *"Ramchandra Keh Gaye Siya Se, Aisa Kalyug Aayega/ Hans Chugega Daana Tinka, Kauva Moti Khayega"* was used in *Gopi* (1970). He was used in the song *'Maati Kahe Kumar Se, Tu Kya Raunde Mohe, Ek Din Aisa Aayega'* (*Adhikar*, 1954). *'Maati Kahe Kumar Se'* was also the opener for the song *'Aas Ka Jhoota Bandhan Toota'* in *Mrig Trishna* (1975) sung by Mehdi Hassan. His *"Lakdi Jal Koyla Bhai/Koyla Jal Bhayo Raakh/Main Paapan (in lieu of 'Baawri') Aisi Jali/Na Koyla Bhai Na Raakh"* was the song opener of *'Mori Bali Re Uumariya'*, sung by Lata in *Chhoti Chhoti Baatein* (1965).

In *'Mohe Bhool Gaye Saanwariya'* (*Baiju Bawra*, 1952) the song began with *"Jo main aisa jaanti preet kiye dukh hoye, nagar dhindora peetti preet na kariyo koye"*—a couplet from Meera. This piece of poetry was used earlier the Shamshad Begum song *'Nirmohi Bansiwaale' (Veena*, 1948).

Does this phenomenon still occur in Hindi film music? *Baaghi 2* (2018) had a song.

'Allah Mujhe Dard Ke Qaabil Bana Diya', which borrowed from the old couplet—*"Betaabiyaan (*the song used *'Bechainniyan'* instead*) Samet Ke Saare Jahaan Ki/Jab Kuchh Naa Ban Sakaa Toh Mera Dil Banaa Diya"*, credited to Najmi Naginvi though it is also often credited to Jigar Moradabadi.

Kabir's *"Jako Rakhe Saiyan Maar Sake Ka Koe"* was used in *Batla House* (2019) in the song *'Nigaahein Rakh Aasmaan Pe, Ghumade Tu Rukh Dariya Ke'*. However, contrary to the extant film industry conduct, Varun Grover wrote a song *'Tu Kisi Rail Si Guzarti Hai'* (*Masaan*, 2015) based on Dushyant Kumar's poem *'Main Jisse Odhta-Bichhata Hun/Woh Ghazal Aapko Sunata Hun'*, in which the line appears. Grover acknowledged it. So did Irshad Kamil. The song *'Aaj Din Chadiya' (Love Aaj Kal*, 2009), for which Irshad Kamil won his first Filmfare Award, centred on the words written by late poet Shiv Kumar Batalvi—*"Aaj Din Chadeya Tere Rang*

Warga". He took permission from Batalvi's wife. The audio CDs gave credit to the poet and Kamil also dedicated his Filmfare Award to Batalvi.

Incidentally, in *'Nadaan Parindey' (Rockstar*, 2011), Kamil had borrowed lines from the 12th-century Sufi saint Baba Farid—*"Kaga Sab Tan Khaiyo, Mera Chun Chun Khaiyo Maas/ Do Naina Mat Khaiyo, Mohe Piya Milan Ki Aas"*.

In his book of essays, *The Sacred Wood*, poet TS Eliot said: "One of the surest tests [of the superiority or inferiority of a poet] is the way in which a poet borrows... The good poet welds his theft into a whole of feeling which is unique, utterly different than that from which it is torn; the bad poet throws it into something which has no cohesion." What would he have said of such Hindi film songs, had he been around?

10

The Woman Who Broke the Glass Ceiling

Usha Khanna

An abiding mystery for several decades in the Hindi film music industry is the almost complete lack of female composers. Nobody has the answer. Is there a barrier to their entry by filmmakers and male composers? Do the females lack the talent and the smarts to become composers? Do they find other sectors of film music, such as singing, more glamorous or fulfilling?

Do they feel that they will not be taken seriously by the filmmakers, singers and musicians? Do they feel that the sector is too competitive? Do they feel that talent is not enough, and networking and kowtowing would also be required—something that they are not comfortable with?

Is it because they are coy about interacting with men at all levels of the food chain—the filmmaker, the lyricist, the clarinet player, the percussionist—and taking their language, their jokes in stride? Is it because they don't have the patience for the endless hours of 'sittings' before a tune is okayed and they rather take the easy route to fame? Is it a demand-side issue or a supply-side phenomenon? Your guess is as good as mine.

Usha Khanna.

The third woman music director, after Jaddanbai (in the '30s) and Saraswati Devi (from the '30s to '50s), she has been the lone female representative in the 'men's only' club since 1959. She has been active for four decades and this longevity speaks volumes of her talent and tenacity.

By her own account, she did not face any opposition from any quarter and is herself stupefied by the mystery of the missing female baton. She has claimed that all the artists were very good to her. Nobody tried to put her down or patronize her. They would always appreciate good music. However, she did face many challenges. She was only seventeen when she entered the recording studio. On the very first day, she was whistled at. But when the musicians were informed that she was the composer, they went quiet. She went up to all the musicians and made it clear that she was the boss of the recording studio. She told them that they were working under her and if any of them felt otherwise, they were free to leave.

Nobody gave her any chance of survival, let alone make her mark. The rumour mills had it that she wasn't really composing the tunes; someone else was composing for her and her name was being given as a publicity stunt. She had to switch over to sarees from frocks to be taken seriously. In the '60s and '70s, film music composing was marked by informality and unstructured method of working. Filmmakers did not think twice before inviting composers for late night sittings; many times, sitting rooms were dispensed with for, say, a trip to Khandala for an uninterrupted session of listening to and approving tunes. And there was the drinking to get into the mood.

Usha was uncomfortable with this method of working and preferred a professional work environment, with work being done at regular hours, which of course did not happen too often. She also had to battle rumours about affairs, her sexual orientation, and drugs. Consequently, she did very few big banner films and had to be content with low budget films. But she motored on, determined to prove herself.

Even after making music for about 250 films, including regional films in Tamil, Telugu and Gujarati, Usha Khanna did not receive the kind of acclaim that she deserved. She never got invited to the high table.

Usha Khanna's father Manohar Khanna used to work for the Maharaja of Gwalior. He was fond of music and wrote poetry. As a youngster, Usha Khanna used to sing his songs after composing tunes for them. She was not a trained musician, and her talent was God-given. After coming to Bombay, Manohar started working in the film company of Jaddanbai as a writer.

The noted lyricist Indeevar was a family friend. Impressed with Usha Khanna's talent, Indeevar took her to meet Sashadhar Mukherjee, the noted filmmaker and founder of Filmalaya Studios. Usha Khanna sang a few songs, but Mukherjee was unimpressed.

Then Indeevar told Mukherjee about her composing skills. He wasn't interested but nevertheless told her to play a few tunes on the harmonium. When he heard her, he couldn't believe the tunes had been composed by her. Indeevar made her compose tunes for some dummy lyrics. After listening to them, Mukherjee asked his sons—Joy and Dev—to join him. He remarked to them that her music sounded just like OP Nayyar's and that she deserved a break. She was asked to come to Filmalaya office for next one year to compose four new tunes daily.

Unbeknownst to Usha Khanna, OP Nayyar, known for his high fees and arrogance, was not Mukherjee's favourite person those days even though he had delivered him a huge musical hit in *Tumsa Nahin Dekha* (1957) a year earlier. Here was Usha composing in OP Nayyar's style at a fraction of his cost. This was a godsend for Mukherjee to have his cake and eat it too. Usha was handed over the musical directorship of *Dil Deke Dekho* (1959). Any listener could be forgiven to mistake the composer to be OP Nayyar. Even OP Nayyar was surprised to hear the remarkable similarity to his own music. When he first saw Usha as a shy teenager, he could not believe that it was she who had composed those songs. He gave her his blessings and called her his *Putri Paathshaala* (daughter-student)!

The songs were a big hit. Just consider this fabulous collection—from the title song '*Dil Deke Dekho*', to '*O Megha Re Bole*' (the first song she recorded), '*Bolo Bolo Kuchh Toh Bolo*' ("*Pyaar ho toh kehdo yes, pyaar nahin toh kehdo no*"—such a matter-of-fact solicitation had never been attempted before), '*Pyar Ki Kasam Hai*', '*Dilruba Meri Neeta*', '*Yaar Chulbula Hai*', '*Bade Hai Dil Ke Kaale*', '*Do Ekum Do*', '*Rahi Mil Gaye Raahon Mein*', and the ultimate romance-soaked '*Hum Aur Tum Aur Yeh Sama*' (after all the songs had already been picturized, Shammi Kapoor asked Usha Khanna to play a new tune for him. After listening to the tune, he told Mukherjee that he wanted that song in the film at any cost and thus was born this song).

The songs were exuberant, feel-good, youthful and created a rage. Usha had arrived. Rafi sang all the songs—solos and duets (with Asha Bhosle) and what a wonderful job he did. Usha Khanna was all praise for Rafi's humility. At the recording of one of the Asha-Rafi duets, she was not fully satisfied with one part of the song but was hesitant about telling him. He sensed it and told her: "*Usha, tumne humse nahin seekhna. Hamein tumse gaana seekhna hai.*"

Rafi and Usha Khanna would make a formidable pairing and have many hits. Post *Aradhana* (1969), Rafi's self-confidence was at its lowest ebb, and it was Usha Khanna who repaid her debt of gratitude to Rafi when Rafi was voted Best Singer by *Film World* magazine for his empathetic rendition of '*Teri Galiyon Mein Na Rakhenge Kadam Aaj Ke Baad*' from *Hawas* (1974). Bombay's Shanmukhananda Hall was jampacked when it came to be announced that Rafi had been voted Best Singer. The moment Rafi was pronounced the winner, he was a man transformed. All of Rafi's shaken singing confidence thus returned in one stroke—it was his first award in years.

Usha Khanna was most active from the '60s to the '80s. Consider some of the songs from her formidable oeuvre—Mukesh's '*Chhodo Kal Ki Baatein*' from *Hum Hindustani* (1961); Rafi's '*Dil Ke Aaine Mein Tasveer Teri Rehti Hai*' from *Aao Pyaar Karein* (1964); '*Maine Rakha Hai Mohabbat Apne Afsane Ka Naam*' and '*Yeh Teri Saadgi Yeh Tera Baankpan*', both from *Shabnam* (1964; written by Javed Anwar, which was the pen name of her father); '*Haye Tabassum Tera*' from *Nishan* (1965; lyrics again by Javed Anwar); '*Hum Tumse Juda Hoke*' from *Ek Sapera Ek Lutera* (1965); Manna Dey's '*Apne Liye Jiye Toh Kya Jiye*' from *Badal* (1966); Mukesh's '*Chaand Ko Kya Maaloom Chahta Hai Usey Koi Chakor*' from *Lal Bangla* (1966); Rafi's '*Teri Galiyon Mein Na Rakhenge Kadam*' from *Hawas* (1974); Yesudas' '*Madhuban Khushboo Deta Hai*' from *Saajan Bina Suhagan* (1978) and '*Dil Ke Tukde Tukde Karke Muskurake Chal Diye*' from *Dada* (1979) which fetched Yesudas the Filmfare Award; Rafi/Manhar/Hemlata's '*Tu Is Tarah Se Meri Zindagi Mein Shaamil Hai*' from *Aap Toh Aise Na The* (1980)—this was her last song with Rafi and he warmly embraced her after the recording and complimented her on the composition.

She gave music for several Sawan Kumar Tak films (she was briefly married to him). He was the writer, producer, director of his movies, so Usha Khanna found it easy to work with him. He also wrote some songs in his films. They both shared a great rapport. In *Souten* (1983), all the songs were chartbusters. '*Shaayad Meri Shaadi Ka Khayal*' became a craze, as did '*Zindagi Pyaar Ka Geet Hai*'. She received a Filmfare Award nomination for the film.

In B-grade films, she found a way of staying inspired and creative. While composing a Mukesh song, she imagined she was composing for Raj Kapoor; for Kishore's songs it would be Dev Anand and for Rafi's numbers, it would be Dilip Kumar. She never compromised on quality.

The one criticism that dogged Usha Khanna throughout her career was the lack of a distinctive signature, a unique identifiable compositional style which all music directors have. She did not develop any style of her own. In her defence, she has stated that she would always try to follow the winning trend. Music director Laxmikant's wife mistook '*Teri Galiyon Mein Naa Rakhenge Kadam*' (*Hawas*, 1974) as her husband's song and, despite Laxmikant's denial, got enlightened when the radio announcer announced Usha Khanna's name as the composer!

The other criticism, which began from her very first film, was that of plagiarism. She claims that she did not plagiarize any tune, just picked up the basic style and tried to add something of her own. *Dil Deke Dekho* (1959) included some songs inspired from popular Western tunes. The title tune was a rip-off of '*Sugar In The Morning*', though the orchestration and the look and feel of the song were her value addition and took the song to another level.

Usha Khanna claimed that she was expressly asked to use that tune by Mukherjee. Usha Khanna was fascinated by Arabic music and used a lot of it in her songs. She felt it was closer to the Indian style as compared to Western music. She sang several songs too but since composing was her main profession, she did not venture much in that direction, lest her composition got adversely affected.

One such song was '*Shaam Dekho Dhal Rahi Hai*' with Rafi in *Anjaan Hai Koi* (1969). Also, remember the brief female humming/singing in '*Pal Bhar Ke Liye Koi Humme Pyaar Kar Le*' with Kishore in *Johnny Mera Naam* (1970)?

Though her main artistes were Rafi and Asha, Lata too did some great songs with her. The first song that she sang for her was '*Majhi Meri Kismat Ke*' (*Hum Hindustani*, 1960).

Later, Lata became quite friendly with her. Sometimes she would just drop in unannounced at her place if she wanted to avoid a recording. Then the composer would call Usha Khanna to ask if Lata was at her place and Usha Khanna would lie that she wasn't. Then the two of them would spend the time chatting and laughing. But before that, there arose a misunderstanding too which lasted 13 years.

Her devotion to Rafi made her encourage and introduce his voice-alike—artists like Vinod Rathod, Shabbir Kumar, Mohammed Aziz, Pankaj Udhas, Sonu Nigam, and Udit Narayan.

I met Usha Khanna at her modest apartment in Mumbai. We spent a memorable afternoon talking about her life and her music. She had just returned from the recording of a song of *Souten 2* with Javed Ali.

Surprisingly, she seemed to have forgotten some of her famous tunes, which I had to then hum for her. She would smile once she remembered and then take over. I was honoured to have heard Usha Khanna sing a few of her popular songs to me.

She had wonderful words for Rafi. She narrated the incident when she felt embarrassed to approach him, when a song hadn't gone to her satisfaction. Rafi found out and asked Usha Khanna why she hadn't ordered a retake. As the music director, she had the right to order him, and he would have abided willingly.

She narrated a very interesting incident involving Kishore Kumar. Once a Kishore recording of '*Zindagi Pyar Ka Geet Hai*' from *Souten* (1983) had been scheduled. All the musicians were ready.

Then Usha Khanna received a phone call from Kishore that he wouldn't be able to come for the recording as he was not feeling well and advised her to record the orchestra track that day. After a few minutes, just when Usha Khanna was getting ready for the orchestra recording, Kishore walked into the studio. He told her that he had listened to a wrong demo-tape from another composer and had felt that the tune was not good and had decided to cancel the recording. But then he had found the actual tape and after listening to it he changed his mind.

About technology, she admitted that while one could record the singer and instrument tracks separately and then mix them together, the effect one got of recording singers together was altogether different. She gave the example of '*Shaayad Meri Shaadi Ka Khayaal*' (*Souten*, 1983), where one could feel that the singers were enjoying singing together.

Lata's "*Arey Nahin Baba*" was done on the spur of moment as a reaction to Kishore's antics. It was not planned but added so much to the song. That element was missing in contemporary songs. Usha has said that behind every successful woman, there is a woman. And that's Goddess Saraswati. Here's hoping that Goddess Saraswati opens the doors of the recording rooms to other female music directors as well. She has already admitted Sneha Khanwalkar, known for her score for the films *Oye Lucky! Lucky Oye!* (2008) and *Gangs of Wasseypur—Part 1 and 2* (2012), and Jasleen Royal, Alokananda Dasgupta, Rachita Arora, Parampura Thakur, and others.

We are grateful to this pioneering and long-lasting wonderful composer for the memorable music that she has given us. Instead of Shammi Kapoor asking Asha Parekh '*Pyar Ho Toh Kehdo Yes*' (*Dil Deke Dekho*, 1959), Usha could well be asking us the same, and the answer is a resounding "Yes".

11

The Ultimate Singer

Lata Mangeshkar

Adjectives don't always do their job—even the superlative ones. They cannot measure the immeasurable; they fail to quantify the unquantifiable; they fall short of encapsulating the borderless. Sometimes the language cannot describe the Colossus. Superb, fantastic, unbeatable, inimitable, the best—they become meaningless.

Lata sang in many languages. But none of them can capture her artistry, her hold over a nation, her sway over the listeners, her embodiment of the country's soul. No paean can adequately portray this symbol of national integration, this incarnation of the nation's fantasies, this repository of several generations' memories.

So, what does one say?

In creative arts, the finishing line cannot remain static. A highly accomplished artiste, even with the helping hand of God, just as he/she approaches it at the end of a gruelling race, sees it shift further ahead. Another attempt, another shift—marginally beyond reach, never within one's grasp. There is no perfection in creativity. Everything can be improved upon.

But Lata was different. She had breached the finishing line very early in her career and became an earthly embodiment of Goddess Saraswati. She became the personification of 'perfection'. She didn't stop running even though she ran alone. She just kept updating the definition of 'perfection'. She was the journey; she was its end. Others could only watch from a distance and watch the ever-growing chasm.

Many were motivated to bridge it as much as they possibly could.

Her voice soothed you when you were in despair, her voice instilled your chest with pride when you faced hostile bullets, her voice filled your heart with romance when you were in love, her voice suffused your soul with spirituality when you were before God. She was with you through thick and thin, from womb to tomb. She was your life's chronicler, the keeper of your memories. She became part of your daily life. She was ubiquitous. You took her for granted. She never let you down even once. From her phenomenal vault, you could summon any song tailormade for your needs, your mood.

Emotions have countless hues, unlimited dimensions, immeasurable shades. She courted every one of those. Perfect singing is not only about technique; it is also investing it with the right colour.

Lata's was a once-in-a-century earthly presence. It was therefore a given that she would become a legend in her lifetime and become THE VOICE. She went beyond music directors, the lyricists. Any tune, any word would be invested with an ethereal attribute. Her genius would ensure it.

Consider her '*O Sajana Barkha Bahaar Aayi*' (*Parakh*, 1960). It is perfect singing. The delivery, the throw, the intonation, the inflection, the ornamentations, the nuances, the emotions. Even the heavens weep in joy when they hear it.

Or '*Rahein Na Rahein Hum*' (*Mamta*, 1966). Even the most cold-hearted stone in the garden would fail to be unmoved. The trees and the flowers would of course sway in approbation, spreading their perfume at the plighting of one's troth.

As a person, Lata was the girl next door; modest to a fault, simple, sincere. Her playfulness, at unexpected moments, brought out her *joie-de-vivre*. She was forthright about her limitations.

It's not that she didn't have her faults. But in the overall context of her extraordinary contribution to the ever-grateful nation and the die-hard devotees, it pales into insignificance.

All the awards that she received were of course her due. Her contribution to film and non-film music is epoch-making, her position on the pedestal fully earned. The Singing Goddess has brought immense joy and happiness to millions of grateful mortals. The planet has become much better for it.

I was very fortunate and blessed to have met her on two occasions. To commemorate India's victory in the 1971 War, Lata gave a public performance at Ramlila Maidan, Delhi in 1972. She sang *'Sarfaroshi Ki Tamanna'* and *'Jayate Jayate Jayate'* composed by Jaidev. A day earlier, Lata along with Usha, Hridayanath and Jaidev, visited my uncle—late Satish Bhatia—music director, for tea, where I had the ultimate pleasure of meeting her.

The second time I met her in the late '90s at the rehearsal room on the ground floor of Prabhu Kunj, her residence at Pedder Road, Mumbai. She was rehearsing for an upcoming show at Kolkata with Udit Narayan. She met me very warmly. It was an opportunity of a lifetime to be present at her rehearsal and witness first-hand her commitment and passion for her craft.

Matthew Arnold, the Victorian poet and critic wrote the poem 'Shakespeare'. He might as well have been writing of Lata though she would have winced in embarrassment:

"Others abide our question. Thou art free.
We ask and ask—Thou smilest and art still,
Out-topping knowledge. For the loftiest hill,
Who to the stars uncrowns his majesty."

Lata's is beyond discussion; she is beyond comparison. Period!

'Tum Jiyo Hazaaron Saal, Saal Ke Din Hon, Pachaas Hazaar' (*Sujata*, 1959) goes the song sung by Lata's sister. It's a formal salutation by way of a birthday greeting, of course not meant to be taken literally. But in Lata's case, it applies squarely. She will live through her songs which will continue to thrill, to motivate, to edify, to console, and everything else in between, for a long, long time. She now sits at the feet of Goddess Saraswati and teaching Her a thing or two!

12

The Song that Made Nehru Cry

"Koyi Sikh Koyi Jat Maratha, Koyi Gurkha Koyi Madrasi,
Sarhad Par Marnewala, Har Veer Tha Bharat Vaasi,
Jo Khoon Gira Parvat Par, Woh Khoon Tha Hindustani,
Jo Shahid Huye Hain Unki, Zara Yaad Karo Qurbaani"

Even as a six-year-old, these rousing words never failed to move me to tears. HMV had released a 78-RPM disc of '*Ai Mere Watan Ke Logon*' in 1963 which was played regularly on our record-changer. Lata Mangeshkar's pathos-filled rendition of Kavi Pradeep's stirring lyrics, set to a soulful melody by C Ramchandra, held, not only me, but the entire nation in thrall.

Even though it has been ages since Lata sang it on 27th January 1963, at the National Stadium, New Delhi, in the presence of Jawaharlal Nehru, the ditty remains the mother of all Indian patriotic songs. Yet, the song may not have had the above stanza.

In fact, except for the opening stanza, the remaining stanzas that appeared in the song may not have been there at all if C Ramchandra had not chosen them from a hundred (yes, a hundred) stanzas penned by Pradeep. The song may have had different stanzas.

The song may have been sung by Asha Bhosle instead of Lata.

Or it could have been a duet of Lata and Asha. The origin of this song—a national institution—is controversial and there exist many versions. In the wake of the Chinese back-stabbing in 1962, and the gloom and despondency that had descended on the country, film producer Mehboob Khan organized a fund-raiser at the National Stadium, New Delhi to augment the National Defence Fund.

The audience included then President S Radhakrishnan, Prime Minister Nehru, Indira Gandhi, Cabinet ministers, and virtually the entire film industry comprising stalwarts like Dilip Kumar, Dev Anand, Raj Kapoor, Rajendra Kumar, and others.

The programme had songs from Naushad (*'Apni Azadi Ko Hum'*, from *Leader*,1964), Shankar-Jaikishan (*'Hothon Pe Sachhai'*, from *Jis Desh Main Ganga Behti Hai,* 1960), Madan Mohan (*'Kar Chale Hum Fida'*, from *Haqeeqat,* 1964) and C Ramchandra, in that order.

According to Ramchandra, even though he had been selected, he had no song with him. All others were presenting their own film songs. He went to Pradeep and requested him to write a song. Pradeep jokingly responded, "*Phokat ka kaam ho toh aate ho.*" But he did write 100 stanzas of which Ramchandra selected five–six.

In fact, the opening stanza struck Pradeep when he was walking on the Mahim beach in Mumbai. He borrowed a pen from a fellow walker, ripped out the foil from his cigarette packet and penned it down.

They had decided to keep the lyrics a secret. All the earlier songs were fast-paced, forceful and about valour and bravery. Only Pradeep's song spoke about the sacrifices jawans made and how much they suffered. If this concept was revealed, there would have been no element of surprise.

Also, a sad, patriotic song may not have been acceptable to many. The song which was given for the souvenir was deliberately a differently worded song. Hridaynath Chattopadhyay translated the song in English and put his own name, without mentioning Pradeep's.

Asha was chosen by Ramchandra to sing the song, not Lata because he was not on speaking terms with Lata owing to a rift between the two. Asha had also started rehearsals.

Six days before the program, Pradeep called up Ramchandra saying that Lata was ready to sing the song. Ramchandra told him that Asha would be singing. When Pradeep insisted, he relented on the condition that both would sing it as a duet. Pradeep informed Lata and she agreed.

Two days later, he called up Asha and Lata, gave them the song and was about to begin rehearsals when Asha informed Ramchandra that she was not well and would not be able to go to Delhi. In spite of his entreaties, Asha refused to relent and walked out of the project.

Raju Bharatan, the eminent music historian, has a different take on the matter. Lata, who was not on good terms with Ramchandra, agreed to give her voice only on one condition that it would be recorded as a solo. Ramchandra had actually tuned the song into a duet.

Lata, out of the blue, called Pradeep at around six one morning to express her keenness to sing the song provided she could do it as a solo.

Asha had even rehearsed with the composer but was dropped when Lata insisted to record it solo. Pradeep found Ramchandra too to be jumping at this chance to have his very own Lata back to render such a hallmark number. Forgotten in a trice were Ramchandra's long-spread rehearsals with Asha.

The truth according to Lata is, however, different. She stated in an interview that she had initially refused to be a part of the project. It was Pradeep who had approached her to sing the song. She declined because there was no time to rehearse. At that time, she was working round-the-clock and to give special attention to one song seemed impossible. But Pradeep insisted.

Lata revealed that she wanted to sing it with sister Asha, but that didn't happen.

Pradeep wanted it to be a solo. Asha too opted out. Lata tried to convince her to change her mind arguing that her name had even been printed in the newspapers as one of the singers. But Asha did not agree. The singer revealed that she couldn't even rehearse the song properly before performing it in front of the distinguished gathering.

Ramchandra had to be in Delhi at least four days ahead of the performance so he was unable to rehearse the song with Lata. Instead, he gave her a tape of the song. Lata picked up the tune from the tape and flew to Delhi on 26th January 1963, one day before the function.

During the program, Mohammad Rafi's '*Apni Azaadi Ko*' from Dilip Kumar's *Leader* (1964) took the people by storm. It looked as if the show had been stolen by Rafi.

Ramchandra finally took centre stage, with lively rhythmic beats of drums playing in the background. As the sound of the drumbeats faded, the prelude started with Basu Manohari's flute. Then Lata began.

At the end when the chorus sang '*Jai Hind...Jai Hind Ki Sena*', people started looking for the source of the sound, but Ramchandra had hidden the chorus behind the curtain for echo effect and to create an effect of the entire country singing together. The effect was electrifying! Till the song climaxed there was pin drop silence all around. When the song ended, the stadium vibrated with the thunderous sound of claps, whistles and applause.

According to Lata, she was very nervous before the performance and said she was much relieved to get it over with. After she finished, she went backstage to relax with a cup of coffee. Mehboob Khan then came looking for her saying, "*Chalo, Panditji ne bulaya hai.*" Lata stated that Nehru liked the song very much. The song had touched a chord not only with him, but the entire nation traumatized by the Himalayan debacle. Pradeep was not invited to the function. When Nehru visited Mumbai two months later, he sang it especially for him at a function at RM High School and also presented the original handwritten poem to him.

Incidentally, Lata sang nine years later in 1972, again at a public function—this time at the Ram Lila Maidan in Delhi. Except this time, it was against the backdrop of the nation's resounding victory in the 1971 war with Pakistan when the mood of the nation was upbeat.

Under Jaidev's baton, she sang *'Sarfaroshi Ki Tamanna'* and *'Satyamev Jayate'*. I was very fortunate to have met her and Jaidev, along with Usha Mangeshkar and Hridaynath Mangeshkar a day earlier when they had dropped in for a cup of tea at my uncle—the late music director Satish Bhatia's residence.

The Hindi film industry is replete with what ifs, maybes and what might have beens. If SD Burman and Lata had not had a tiff, maybe Asha wouldn't have got to sing his songs during that phase. If Rafi and Lata had not had their tiff, maybe Suman Kalyanpur wouldn't have sung duets with him.

If OP Nayyar and Rafi had not had their tiff, maybe Mahendra Kapoor wouldn't have been allowed inside OP Nayyar's recording studio. What matters is the final product. I can't imagine Lata crooning *'Deewana Mastaana Hua Dil'* (*Bombai Ka Babu,* 1960) with Rafi, nor singing *'Na Na Karte Pyaar Tumhi Se'* (*Jab Jab Phool Khile,* 1965) with Rafi, nor Rafi doing *'Badal Jaaye Agar Mali'* (*Baharen Phir Bhi Aayengi,* 1966). Asha, Suman, and Mahendra Kapoor are well and truly entrenched in our psyche with respect to these songs.

Just as Lata is with this iconic song! Never mind the history. The song still retains its relevance to this day and applies in equal measure to jawans of the armed forces, and paramilitary forces, who not only fight enemies on the border but within the country too.

These jawans sacrifice their lives and in return desire nothing but dignity and respect. If the song doesn't stir us to acknowledge the society's debt towards them, then the song runs the danger of degenerating into a shibboleth, dusted off and polished up on national days. And that would be a tragedy of Himalayan proportions!

13

The Brother Duo

Kalyanji-Anandji

I have a question for people who grew up listening to Hindi music in the 1960s, particularly those who played *antakshari*. Please answer honestly. Which song did you sing when you got the letter 'D' (pronounced as in Delhi)? *'Dum Dum Diga Diga'* (*Chhalia*, 1960)? And which song came straight out of your mouth when you got 'N'? *'Na Na Kar Ke Pyaar Tumhi Se Kar Baithe'* (*Jab Jab Phool Khile*, 1965)? Who composed these songs?

The entire country loves the song *'Man Dole Mera Tan Dole'* from *Nagin* (1954) composed by Hemant Kumar, who achieved a meteoric rise in popularity because of the film. But the main attraction which has made the song iconic is the *been*. The melody of the *been* is deeply entrenched in our national consciousness. It has been the anthem of the snake charmers (now an almost extinct breed). If snakes could hear, they would have loved it and swayed from side to side even if their handler sat still. However, the *dhun* was not played on the *been* but on the clay violin (an early version of the synthesizer). Who played the instrument?

Who composed one the greatest patriotic songs— *'Mere Desh Ki Dharti'* in *Upkar* (1967), earning Manoj Kumar the tag of Mr Bharat? And while on the song, who can forget the seamless slide of the interlude music from the nightclub to the rustic when showing the different trajectories of Manoj Kumar and his younger brother Prem Chopra!

Who composed the song *'Kasme Vaade Pyar Wafa Sab'* (*Upkar*, 1967) that changed the image of Pran, and fetched him the Filmfare Best Supporting Actor, not as a villain but for his first positive character role?

Who can forget the song *'She's Very Pretty; Pretty Pretty Priya'* (*Priya,* 1970)? One of the first Hindi songs with the *mukhra* entirely in English and with such a catchy tune. Composer?

Which music director gave us Shammi Kapoor singing not in one, not in two but in four voices (including female) in *Bluff Master* (1963)?

Which music director gave us *'Govinda Ala Re'* (*Bluff Master,* 1963)—a must-play song during the Dahi-Handi festivities?

Who got actors to sing at least one song in their films—Nanda (*'Ek Tha Gul Aur Ek Thi Bulbul'*, *Jab Jab Phool Khile,* 1965); Hema Malini (*'Peene Wale Ko Peene Ka Bahana Chahiye'*, *Haath Ki Safai,* 1974); Nutan (*'Boli Sawan Ki Raat Badi Paawan Hai Baat'*, *Yaadgaar,* 1970); Mehmood (*'Yeh Duniya Motorgadi…Puncture'*, *Kangan,* 1972); Amitabh Bachchan (*'Mere Angane Mein'*, *Lawaris,* 1981), Mala Sinha (*'Mere Mehboob'*, *Lalkaar,* 1972)?

The answer to all the above is Kalyanji-Anandji.

Kalyanji Virji Shah and Anandji Virji Shah hailed from the traditional trading community of the Kutchis. They started their career by way of film orchestras and conducting live bands. Kalyanji was Hemant Kumar's assistant. Later, he turned independent, and his first composing assignment was *Chandragupta* (1955). In 1958, he had his first hit with Hemant-Lata in *'Neend Na Mujhko Aaye'* (*Post Box 999*). Then he teamed up with his brother Anandji to create another Hemant-Lata melody *'Tumhe Yaad Hoga'* (*Satta Bazaar,* 1959).

Their first hit film was *Chhalia* with memorable songs such as *'Dum Dum Diga Diga'*, *'Mere Toote Hue Dil Se Koi Toh Aaj Ye Poochhe'*, *'Chhalia Mera Naam'*, *'Baje Payal*

Chham Chham Hoke Beqaraar' and *'Teri Rahon Mein Khade Hai Dil Tham Ke'* (this song also featured in the Pakistani play *Humsafar* starring Fawad Khan and Mahira Khan). Incidentally, the word *'Chhaliya'* (cheat) used in the title song of *Chhaliya* was disapproved by the Censor Board. The phrase *'Chhalna Mera Kaam'* had to be replaced with *'Chhaliya Mera Naam'*.

Some films that followed were *Dulha Dulhan* (1964); *Himalaya Ki God Mein* (1965)— songs such as *'Main Toh Ek Khwaab Hoon'* and *'Chand Si Mehbooba Ho Meri'* (winning the duo the Cine Music Directors Association Award for best musical score); *Jab Jab Phool Khile* (1965) with songs such as *'Ek Tha Gul Aur Ek Thi Bulbul', 'Pardesiyon Se Na Ankhiyan Milana', 'Yahan Main Ajnabi Hoon', 'Ye Samaa, Samaa Hai Ye Pyaar Ka', 'Na Na Karte Pyaar Tumhi Se Kar Baithe'*; *Upkar* (1967); *Raaz* (1967).

With *Saraswatichandra* (1968), they reached their zenith—*'Chandan Sa Badan', 'Main Toh Bhool Chali Babul Ka Des', 'Chhod De Saari Duniya Kisi Ke Liye', 'Phool Tumhe Bheja Hai Khat Mein'*. They deservingly won the National Award—the first music directors in Hindi cinema.

The year 1970 saw *Johny Mera Naam*—*'Pal Bhar Ke Liye Koi Humen Pyar Karle', 'O Mere Raja'*. In *Safar*—with songs such as *'Zindagi Ka Safar'* and *'Jeevan Se Bhari'*, they brought out the serious singer in Kishore Kumar, a facet under-utilized in his career. Then *Purab Aur Paschim*— *'Koi Jab Tumhara Hriday Tod De'*.

The 1970s saw *Zanjeer* (1973)—*'Yaari Hai Imaan Mera'*; *Blackmail* (1973)—*'Pal Pal Dil Ke Pass'*; *Kora Kagaz* (1974)—*'Mera Jeevan Kora Kaagaz'* (which fetched them their only Filmfare Award); *Don* (1978)—*'Khaike Paan Banaraswala'*; *Muqaddar Ka Sikander* (1979)—*'O Saathi Re'*.

The 1980s began with a bang—*Qurbani* (1980)—*'Laila O Laila'* (they took the inclusion of Nazia Hassan's *'Aap*

Jaisa Koi' composed by Biddu in their stride though they certainly were hurt); *Vidhaata* (1982), *Laawaris* (1982), *Jaanbaaz* (1986). By the end of the decade, they realized their time was over.

They innovated with rhythms to create rhythmic interest. Say, *'Nafrat Karnewalon Se'* (*Johnny Mera Naam*, 1970). Here the stanza is recited or spoken before it is rendered as a song. This breaks the mechanical progression of the fast pace and makes the song textured and interesting. Similarly, in *'Na Na Na Karte'* (*Jab Jab Phool Khile*, 1965), there is recourse to conversational interjections in between the fast tempo.

The sedate rhythms, soothing mix of strings, santoor, piano, guitar, saxophone in the slower compositions was their forte. Their use of simple tunes and basic rhythms were often mistaken for lack of musical intricacy, but their songs had an extraordinary mood-building ability.

It was in Mukesh's voice that Kalyanji-Anandji would find their identity. The true range and depth of Mukesh as a singer came in their compositions. The songs Mukesh sang for them rank among their best compositions. Kalyanji-Anandji were gracious enough to acknowledge that Mukesh was their ladder of success and recognition in the 1960s.

They were the finest exponents of the tandem/twin song genre. For example, Lata's version of Mukesh's *'Mujhko Is Raat Ki Tanhai Mein'* (*Dil Bhi Tera Hum Bhi Tere*, 1960) and *'Humne Tujhko Pyar Kiya Hai Itna'* (*Dulha Dulhan*, 1964); or Rafi's *'Dil Beqaraar Sa Hai* '(*Ishara*, 1964) and '*Pardesiyon Se Na Akhiyaan Milana'* (*Jab Jab Phool Khile*, 1965).

Sometimes the same singer would sing the happy and sad versions. Lata sang both versions of the *'Mehendi Lagi Mere Haath'* title song (1962). Sometimes they pitted a romantic duet version against a sentimental solo version: Rafi-Lata's romantic *'Mere Mitwa Mere Geet Re'* (*Geet*, 1970) against Rafi's sentimental solo version.

Sometimes they presented two versions with different refrains and totally opposite lyrical themes—Lata's joyous *'Ik Tu Jo Mila Sari Duniya Mili'* and her emotional *'Ek Tu Na Mila Sari Duniya Mile Bhi Toh Kya Hai'* (*Himalaya Ki God Mein*, 1965).

They remained well-versed with changing musical trends. Their understanding of traditional forms of Indian music was exceptional. They had a fine flair for regional folk music, catchy dance numbers, soulful devotional songs, children's songs—you name it.

Yet, they were not trend-setters, never demanded their listener's attention nor shocked them into a new musical consciousness. They created simple tunes that appealed to everyone. No complex melodies or rhythms. Lot of importance to words and making music appropriate to the situation in the film. Their songs became very popular, good hummable tunes.

They composed from 1959 to 1991, a total of about 260 films. Their best work happened between 1960 and 1970. However, during the 1980s, when mainstream film music hit an all-time low, Kalyanji-Anandji, like others, succumbed to the Bappi Lahiri phenomenon, churning out banalities like *'Saath Saheliyan Khadi Khadi'* (*Vidhata*, 1982).

Their success during the three decades they were active came without resorting to any manipulative tactics. They had their heads on their shoulders, winning them respect and affection from the film industry. They were also recipient of the Lata Mangeshkar Award and were conferred with the Padma Shri.

They introduced many new singers—Manhar Udhas, Udit Narayan, Anuradha Paudwal, Sadhna Sargam, Alka Yagnik, Kanchan, Sunidhi Chauhan.

Kalyanji-Anandji were the first music directors to organize stage shows in India and abroad from the 1970s onwards. They conducted thousands of successful shows in which the who's who of Bollywood participated. Later, after the ill health of Kalyanji, Anandji would conduct the orchestra. In the 1990s, Anandji began Little Stars—a platform for talented youngsters.

In the late 1990s and early 2000s, their work was introduced to a young Western audience by three albums—*Bombay the Hard Way: Guns, Cars and Sitars* (in which their songs were given a funky re-mix); *Bollywood Funk* (which, among other music directors, also had six of their tracks); and *The Beginner's Guide To Bollywood* (which had some of their tracks). Their composition '*Pal Bhar Ke Liye*' was used in an episode of *The Simpsons*.

On 24th August 2000, Kalyanji breathed his last. A chowk in Malabar Hill called Kalyanji Virji Shah Chowk, named in his honour, is not very far from where I lived when I was in Mumbai. I had the good fortune of meeting Anandji at his Peddar Road residence. Sadhna Sargam was also present, and it was fascinating to discuss his glorious stint in the Hindi film industry and the work he was doing regarding Little Stars.

'*Aaja Tujhko Pukare Mere Geet Re*' (*Geet*, 1970) goes one of their popular songs. The outstanding oeuvre that the brothers have given to the country will ensure just that!

14
The Brown Blues Singer

Mukesh

If Mukesh had applied for audition at the All India Radio, he probably would have failed. Or, if he were lucky, perhaps got a B grade—the lowest grade awarded to artists based on the performance quality adjudged by a Committee of Eminent Musicians and Experts (B-High, A, and Top being the other grades).

At some places in the song, he may have been found to be *be-sura*, or, perhaps, out of beat. The Committee would have found his diction to be wanting in some parts. The judges would have found his range to be limited, his voice nasal. They would have discovered that he had no classical training and could not do an *alaap*—forget the *alankars*. He would not have ticked most boxes in the judges' scoring sheet as laid down by the State-owned broadcaster. The judges' hands would betied.

But they would have gone home and felt very uneasy, very guilty. The singer may have been imperfect, may not have had the technique, but he had touched their hearts. They could feel the pathos in his voice, the sincerity in his rendition, the innate sadness in every word that was sung.

There was directness in his approach; there were no filters in his outpouring. His singing was primal, unadulterated, simple, and appealing to the soul.

At the audition, they had used their minds and failed him. At home, they were using their hearts, and would have passed him with flying colours.

A gem is a gem, polished or not.

In the early 1920s, HMV had rejected SD Burman for his nasal twang. KL Saigal also met the same fate.

It is a good thing that Mukesh did not venture close to AIR but carved an independent path right from day one. In any case, since he started off as an actor-singer, radio was not on his 'to-do' list.

My own maternal uncle, the late Satish Bhatia, who retired as a Chief Producer (Light Music), AIR, and must have sat on many such auditions, himself used Mukesh when he composed music for V Shantaram's '*Boond Jo Ban Gay Moti*' (1967). The song, '*Yeh Kaun Chitrakar Hai*', which became a huge hit, could not have been delivered by any of the AIR-empanelled singers with the same emotion and feeling that Mukesh brought to it.

My mother, Usha Bhatia, herself a radio artist, sang at a live show alongside Mukesh and Geeta Roy at Odeon Theatre in the early 1950s. So impressed was Mukesh with her singing, that he presented her a Saima Swiss watch, which she has still preserved as a prized memento.

To express tiredness and disappointment with society, a distinctive kind of voice is required. A rich baritone works great. If the voice has no frills and is sourced not from the lungs, but straight from the heart, it summons up something that is ethereal and soulful. If the voice can convey life's truths with a feeling of longing and tenderness, it can move even an obstinate boulder. If the voice is filled with character, originality and straightforwardness, it can bring tears to the eye.

That would be Mukesh.

He communicated emotion—especially the sadder variant—in a way that was unparalleled. He conveyed the *dard* to his audience. He was a blues singer who wore a brown skin and sang in Hindi.

He was a singer who thoroughly internalized the words of the songs he sang, becoming the messenger of the poet. The simple packaging of the words ensured their optimal registration in the minds of the listeners. The simplicity may have been mocked by some, but it served the purpose of the song. He was truly a man of the masses.

Comparisons are odious, yet, to understand his impact, it is nevertheless necessary. Let us see how Mukesh (who was not even considered worthy of Padma Shri) stacks up against Bharat Ratna Lata Mangeshkar—the complete singer, the perfect nightingale—in twin or tandem songs (same or similar song sung by two different singers).

Decide for yourselves.

Take *'Aa Laut Ke Aja Mere Meet'* (*Rani Rupmati*, 1957). Can you imagine any other singer doing justice to this song, Lata included?

In *'Mujhko Is Raat Ki Tanhai Mein'* (*Dil Bhi Tera Hum Bhi Tere*, 1960)—Mukesh wins with a massive public approbation. Then there are songs like—*'Humne Tujhko Pyar Kiya Hai Jitna'* (*Dulha Dulhan*, 1964), *'Jyot Se Jyot Jagate Chalo'* (*Sant Gyaneshwar*, 1964), *'Jis Dil Mein Basa Tha Pyar Tera'* (*Saheli*, 1965), and so on. Of course, in some songs, the honours were even but never inferior—*'Raat Aur Din Diya Jale'* (*Raat Aur Din*, 1967) and *'Chandan Sa Badan'* (*Saraswatichandra*, 1968).

Let us see how Rafi compares with Mukesh. Consider *'Saranga Teri Yaad Mein'* (*Saranga*, 1961). The composition of the song was such that only the 'Emperor of Melancholy' could do full justice to it. No other male singer, including Rafi in this case, could even come close. Many do not know that Rafi also rendered this song; his version is relatively unknown.

Even Manna Dey could not best Mukesh's heart-touching rendition of *'Zindagi Khwaab Hai'* (*Jaagte Raho*, 1956). Mukesh invested the song with such intensity and emotion, and with such consummate ease—he did not even have to try—his voice was suffused with it by default. But Manna's version, otherwise technically the best Hindi film singer, seemed contrived.

Forget twin songs. Even in films where he got only one song to sing, he normally outshone the other male songs. '*Chal Ri Sajni*'—a background song in *Bombai Ka Babu* (1960) was a huge hit besting Rafi's '*Saathi Na Koi Manzil*'. Mukesh got the song only because Kishore Kumar turned it down, since the song was not picturized on Dev Anand whose main voice in the film was Rafi.

SD Burman had many misgivings about entrusting the song to Mukesh. If the Mukesh recording turned out to be unsatisfactory, SD Burman had threatened to scrap the song. However, such was the spell cast by Mukesh, that the song was retained. The "not a good singer" (as SD Burman rated him) had weaved his magic.

In *Bandini* (1963), Mukesh was again summoned by SD Burman for the atmospheric number '*O Jaane Waale Ho Sake Toh Laut Ke Aana*'. SD Burman—the Bengali folksinger par excellence that he was—also sang '*O Re Maajhi… O Re Maajhi*'. But Mukesh eclipsed him in popularity with his rendition.

Salil Chowdhury wanted '*Suhana Safar Aur Ye Mausam Haseen*' on Dilip Kumar in *Madhumati* (1958) to be sung by Hemant Kumar. Could Hemant Kumar have—even with the allure of temple bells in his voice—done a better job than Mukesh? You decide.

Dilip Kumar initially wanted Talat Mehmood for both '*Suhana Safar*' and '*Toote Hue Khawabon Ne*'. Could Talat have delivered the goods? Rafi ultimately sang '*Toote Hue Khawabon*'. Yet, did Rafi's '*Toote Hue*' displace Mukesh's '*Suhana Safar*'? You decide.

And there is no dearth of such instances, where just one song by Mukesh in a film, emerged on top.

It's not that Mukesh was not aware of his limitations; nor was he averse to criticism. But he took it in his stride.

Sometimes, while singing 'live' with Lata, he would jocularly ask the audience whether they knew why Lata was the greatest singer—it was only because she had such an out-of-tune singing partner like him! And this from a singer who had rendered absolute top-drawer duets with Lata like '*Bade Armaano Se Rakha Hai Kadam*' (*Malhar*, 1951), '*Dekho Mausam Kya Bahaar Hai*' (*Opera House*, 1961), '*Dil Tadap Tadap Ke Keh Raha Hai*' (*Madhumati*, 1958), '*Sawan Ka Mahina*' (*Milan*, 1967), '*Phool Tumhe Bheja Hai*' (*Saraswatichandra*, 1968), '*Ek Pyaar Ka Naghma Hai*' (*Shor*, 1972), '*Kabhi Kabhi Mere Dil Mein*' (*Kabhi Kabhie*, 1976), and so many others.

However, to assign only the melancholy slot to Mukesh would not be correct. He could also belt out light numbers with consummate ease. Songs like '*Ruk Jaa O Jaane Wali Ruk Jaa*' (*Kanhaiya*, 1959), '*Aasman Pe Hai Khuda*' (*Phir Subah Hogi*, 1958), '*Itna Husn Pe Guroor Na Kijiye*' (*Mohabbat Isko Kehte Hain*, 1964), and others are a testimony to this facet of his oeuvre.

Born in Delhi on 22nd July 1923, Mukesh left for Bombay soon after finishing Matriculation to try his hand at acting. At the age of 18, he made his film debut as a hero opposite Nalini Jaywant in Ranjit Movietone's *Nirdosh* (1941). A strong recommendation from his relative, noted actor Motilal, gave Mukesh this opportunity. He also sang his first movie song '*Dil Hi Bujha Hua Ho Toh*', composed by Ashok Ghosh.

Both the movie and the song sank without any trace. His other acting ventures also met with the same fate. Hence, acting had to be given up and full-time playback singing had to be taken up to keep body and soul together.

His first singing success came in *Paheli Nazar* (1945) under the baton of Anil Biswas. Mukesh wanted to be the second KL Saigal. So, Anil Biswas cast him in the mould of KL Saigal through the poignant '*Dil Jalta Hai to Jalne De*'. The song was a massive hit.

Who could have known that a slap could change the destiny of a man and that of the film industry? Indeed, without that slap, Mukesh would not have been the Mukesh we know.

During the rehearsal, Mukesh could not grasp the complexities of the song. When he kept failing, Anil Biswas told him that he would sing the song himself. Reportedly, Mukesh complained to some people that if composers started singing their own songs, what would happen to singers?

Anil Biswas heard about it and agreed to let Mukesh sing. On the day of the recording, the musicians had finished, and Mukesh had not arrived. Anil Biswas got very upset. He was informed that Mukesh was drinking at a bar because he was very nervous and felt that he will not be able to sing.

Anil Biswas went to the bar and picked him up by the collar. He did his best to shake him out of the haze by putting his head under the tap and giving him a glass of black coffee. When a sobered-up Mukesh expressed his inability to bring pain into his singing, Anil Biswas reportedly slapped him hard and asked him to bring that very pain into the recording room.

Mukesh could have objected and walked out of the song, and, effectively, the film industry. But he chose not to and never held a grudge against Anil Biswas for the rest of his life.

Anil Biswas told Mukesh that they had both proved that they could do a KL Saigal. Now they had to prove that Mukesh was Mukesh, the authentic product, not just an imitation of KL Saigal. Instead, he advised him to develop his own style.

Anil Biswas' *Anokha Pyar* (1948) and Naushad's *Mela* (1948) and *Andaz* (1949) presented Mukesh in his own original style as Dilip Kumar's voice. Songs like '*Gaaye Ja Geet Milan Ke*', '*Dharti Ko Aakash Pukare*', '*Main Bhanwara Tu Hai Phool*' and '*Mera Dil Todne Wale*' from *Mela* (1948); '*Jhoom Jhoom Ke Naacho Aaj*', '*Tu Kahe Agar*', '*Toote Na Dil Toote Na*', and '*Hum Aaj Kahin Dil Kho Baithe*' from *Andaz* (1949) became a rage.

Naushad too had a role to play in the transformation. Mukesh had a drinking problem in his initial years as a singer. One day Naushad caught him drunk during the daytime and told him that he had already proved with '*Dil Jalta Hai*' that he could do a KL Saigal. What was it that he was now trying to prove—that he could out-do Saigal in drinking too?

Mukesh was in tears. Naushad demonstrated to him that he had a voice identifiably his own, which would prove his vocal credentials.

The association with Dilip Kumar was short-lived as Dilip Kumar switched over first to Talat and then to Rafi as his playback.

However, you cannot keep a good talent down. Raj Kapoor stepped in. In *Aag* (1948), Mukesh sang '*Zinda Hoon Is Tarah*' for Raj Kapoor and a life-long partnership came into existence. Mukesh's voice was tailor-made for Raj Kapoor's screen image of a tragicomic tramp, prompting Raj Kapoor to state that he was just a body, and Mukesh was his soul.

The role of Raj Kapoor in making Mukesh a star was huge. Raj played the role of an impoverished simpleton who only Mukesh could best articulate. In post-Independence India, where innocence clashed with the harsh hurly-burly of reality, the resultant despondency required a voice and who better than Mukesh to convey pain and angst, yet never losing hope.

Backed with Shankar-Jaikishan's outstanding music, the message went through. The songs, right from *Barsaat* (1949) to *Mera Naam Joker* (1970) are many and well-known and do not require any detailing.

Kalyanji-Anandji were also firmly in Mukesh's corner and served the listeners some delectable numbers such '*Chhalia Mera Naam*', '*Mere Toote Hue Dil Se*', '*Dum Dum Diga Diga*' (*Chhalia*, 1960), '*Mujhko Is Raat Ki Tanhai Mein*' (*Dil Bhi Tera Hum Bhi Tere*, 1960), '*Hum Chhod Chale Hain Mehfil Ko*' (*Ji Chahta Hai*, 1964); '*Main To Ek Khwab Hoon*', '*Chand Si Mehbooba Ho*' (*Himalaya Ki God Mein*, 1965); '*Waqt Karta Jo Wafaa*' (*Dil Ne Pukara*, 1967), '*Deewanon Se Yeh Mat Poochho*' (*Upkar*, 1967), '*Chandi Ki Deewar*' (*Vishwas*, 1969), '*Koi Jab Tumhara Hriday Tod De*' (*Purab Aur Paschim*, 1970), and so many others.

Laxmikant-Pyarelal also had Mukesh's back. Consider some of the songs—'*Saawan Ka Mahina*' and '*Ram Kare Aisa Ho Jaaye*' (*Milan*, 1967), '*Ek Pyar Ka Naghma Hai*' (*Shor*, 1972), '*Mai Na Bhoolunga*' (*Roti, Kapada Aur Makaan*, 1974).

Similarly, Roshan also swore by him and produced outstanding songs: '*Tum Agar Mujhko Na Chaaho Toh*' (*Dil Hi To Hai*, 1963), '*Baharon Ne Mera Chaman*' (*Devar*, 1966), '*Oh Re Taal Mile Nadi Ke Jal Mein*' (*Anokhi Raat*, 1968).

Likewise, with Salil Chowdhury, Mukesh sang such immortal songs: '*Maine Tere Liye Hi Saat Rang Ke*' and '*Kahin Door Jab Din Dhal Jaaye*' (*Anand*, 1971), and '*Kayee Baar Yoon Hi Dekha Hai*' (*Rajnigandha*, 1974).

Mukesh was a creature of the laidback, idealistic, and empathetic times of the 1950s and '60s. He helped shape these times. But with Hindi film themes changing tack from the mid-'70s, with social themes being supplanted by revenge and gore, with *dard* not the flavour of the season, with simpletons being classed as losers, Mukesh's role began diminishing, though even the few songs he did continued to be chartbusters.

He died at the young age of 53, during a tour of the USA in 1976 along with Lata.

Singers like Mukesh are rare. His output was miniscule compared to his peers. But each song is outstanding.

Mukesh will be remembered as a singer who left an indelible imprint on the national consciousness by his charismatic voice, his simplicity in singing, his abiding humility, his emotional depth, and his art of communication.

He may have lacked in technique but not in his best impulses. His vulnerability, his imperfections, made him accessible to the listener. His sincerity of spirit aimed straight at the heart.

"Sab Kuchh Seekha Usne, Na Seekhi Hoshiyari, Sach Hai Duniyawalo Ki Woh Tha Anari."

That is why Mukesh will live on forever.

15

When Actors Outsource Their Songs to Buskers

Amitabh Bachchan's breakout film, *Zanjeer* (1973), has a duet *'Deewaane Hain Deewano Ko Na Ghar Chaahiye, Muhabbat Bhari Ik Nazar Chaahiye'*. But the song is not sung on screen by Amitabh and Jaya Bhaduri. Amitabh's role in the film is too serious—of an angry young man—to warrant a song and dance routine, though Jaya has no such issues, having sung *'Chakku Chhuriyan Tez Kara Lo'* earlier in the film. So how is the budding romance between the two protagonists to be depicted on screen, when the male lead has been forbidden to do so by the film's script? Enter the buskers Gulshan Bawra (playing the harmonium), also the film's lyricist, and a minor actress Sanjana. They sing with gay abandon on behalf of Amitabh and Jaya, expressing the emotions raging inside the hero and heroine, as they watch the street song from Amitabh's house while simultaneously exchanging coy glances at each other.

Incidentally, singer Mohammad Rafi had been fasting and was a bit irritable during the song's recording. One 'take' of the song had been okayed by the music directors Kalyanji-Anandji, but co-singer Lata Mangeshkar wanted a retake. Uncharacteristically, Rafi refused. Gulshan Bawra followed him out of the studio and told him that he was going to enact this song on screen. Rafi came back and gave two 'takes' and sang it in a way that suited Gulshan Bawra's persona.

A year later, in *Majboor* (1974), Amitabh would step out of the room and try to placate Parveen Babi through the good offices of the beach buskers (in the voice of Rafi and Asha Bhosle)— harmonium and all—in '*Roothe Rab Ko Manana Aasaan Hai, Roothe Yaar Ko Manana Mushqil Hai*'.

Buskers in India, like their Western counterparts in markets, metros, pavements, street corners, beaches, waterfronts, railway stations, entertain the public. But unlike the western counterparts, they also play a role in films by vicariously conveying the feelings of the actors who cannot or will not do it themselves. These buskers play the role of their surrogate—they deputize for them to ensure that film story continues its journey.

Hindi films are replete with this fascinating cinematic device.

A similar song was enacted in *CID* (1956) with a harmonium-slung Shyam Kapoor (Rafi) and flautist Sheila Vaz (Shamshad Begum), singing '*Leke Pehla Pehla Pyar*' on behalf of Dev Anand and Shakila. The debonair, and clearly love-struck, Dev would have done the honours himself, but his love-interest is in no mood. Enter the buskers as the outsourced service providers. The lady dancer confronts Shakila—"*Mukhde pey daley hue zulfon ki badli, chali balkhati kahan ruk ja o pagli*". In the later stanza, she continues—"*Dekha aisa mantar maar, akhir hogi teri haar, jadunagri se aaya hai koi jadugar*". All this while, Dev walks behind Shakila, egging the buskers on. The experiment works and the lady eventually, whilst at her house, melts. The buskers having done their job and left the screen, she (in the voice of Asha Bhosle) laments—"*Uski deewani haai kahun kaise ho gayi, jadugar chala gaya main toh yahan kho gayi*".

The harmonium again appears (street-singers cannot do without it) in the song '*Bichhde Hue Milenge Phir, Kismet Ne Gar Mila Diya*' (*Post Box 999*, 1958). There is a dholak player too, and a female dancer. Shakila (unamused) and Sunil Dutt (smiling) are amongst the audience. The song not only takes care of them, but Leela Chitnis too, craning her neck—the song articulating her conviction that those separated would meet again one day.

Sheila Vaz reprises her role as a busker in *'Jab Hum Tum Dono Razi, Toh Kya Karega Qazi'* in *Bade Sarkar* (1957). The ubiquitous harmonium, along with the dholak, is in attendance. Kishore Sahu and Kamini Kaushal have had a lover's tiff. Vaz (in the voice of Asha) proclaims—*"Kyun duniya ke pichhe bhage, kuchh nahin duniya dil ke aage, dekh nazara pakad ke hath humara, samajh le dil ka ishara, jamaa le rang zaraa"*.

In *Dil Apna Aur Preet Parai* (1960), the minor actor Raj Kishore wields the guitar, while a female extra plays the harmonium, and a male extra, the dholak. Raj Kishore (in Rafi's voice) sings *'Jaane Kahan Gayi, Dil Mera Ley Gayi Woh'*, echoing Raj Kumar's anguish at his doomed love affair with Meena Kumari (all works out well in the end though). A dejected Raj Kumar, sitting on a rock next to the sea, could not have been expected to sing the song of separation; it did not suit his character. Enter the trio and sing on his behalf.

This phenomenon is as old as the films. As long back as in 1937, *Izzat* had a song—*'Prem Dor Mein Baandh Hume, Kit Chale Gaye Girdhari'* sung by minor actors in the voice of Ashok Kumar and Devika Rani (music by Saraswati Devi) for Devika Rani pining for Ashok Kumar. For a brief period during the song, she dreams of herself singing it with Ashok Kumar. Even the actress credited with the longest kiss in Hindi films (in *Karma*, 1933) could be coy and let others emote for her!

And the list goes on. *'Mohabbat Ka Haath, Jawani Ka Palla'* in *Howrah Bridge* (1958) on Ashok Kumar and Madhubala; *'Ek Bewafa Se Pyar Kiya'* in *Awara* (1951) on Nargis; *'Nain Khoye Khoye'* in *Munimji* (1955) on Dev Anand and Nalini Jaywant; *'Nigahon Ka Ishara Hai'* in *Night Club* (1958) on

Ashok Kumar and Kamini Kaushal; *'Dhalti Jaaye Raat, Kehde Dil Ki Baat'* in *Razia Sultana* (1961) on Jairaj and Nirupa Roy.

It is not only the buskers who put to song the emotions heaving inside the hearts of the main actors. There is another equally important category—the boatman. He not only plies his trade in ferrying people across the river, but also creates the atmosphere, the mood, the ambience by singing (usually) a philosophical ditty. And, sometimes gives voice to the innermost feelings of the main cast.

The iconic *'Sun Mere Bandhu Re'* in *Sujata* (1959) is one such song. If Hemant Kumar is considered the voice of God, SD Burman, who also composed the song, is the ghost voice of all Bengali boatmen. His voice was plaintive, serene, slow and melodious. In this song, picturized on the romancing Sunil Dutt and Nutan, the song evocatively captures their mutual feelings for each other.

In *'Ulajh Gaye Do Naina'* from *Ek Saal* (1959), Ashok Kumar and Madhubala are in love, and it shows. But they have inhibitions in declaring it to each other. How to overcome the reserve and communicate their feeling? Enter the boatman and his wife to shoulder the responsibility. The couple is relieved.

In *'Kho Gaya Hai Mera Pyaar'* from *Haryali aur Raasta* (1962), the boatman ferrying Mala Sinha away from Manoj Kumar, who watches it sail away from the riverbank, understands what Manoj Kumar is going through and breaks into the song, very apposite in the circumstances. The boatman is also prescient enough to sing in the voice of Mahendra Kapoor who would be a very successful ghost voice of Manoj in later films, though in this film Mukesh does the honours in other songs.

There is also a song, not sung by, but addressed to a boatman: *'O Mere Majhi, Mere Sajan Hain Us Paar'* in *Bandini*

(1963). SD Burman's pathos-soaked voice (who also composed the song) suited Ashok Kumar's melancholia perfectly. The song is set on a riverbank with a steamer about to depart, and evocatively captures the struggle of Nutan to choose between the ailing love of her life Ashok Kumar and the young doctor who loves her and could give her a comfortable life (Dharmendra). The entreaty works eventually—Nutan abandons the train which is about to depart and makes it to the steamer in the nick of time on which Ashok Kumar is travelling. Incidentally, most songs of SD Burman were about creating the atmosphere, and not as a vicarious platform. But the song such as this was an exception.

Mukesh too, with his unique voice, served as the voice of boatman. *'Kaise Manau Piyawa'* in *Char Diwari* (1961) beautifully captures the emotions of Shashi Kapoor for Nanda on their wedding night.

Then there are itinerant singers, such as *baul* singers, who do the needful.

'Aaj Sajan Mohe Ang Laga Lo' from *Pyasa* (1957) is one such song where the *baul* singer (in the voice of Geeta Dutt) echoes Waheeda Rehman's yearning for Guru Dutt.

Or they could be villagers in a pastoral setting, or people in slums, or fishing villages or tribal people singing what the actors would want to sing.

In *'O Meri Pran Sajni, Champawati Aaja'* from *Annadata* (1972), a village couple—Gopi Krishna (the dance maestro) and Madhumati—express their love for each other on behalf of Anil Dhawan and Jaya Bhaduri whose shyness prevents them from taking matters in their own hands.

In *'Mere Jeewan Mein Kiran Bankey Bikharney Walley, Bolo Tum Kaun Ho'* from *Talaq* (1958), the villagers sing on behalf of Rajendra Kumar and Kamini Kadam.

'So Rahe Hain Bekhabar, Sonewale Gaon Mein, Aan Milo Balma Taron Ki Chhaon Mein' in *Hulchul* (1951) deals with

Nargis' feelings for Dilip Kumar. Dilip wants to reciprocate but unfortunately there is no male amongst the bevy of female villagers.

'Laagi More Man Ki O Sajana, Zara Yaad Rakhna' from *Shabab* (1954) has villagers sing for Bharat Bhushan and Nutan.

'Mose Rooth Gaye More Ram Re' in *Karigar* (1958) is sung by temple singers on behalf of Nirupa Roy for Ashok Kumar.

'Ho Jab Se Mili Tose Ankhiyan' in *Amaanat* (1955) is sung by villagers for Bharat Bhushan and Chand Usmani.

'Ab Toh Ji Hone Laga Kisi Ki Surat Ka Saamna, Gori Gori Goriyon Ko Padey Na Kahin Re Dil Thaamna' in *Mr. and Mrs. 55* (1955), is sung by a wandering woman seller with her son, while a coy Guru Dutt and Madhubala look on approvingly.

'Kit Gaye Ho Khewanhaar, Naiyaa Doobti' in *Achhut Kanya* (1936) is sung by a wandering old woman woodcutter (in the voice of Saraswati Devi, who was also the composer) for Devika Rani, in love with Ashok Kumar (who makes an appearance at the end of the song). The same song and footage are used for another sequence in the film, when Devika Rani is married to Anwar. When one song and its picturization can work for two diametrically opposite situations, why re-shoot?

A farmer's wife sings *'Chhodo Chhodo Mori Baiyan Saanwre'* in *Miya Biwi Raazi* (1960) for Kamini Kadam (and Shreekant).

Sometimes a radio artist steps in. *'Hum They Jinke Sahare, Woh Hue Na Hamare, Doobi Jab Dil Ki Naiyya, Saamne They Kinare'* from *Safar* (1970) is sung capturing Sharmila Tagore's heartbreak at Rajesh Khanna's cancer. Similarly, *'Humne Dekhi Hai In Aakhon Ki Mehekti Khushboo, Haath Se Chhooke Isse Rishton Ka Ilzaam Na Do'* from *Khamoshi* (1969) is being sung representing Waheeda Rehman.

A song may be sung in a music gathering. *'Kya Karun Sajni Aaye Na Baalam'* in *Swami* (1977) is sung by Dheeraj Kumar on behalf of Shabana Azmi.

'Unke Khayal Aaye Toh Aate Chale Gaye' from *Lal Pathar* (1971) is sung by GM Durrani (in the voice of Rafi—ironical because Durrani was a big singer during his heyday) on the tanpura, and Raj Kumar (on whose behalf the song is intended) playing the table.

A song may be sung by a friend. *'Salaam-E-Hazrat Qubool Kar Lo'* from *Babar* (1960) is sung by Shubha Khote for Azra, though Azra seems quite capable of singing herself, having asked Shubha why she had stopped the song after the introductory humming.

Sometimes the singers at the wedding *sangeet* take over and express the feelings of the groom and the bride—all fun and games of course. *'Mere Banne ki Baat Na Poochho'* from *Gharana* (1961) sung in support of Rajendra Kumar and Asha Parekh.

Sometimes, these songs are not directed at one person, but a whole community who are thinking the same thing. *'Ab Ke Baras Bhejo Bhaiya Ko Babul'* from *Bandini* (1963) is one such song where a woman prisoner sings this doleful song for all fellow inmates including Nutan.

Sometimes it can be an inanimate object like a record player. *'Main Jab Bhi Akeli Hoti Hun, Tum Chup Ke Se Aa Jate Ho'* from *Dharmputra* (1961) is one such song pictured on Mala Sinha. *'Kitni Akeli Kitni Tanha Si Lagi, Tumse Mil Ke Main Aaj'* from *Talash* (1969) is another song where the feelings of Sharmila Tagore for Rajendra Kumar are outsourced to the turntable. *'Dil Ka Diya Jala Ke Gaya, Yeh Kaun Meri Tanhai Mein'* in *Akashdeep* (1965) expresses Nimmi's blossoming love for Ashok Kumar. She may have sung it herself, but for the fact that she is mute.

Sometimes film stars on screen do the job for the actor(s) sitting in the audience. *'Jaaneman Jaaneman Tere Do Nayan'* in *Chhoti Si Baat* (1975) has Dharmendra and Hema Malini singing on behalf of Amol Palekar and Vidya Sinha up to a point. Then Amol Palekar imagines Vidya Sinha on the screen with Dharmendra, and then eventually slips into Dharmendra's role—all in his imagination, of course. So, it is a quasi-vicarious song at best.

The list continues. The number of such songs since the last few decades has come down drastically, though they do happen occasionally. *'Chhupana Bhi Nahi Aata, Jatana Bhi Nahin Aata, Humein Tumse Mohabbat Hai, Batana Bhi Nahin Aata'* in *Baazigar* (1993) is sung by Vinod Rathod at a party for Siddharth who watches helplessly at Shah Rukh Khan and Kajol. *'Pardesi Pardesi Jaana Nahin, Mujhe Chhod Kar, Mujhe Chhod Kar'* from *Raja Hindustani* (1996) is sung by female singers/dancers in front of a roadside *dhaba* echoing the sentiments of Aamir Khan and Karisma Kapoor. Aamir, unable to resist, joins in a little later.

The present-day films, with their scripts and storylines, reflecting the mores of society at large, hardly have any scope for diffidence or bashfulness or reservations or inhibitions. If you feel something, then articulate it yourself—no delegation allowed. Power of attorney does not work anymore. Another glorious genre of Hindi film music has been consigned to the realm of nostalgia.

16

Debt of Gratitude

What ifs, maybes and might-have-beens are replete in the Hindi film music industry. This is particularly so in the case of SD Burman.

What if the music of *Mashaal* (1950) had flopped and SD had packed his bags and left for Kolkata, would the music world have suffered immeasurably; what if the tiff between SD Burman and Sahir Ludhianvi over *'Tadbeer Se Bigdi Hui'* (*Baazi*, 1951) had not been resolved and they had parted, would the film's music have been poorer by the lack of their formidable collaboration?

What if SD Burman and Sahir had not fought again and parted ways on whether the success of *Pyaasa* (1957) rode on the music or the lyrics, would there have been more *'Pyaasas'*; what if SD Burman had not had a tiff with Shailendra during the making of *Bandini* (1963), would Gulzar ever have been discovered?

What if there had been no misunderstanding between SD Burman and Lata Mangeshkar, would Asha Bhosle ever have stepped into SD Burman's studios to the extent she did from 1957 to 1962; what if RD Burman had not become the music director of *Chhote Nawab* (1961), which led to the reconciliation between SD Burman and Lata, would SD Burman and Lata ever have patched up and given us memorable songs?

What if SD Burman had refused to change the tune of *'Din Dhal Jaaye'* as requested by Dev Anand and Goldie Anand, would the original tune have been as moving as the tune that was changed; what if SD Burman had consented to sing for other music directors (almost all his songs were composed by him), would we have had more unique becalming, nasal songs to relish?

These questions are, of course, all moot. Whatever happened, happened for the best and we can't imagine it any other way.

Whenever Asha's songs are discussed, only two composers are mentioned—OP Nayyar and RD Burman. And rightly so. OP Nayyar gave her self-confidence, made her realize her self-worth, smoothened her rough edges, trained her, removed her from out of the shadow of her sister; RD Burman continued the journey forward.

He expanded her musical horizon, made her a youth icon, opened new territories, further developed her vocal line.

However, SD Burman's contribution is never acknowledged. Once she entered his studios, even though she was not his number one choice, he groomed her, honed her skills and exploited the entire gamut of her singing range—the breezy, the mischievous, the pathos, the romantic. He, along with OP Nayyar and RD Burman, was also responsible for making her a complete singer.

Let's consider her songs in this era.

'Kali Ghata Chhaye Mora Jiya Tadpaye', *Sujata* (1959)

Composed in Raag *Pilu*, Asha surpassed herself with this gem of a song. SD Burman had the uncanny capacity to create songs in different voices in the same film, each of which became masterpieces—his own *'Sun Mere Bandhu Re'*, Talat Mahmood's *'Jalte Hain Jiske Liye'*, Geeta Dutt's *'Nanhi Kali Sone Chali'* and this song of Asha's.

'Tum Jiyo Hazaron Saal Saal Ke Din Ho Pachaas Hazaar', *Sujata* (1959)

From the same film, this evergreen song has become a staple in birthday greetings. I myself convey my greetings to friends and relatives by singing this nugget which everyone knows and loves.

'Sach Hue Sapne Tere Jhoom Le O Man Mere', Kaala Bazaar (1960)

Asha's singing to SD Burman's music makes your heart sway.

'Dekhane Mein Bhola Hai Dil Ka Salona', Bombai Ka Babu (1960)

A gaggle of giggling girls teases a city-bred dandy. What a wonderful job Asha did in bringing in the element of harmless ragging and poking fun.

'Koi Aya Dhadkan Kehti Hai', Lajwanti (1958)

An extraordinary song of wait and anticipation.

'Chanda Re Chanda Re Chhupe Rehna', Lajwanti (1958)

The same film had another outstanding Asha song—a melodious *lori* (lullaby).

'Dil Laga Ke Kadar Gayi Pyari', Kala Pani (1958)

One of the greatest *mujra* songs with beautiful picturization. Dev Anand interspersed the courtesan's song with *bols* of tabla (in the voice of SD Burman himself).

'Nazar Lagi Raja Tore Bangle Par', Kala Pani (1958)

SD Burman created another iconic *mujra* song in the same film.

'Ab Ke Baras Bhej', Bandini (1963)

Even though Lata had returned to his fold, SD Burman had room for two great songs by Asha. *'Ab Ke Baras Bhej'* was sung by the solitary female prisoner on the grinding wheel, singing this heart-rending song of hopelessness. SD Burman asked Asha to imagine that she had not been allowed to visit her parents by her in-laws. As a result, he got just the emotions he was seeking. The song was also in Raag *Pilu*.

Asha by now had become an expert in this raag, having sung songs in this raag in *Phagun* (1958), five years earlier, under OP Nayyar's baton.

'O Pancchi Pyare', *Bandini* (1963)

This song, from the same film, was by a group of female prisoners, engaged in a variety of chores—grinding, pounding, sowing, washing—to relieve the tedium. Real rice and real wheat, and a real bamboo *'chaaja'* were used to create the real word sound of grain sorting. This one was effusive on the surface, but melancholic under the surface. Presenting two contrasting songs by Asha was something only SD Burman could have done.

The duets she sang with Rafi are unforgettable.

'Deewana Mastana Hua Dil' (*Bombai ka Babu,* 1960); *'Chand Sa Mukhda Kyun Sharmaya'* (*Jaag Utha Insaan,* 1959); *'Achha Ji Main Haari Chalo Maan Jaayo'* (*Kala Pani,* 1958); *'Kali Ke Roop Mein Chali Ho Dhoop Mein'* (*Nau Do Gyarah,* 1957); *'Aaja Panchhi Akela Hai'* (*Nau Do Gyarah,* 1957); *'Dil Toh Hai Deewana Na'* (*Manzil,* 1960); *'Dilwale Ab Teri Gali Tak Aa Pahunche'* (*Kala Pani,* 1958); *'San San San Woh Chali Hawa'* (*Kaagaz ke Phool,* 1959).

Her duets with Kishore Kumar were no less memorable. Songs from *Chalti Ka Naam Gaadi* (1958)—*'Haal Kaisa Hai Janaab Ka'*, *'Paanch Rupaiya Baara Anna'*; *'Aankhon Main Kya Ji'* (*Nau Do Gyarah,* 1957); *'Chhod Do Aanchal'* (*Paying Guest,* 1957). In *'O Nigaah-e-Mastaana'* (*Paying Guest,* 1957), Asha only hums at strategic points, but what a wonderful contribution she brings to the song.

After the return of Lata, SD Burman made her his *numero uno* singer. Lata was after all his favourite. But he didn't forget Asha. In *'Raat Akeli Hai Bujh Gaye Diye'* (*Jewel Thief,* 1967), Asha's voice flows seductively through low notes and then powerfully through very high notes, without any effort (SD Burman had told her to sing the song as if she were going to whisper in somebody's ear, but then decided to shout instead).

'Arey Yaar Meri Tum Bhee Ho Gazab' (*Teen Devian*, 1965) is a foot-tapping, upbeat song.

Asha, unfortunately, normally does not give any credit to OP Nayyar. There is a personal animus involved, so she may think she is doing the right thing. It's only RD Burman as far as she is concerned. But her late father-in-law also deserves a salute—at least a mention in dispatches, if not a full-fledged award.

17

The Full-Throated Singer

Mahendra Kapoor

"O Mary, go and call the cattle home, And call the cattle home, And call the cattle home, Across the sands of Dee."

I was reminded of this poem by Charles Kinsley when I heard Mahendra Kapoor sing on a winter evening in Chelmsford Club lawns, New Delhi in the early 1990s. He started the program with the title song of BR Chopra's *Mahabharat* TV serial which had created a sensation in the country when it was aired from 1988 to 1990. *"Atha Shri Mahabharat Katha/Mahabharat Katha/Katha Hai Purusharth Ki Yeh/Swarth Ki Parmarth Ki"*, he sang the Raj Kamal composed serial introduction with no holds barred. It was a full-throated voice, without filters, emanating from the pit of the stomach and demanding everyone's focused attention. The audience was still, the bearers stood at attention, the club suspended its service. Kapoor did not need a sound system. But there was one, of course, and because sound travels farther in chilly weather, most of Lutyens' Delhi would have heard him.

This sound quality, this timbre, this pitch, this loudness was Kapoor's default setting. That is the way he normally sang. That is why he was so good in patriotic songs—songs that trigger passion, stir the fervour for the country, move the throng. I once saw the Indo-Pak Retreat Ceremony at Hussainiwala Border, Ferozepur. '*Sandese Aate Hain*' from *Border* (1997) was being played on a loop on the Indian side. The effect on the Indian audience was tepid. Kapoor's '*Mere Desh Ki Dharti*' from *Upkar* (1967) was the tonic required to work the crowd into a frenzy. The song is timeless. Patriotic songs do not have a shelf life and this song is among the best, never mind that it was released in 1967. He has more in his armoury, from '*Jaagega Insaan Zamana Dekhega*' (*Aadmi Aur Insaan*, 1969), '*Hai Preet Jahaan Ki Reet Sada*' (*Purab Aur Paschim*, 1970), '*Mera Rang De Basanti Chola*' (*Shaheed*, 1965), and many others.

Similarly, his unrestrained voice suited religious songs to stir religious ardour amongst the devotees. Every episode of *Mahabharat* was incomplete without a four-line verse in his voice, summing up important situations occurring in the episode. His devotional oeuvre is impressive. My wife insists on playing his '*Om Jai Jagdish*' at the Diwali Puja. He was a congregation singer—be it patriotic or religious, be it a parade ground or a *Mata ki Chowki*. His stentorian voice was what the good doctor had ordered to rouse people.

At an open-air Income Tax Sports function in Mumbai (I was the President of the Tax Sports Club), he was the Chief Guest. He sang '*Mere Desh Ki Dharti*' at full throttle bringing the house, consisting of hundreds of officers and men, down. His muscular voice had that ability. Yet that very voice and that unbridled style was his undoing. It did not work in mainstream songs.

That is why Kapoor remained on the fringes of the Hindi film music industry. His output may have been prodigious but the respect and recognition that his peers got came his way only in modest measures. He never got a seat at the high table. The Department of Posts issued 'Legendary Singers of India' stamps in 2016 to commemorate (amongst Hindi film singers) Rafi, Kishore Kumar, Mukesh, Hemant Kumar, Manna Dey, Shamshad Begum, Geeta Dutt, Bhupen Hazarika and Talat Mehmood. Kapoor was missing. Each of these singers had their own distinctiveness. Each had a place in the musical scheme of things. Each was different. Each sang with sensitivity. Each used an in-built modulator. Most importantly, each was mainstream. Kapoor was superficially close to Rafi in the voice department, but a very distant second. In terms of versatility, he always remained in the shadow of Rafi.

The softness and the balminess were missing in his voice. Only the triumvirate of BR/Yash Chopra, Sahir Ludhianvi and music director Ravi (and to some extent, N Datta) could rein him in. In their hands, he was gentle, even in high-pitched songs. Songs from *Gumrah* (1963) (*'Chalo Ek Baar Phir Se'*, *'Aap Aaye To Khayal-e-Dil-e-Nashaad Aaya'*, *'Tujhko Mera Pyaar Pukare'*), *Waqt* (1965) (*'Hum Jab Simat Ke Aapki'*, *'Din Hain Bahaar Ke'*, *'Maine Ek Khwab Sa Dekha'*), *Humraaz* (1967) (*'Neele Gagan Ke Taley'*, *'Kisi Pathar Ki Moorat Se'*, *'Tum Agar Saath Dene Ka'*), *Aadmi Aur Insaan* (1969) (*'Neele Parbaton Ki Dhara'*, *'Zindagi Ittefaq Hai'*), *Dhund* (1973) (*'Sansar Ki Har Shae Ka'*) are some examples.

N Datta (with BR/Yash Chopra and Sahir) composed one of the gentlest romantic songs *'Aaj Ki Raat'* (*Dharamputra*, 1961) for Kapoor. Even *'Tere Pyar Ka Aasra Chahta Hun'* (*Dhool Ka Phool*, 1959—made with the same team) which Kapoor sang with Lata, otherwise in the high octave, has a pleasant, endearing quality about it.

In *'Yeh Hawa, Yeh Fiza, Aa Bhi Ja'* from *Gumrah* (1963), Kapoor opens the song as loud as is humanly possible, but with honey-soaked wool wrapped around it. The stanza is in the upper regions but could lull a baby to sleep. That was the genius of Ravi; that he could put brakes on the runaway wild horse that critics dismissed Kapoor as. Ravi was also responsible for Kapoor's first two Filmfare Best Singer awards for *'Chalo Ek Baar'* (*Gumrah*), and *'Neele Gagan Ke Taley' (Hamraaz)*. This was at a time when Rafi was at his peak. Incidentally, Rafi's first Filmfare Award for *'Chaudvin Ka Chand'* (*Chaudvin Ka Chand*, 1960) was also Ravi's doing.

Unfortunately, the other music directors failed to tame him except in a few songs. OP Nayyar, whom I knew personally, never a Kapoor fan, had to perforce use him when he had a fallout with Rafi. Most of the Kapoor songs of OP Nayyar's would have gone to Rafi, had the fight not taken place. OP Nayyar's music usually had the Punjabi robustness, so the songs were ideal for Kapoor, a Punjabi. But the warmth was missing. The songs were clinical, devoid of soul. OP Nayyar, otherwise a martinet in the studios, could do nothing. He would tell me how frustrating the experience would be. He would give me the example of *'Tareef Karoon Kya Uski'* (*Kashmir Ki Kali*, 1964). It is a song that can be heard all over Dal Lake and beyond. But Rafi eschewed rawness in his serenading, never mind the volume. With Kapoor, Sharmila Tagore would have pushed Shammi Kapoor off the *shikara*.

Take the case of Manoj Kumar whose ghost voice was Kapoor. Manoj was Kapoor's strong advocate, so much so, that he pressured even a Naushad to replace Talat Mahmood with Kapoor in the duet with Rafi—*'Kitni Haseen Aaj Bahaaron Ki Raat Hai'* (*Aadmi*, 1968)—even after this duet's disc had been released. But even Manoj knew Kapoor's limited area of expertise. In *Upkar* (1967), when he wanted a sturdy voice, he took Kapoor (*'Mere Desh Ki Dharti'*), but when he wanted gentle emotions and pathos, he took Mukesh who had been doing playback for Manoj since Manoj's entry into the film industry (*'Deewano Se Yeh Mat Poochho'*). In *Purab Aur Paschim* (1970) he did likewise—rabble-rousing *'Hai Preet Jahan Ki Reet Sada'* with Kapoor and the plaintive *'Koi Jab Tumhara Hridaya Tod De'* with Mukesh. It happened in *Shor* (1972) with the rousing *'Jeevan Chalne Ka Naam'* with Kapoor and the emotional *'Ek Pyaar Ka Naghma Hai'* with Mukesh and Lata. In *Roti, Kapda Aur Makaan* (1974), Kapoor sang the accusatory *'Aur Nahin Bas Aur Nahin'* (which fetched him his third Filmfare Award) and Mukesh (with

Lata)—*'Main Na Bhooluga'*. In *Kranti* (1981) he kept Kapoor for the religious-nationalistic *'Ab Ke Baras Tujhe Dharti Ki Rani Kar Denge'* but kept Mukesh's son Nitin Mukesh for *'Zindagi Ki Toote Na Lari'*.

So, Manoj too, despite his unstinted support to Kapoor, knew which songs to use him for. The ones, where Kapoor did not fit the bill, were usually given to Mukesh.

No song can depict this contrast more starkly than *'Jo Chala Gaya Use Bhool Ja'* (*Saathi*, 1968). The song begins with *'Bhool Ja, Bhool Ja'* sung at a high pitch preceded and accompanied by dramatic eerie music, followed by Mukesh's contemplative *'Jo Chala Gaya'*. Kapoor got pigeon-holed in such categories of songs.

So, there you have it—a great singer in the patriotic/devotional genre, an outstanding singer when in the magic hands of Ravi (and N Datta) for all genres, but not quite fitting the requirements of the other category of songs. That is why most of the music directors kept away. When you had the choice of a thoroughbred like Rafi, why take a workhorse?

Not that he was not a trained singer. Born in Amritsar to a family of cloth dealers, they shifted to Bombay when he was still very young. Interested in music since childhood, he trained under Ustad Meherji, Ustad Niyaz Ahmad Khan and Pandit Tulsidas Sharma. He auditioned for All India Radio but was rejected! However, he got his first break when Music Director Snehal Bhatkar got him to sing *'Tere Dar Ki Bheekh Maanti Hai Daata'* (*Diwali Ki Raat*, 1956). That year he also sang a song in *Lalkar* (1956)—*'Is Man Ki Nagaria Se'*. However, his career did not take off.

Then lady luck smiled. Kapoor and Arati Mukherjee became winners of the 1957 Metro-Murphy Singing Contest which required all participants to sing only non-film songs (in the open-air ground adjoining Mahalaxmi Racecourse).

The judges were Anil Biswas, Naushad, C Ramchandra, Vasant Desai and Madan Mohan.

Let us see how the judges treated him thereafter. Under Naushad, Kapoor took a start with *'Chaand Chhupaa Aur Taare Doobe'* (*Sohni Mahiwal*, 1958). However, the other songs were in Rafi's voice. Naushad explained that he needed to give a chance to Kapoor having picked him up as a winner. Thereafter, offers dried up.

C Ramchandra was, by 1957, visibly anti-Rafi and provided Kapoor with a big breakthrough in V Shantaram's *Navrang* (1959)—*'Yeh Maati Sabhi Ki Kahani Kahegi'*, *'Shyamal Shyamal Baran'* and the duet with Asha—*'Aadhaa Hai Chandrama'*. He gave Kapoor other songs too—*'Gaa Rahee Hai Zindagi'* (*Aanchal*, 1960) and *'Dil Lagaa Kar Hum Yeh Samjhe'* (*Zindagi Aur Maut*, 1965). By 1967, Kapoor had already been slotted in the ear-splitting bracket and the same V Shantaram in his film *Boond Jo Ban Gayi Moti* (1967), whose music was composed by my late uncle Satish Bhatia, used Kapoor for a thunderous dance number (with Asha)—*'Lovely Lovely Hai Samaa'*. The softer songs—*'Yeh Kaun Chitrakar Hai'* and *'Haan Maine Bhi Pyaar Kiya'* went to Mukesh.

Vasant Desai used Kapoor in songs such as *'Maanjhi Re Himmat Na Haar'* (*Samrat Prithviraj Chauhan*, 1959) and the delightful *'Kalpana Ke Ghan Baraste'* with Lata (*Amar Jyoti*, 1965).

Anil Biswas gave Kapoor a duet *'Stella O Stella'* with Meena Kapoor (*Return of Superman*, 1960).

Madan Mohan, the junior-most among those five judges, never tuned with Kapoor.

Shankar-Jaikishan did not use him much. The song *'Har Dil Jo Pyar Karega'* (*Sangam*, 1964) where Kapoor sings for Rajendra Kumar (whose playback was normally done by Rafi) has an interesting history. Raj Kapoor had grown very fond of Kapoor during a tour of Russia and promised him a chance to sing for the second lead in his films. Kapoor remarked that Raj would forget his promise once he reached India, but Raj took the cigarette he was smoking and burnt his hand and said the mark would remind him. But nothing else came his way after this song even though Kapoor did a great job.

Roshan, SD Burman and RD Burman hardly used him.

His bread and butter came from Kalyanji-Anandji, Ravi and OP Nayyar and other assorted music directors.

As a person, he was a thorough gentleman. Not once did Kapoor offend even the humblest composer, be it Chitragupta or Usha Khanna. He was the quintessential Mr Nice.

Kapoor sang in many Indian languages including Gujarati, Punjabi, Bhojpuri, and Marathi movies. In Marathi movies, he was the voice of Dada Kondke.

He was asked by the group Boney M to sing their songs in Hindi with Mussarat from Pakistan, which resulted in the Pop Album *M-3* (1981).

Looking at the calibre of competition he faced throughout his career in films, Kapoor managed to accomplish a fair amount. But he deserved more. The composers other than Ravi/N Datta could not or would not draw out his softer side. Perhaps he had been typecast in the patriotic/devotional/boisterous genre too deeply for them to experiment with him. Perhaps he consciously let himself be compartmentalized to differentiate himself from others, especially Rafi.

Every singer has a signature song. Kapoor has two—each representing his two musical facets: '*Mere Desh Ki Dharti*' (*Upkar*, 1967)— the ultimate ode to the '*Jai Jawan Jai Kisan*' slogan; and '*Chalo Ek Baar Phir Se*' (*Gumrah*, 1963)—the ultimate break-up song.

18

Being a Muse Didn't Help

OP Nayyar and I became friends when I was posted in Mumbai during the '90s. I used to visit his PG digs in Thane very often and many a drunken evening has been spent reminiscing about his film industry days.

During one such evening, he mentioned that he had great respect for RD Burman's talent and viewed him as a kindred spirit. Both were trendsetters; both defied the existing musical mores; both used musical instruments innovatively; both were rhythm masters.

And both had Asha Bhosle as their muse!

Then came the shocker from him—he claimed that irrespective of Asha being firmly ensconced in RD Burman's studio and heart, RD Burman gave his best songs to Lata!

Let's analyze.

It had been a general rule, with exceptions of course, that melodious and semi-classical songs went to Lata. The frothy, fun-filled, rhythm-oriented ones to Asha.

Take RD Burman's first film itself—*Chhote Nawab* (1961). The Raag *Malgunji* based '*Ghar Aaja Ghir Aayi Badarwa Sanwariya*' created a sensation and is still fresh and timeless.

The songs listed below are only representative. But it will give you the drift. *Amar Prem* (1972) had two gems—'*Raina Beeti Jaaye*' based on Raag *Lalit*, and '*Bada Natkhat Hai*' based on Raag *Khamaj*.

Yet, for all his talent, '*Bada Natkhat*' would have been a run-of-the-mill bhajan had the ever-watchful SD Burman not admonished his son for not exploiting his creative juices adequately in failing to express the nautch-girl's agony in not being able to be a mother.

A chastened RD Burman paid heed, composed a new tune packing it with the right shades of emotion, got Lata to use her dulcet voice to convey the playfulness of Krishna and his association with Yashoda, bed rocked on Sharmila Tagore's pathos, albeit in a refreshingly upbeat format.

Consider the songs from *Baharon ke Sapne* (1967)—'*Aaja Piya Tohe Pyaar Dun*', '*Kya Jaanu Sajan*', and '*Chunri Sambhaal Gori*' (with Manna Dey). These songs are evergreen.

And who can forget *Aandhi* (1975)—'*Is Mod Se Jaate Hain*', '*Tere Bina Zindagi Se*', and '*Tum Aa Gaye Ho*'—all with Kishore.

Consider these songs—'*Vinati Karun Ghanashyam*' in Raag *Jogiya* (*Pati Patni,* 1966), '*Karvate Badalte Rahen*' in Raag *Pahadi* (with Kishore in *Aap Ki Kasam,* 1974), '*Mere Naina Sawan Bhadon*' in Raag *Shivranjani* (with Kishore in *Mehbooba,* 1976), '*Beeti Na Betayi Raina*' in Raag *Bihag* (with Bhupinder in *Parichay,* 1972).

I can go on and on. *Caravan* (1971)—'*Dilbar Dil Se Pyaare*' would normally have been sung by Asha. Lata got into the mood of the song with total abandon and showed that she could encroach Asha's genre with equal felicity.

Her duet from the same film with Rafi—'*Kitna Pyaara Wada Hai*' was melody all the way. In another song that was in Asha's mould—breezy and raunchy, Lata showed that she had it in her—the '*Kaanta*' number of *Samadhi* (1972).

Then there are songs from *Ghar* (1978)—'*Aap Ki Aankhon Mein*' (with Kishore) and '*Aaj Kal Paaon Zameen Par*'; *The Train* (1970)—'*Kis Liye Maine Pyar Kiya*'; *Padosan* (1968)—'*Sharm Aati Hai Magar*', and '*Main Chali Main Chali*'.

RD Burman's Lata number in *Anamika* (1973), '*Bahon Mein Chale Aao*' was such a delectable song. The impishness was conveyed very dexterously by Lata's velvety, whispery voice.

Consider the stunning song from Gulzar's *Libas* (1988)—a film that was never released—'*Sili Hawa Chhoo Gai, Sila Badan Chhil Gaya*' or her song '*Kuhu Kuhu Koyaliya*' from Gulzar's still-born *Devdas* (1976) which saw shooting for only 10 days with two songs recorded.

And so on.

If Lata got the pick of the litter, where did that leave Asha? The fact is that RD Burman had two generally recognizable divisions in his musical repertoire. The melody-based songs were normally assigned to Lata and the rhythm-oriented ones to Asha.

Of course, Asha did melody-based songs too—songs of *Ijaazat* (1987) are usually trotted out by the Asha apologists, but these were glorious exceptions. You and I could like one or both the genres. There is no right or wrong. But when posterity tabulates the 'best' of any music director, the melody-based tunes ordinarily trump the other category.

Asha's songs may have been very popular during their time and are still popular now especially with the younger generation, but history will not record these songs as RD Burman's best.

RD Burman himself admitted that Lata was a better singer. In *The Times of India*, Bombay, 29 September 1985, he said, "...there is no doubt that Lata-*ji* is supreme. When she sings, she forgets about herself, her home, and there's a complete changeover of personality. Though she may not admit this, she becomes a mother, or a sweetheart before the microphone."

So, while the nation enjoys and dances to '*Monica, My Darling*' (*Caravan*, 1971), most would probably rate '*Naam Gum Jaayega*' (*Kinara*, 1976) as the better song!

19

The Music Director Beyond Compare

Naushad

Shanmukhananda Auditorium in Mumbai cannot be accused of being a small hall. Far from it; it is one of the biggest in Asia with a seating capacity of more than 2,700 people at three levels. If you add the aisles and other spaces on the sides and at the rear, then the audience can swell up to 5,000. About three decades back, I attended a felicitation ceremony for a music director who was no longer active. It was his birthday. The entry was free, and the hall was packed to the rafters. Before the official program began with Dilip Kumar as the main speaker, short clips of his songs were screened on one side of the empty stage. The crowd, mostly on the wrong side of the 50s, was in raptures.

Clips of *Rattan* (1944), *Anmol Ghadi* (1946), *Shahjehan* (1946), *Mela* (1948), *Andaz* (1949), *Dillagi* (1949), *Dulari* (1949), *Babul* (1950), *Deedar* (1951), *Aan* (1952), *Baiju Bawra* (1952), *Amar* (1954), *Uran Khatola* (1955), *Mother India* (1957), *Kohinoor* (1960), *Mughal-e-Azam* (1960), *Ganga Jamuna* (1961), and others played one after the other, segueing seamlessly into the next one, each clip bringing a collective gasp and under-the-breath accompaniment. A hypnotic spell had been cast. The half-hour presentation, and its impact on the audience, encapsulated the genius of the man.

But what was this?

Everyone thought that he had hung up his baton, but the Master of Ceremonies announced during the program that he had just been signed for Akbar Khan's *Taj Mahal—An Eternal Love Story* (it was released a few years later in 2005).

There was thunderous applause. The virtuoso would be weaving his magic a little bit longer!

About 20 years earlier, in 1982, at the same venue, Noor Jehan had sung his '*Awaaz De Kahaan Hai*' from *Anmol Ghadi* (1946), the eternal song of hers sung during a brief tenure in India before Partition, defining her musically in the Indian consciousness. The maestro wielded the baton that day too, 36 years after wielding it in the studio.

Naushad.

His hold over the musical firmament in Hindi films was not commensurate with the number of years he spent in the industry and the meagre number of films (just 65) he had to show for it. But it is the best work that God (and the public) wants, not the dregs of exhaustion. Twenty-six silver jubilees, eight golden jubilees, four diamond jubilees are what Naushad's CV reveals, besides many other things.

Why was his output so low? He insisted on doing only one film at one time. He laboured hard over his compositions, and this required time. When he would construct the superstructure of the song, he would go into the minutest detail every step of the way.

If a particular word did not do the trick, he would ask the lyricist to change it or alternatively, to alter the line—never mind even if the lyricist was Shakeel Badayuni who was indelibly linked with Naushad, having done a large part of his oeuvre. It would take Naushad a minimum of 15 days to compose a single song. Tunes upon tunes would be composed till he eventually settled on a melody that satisfied him, keeping the film's requirements in mind. He had the Midas touch—he was a trendsetter with a long line of musical hits. He was an arbiter of public taste.

He rejected a huge monetary offer for *Azad* (1955) because the producer wanted the songs within a month. Naushad wanted at least a year. C Ramchandra was made the music director and delivered the songs within a week (his condition was that he be paid a rupee extra over the offer made to Naushad). The songs were great hits. But Naushad was cut from a different cloth.

He straddled the two pillars of classical and folk music like a colossus and rode to the pinnacle of popularity during the 1940s, '50s and early '60s.

He was one of the first composers to bring folk music into films. With *Rattan* (1944), he showcased the immense appeal of folk music very early in his career. In later years also, he created several lively songs with a folk base and flavour that made them easy on the lips as well as ears. Some examples are '*Gaadi Wale Gaadi Dheere Haaq Re*' (*Mother India*, 1957), '*Nain Lad Jayi He*' (*Ganga Jamuna*, 1961), '*Mere Pairon Mein Ghungroo Bandha De*' (*Sunghursh*, 1968). He did something unique. Even when a song had a classical base, he introduced elements of folk. The classical blended imperceptibly into folk. His tunes were a rare blend of folk music energy and classical gravitas.

To adapt classical music to film music is a mammoth task. Naushad modernized classical music and added colour and freshness to it. But he never wandered off the limits of the musical boundaries. He believed in the purity of melody and never compromised in inserting an offending note to lend novelty. He never pandered to popularity. He had complete command over classical music and used it to enhance the song's appeal—'*Mohe Panghat Pe*' (*Mughal-e-Azam*, 1960) began in Raag *Pilu* and slipped into Raag *Gaara*. '*Yeh Dil Ki Lagi Kam Kya Hogi*', from the same film, in Raag *Jaijaiwanti* had each *antara* in a different tune—according to the prevailing evening mood. In *Baiju Bawra* (1952), each situation had an appropriate Raag—'*Mohe Bhool Gaye Sanwariya*' (*Bhairav*), '*Bachpan Ki Mohabbat Ko*' (*Maand*), '*Tu Ganga Ki Mauj*' (*Bhairavi*), '*Jhoole Mein Pawan Ke*' (*Basant* and *Pilu*). Even Ustad Bade Ghulam Ali Khan broke his rule of keeping a distance from film music by singing two *bandishes*—*'Shubh Din Aayo'* and *'Prem Jogan Ban Ke'*.

He adorned his pieces with aesthetics which made the songs eternal. Listen to the concluding bars of *'O Duniya Ke Rakhwale'* (*Baiju Bawra*, 1952), the climatic onrush of melody in the second stanza of *'Meri Kahaani'* (*Deedar*, 1951), the choral effects of *'O Door Ke Musafir'* (*Uran Khatola*, 1955), and so many others. His music was all about dignified eloquence and chaste reverence.

For Naushad, the melody was of course important, but the polish, more so. He knew every instrument in his orchestra and the best use for each in different parts of the song. He innovated with their pairing, say the flute with the clarinet, the sitar with the mandolin. He introduced the accordion—listen to *'Ta Ra Ri, Aa Ra Ri'* from *Dastan* (1950), composed on waltz beat, the *been*, the brass instruments and the vibraphone. He was instrumental in improving recording techniques and modernizing the orchestra. His songs were composed and arranged in a manner to bring about a vigorous nod of appreciation by the listener. They demanded a serious ear, not a casual play in the background.

Yet, it was not that the composition and its recording were planned to the last detail before entering the studio. The singers would come to his house for oral rehearsals. Mukesh made 23 trips to Naushad's music room in his house—Ashiana—in Bandra, Bombay to rehearse *'Tu Kahe Agar'* from *Andaz* (1949). But they had no idea what the orchestra would be, which was also being readied separately. When the singer and the instrumentalists eventually came face to face at the time of recording, that was the first time the oral and orchestral integration was achieved. Moreover, at recordings, he would sometimes ask the singer to get experimental.

He believed in the power of the chorus to enhance the song's effect. The chorus was not used merely as filler but as an integral part of the song—*'O Door Ke Musafir'* (*Uran Khatola*, 1955), *'Dukh Bhare Din Beete Re Bhaiya'* (*Mother India*, 1957), *'Aayi Hain Bahaarein'* (*Ram Aur Shyam*, 1967). The song *'More Saiyan Utrenge'* from *Uran Khatola* (1955) has basic instrumentation and is almost entirely carried forward by the chorus, replacing instruments.

He has many other firsts to his name—first to use of a 100-piece orchestra, first to use Western notation in India (the notation of *Aan* was published in a book form in London).

In the 1940s and 1950s, when Naushad led, others followed. So gripping was his hold over the listeners' imagination that film distributors would stand to attention whenever his name was mentioned. In the honours list in the film credits, his name would appear after the main hero and heroine. He would charge Rs 1 lakh, plus Rs 10,000 for orchestral charges. The producer could be present during the song recording, but not open his mouth. There was so much aura surrounding him that the trailer of *Dastan* (1950) showed how he composed music for the film while hailing "Naushad, Naushad, *chaalis karor mein ek hi* Naushad". His musical clout was unmatched.

The four songs in *Andaz* (1949) sung by Mukesh and pictured on Dilip Kumar: *'Hum Aaj Kahin'*, *'Tu Kahe Agar'*, *'Toote Na'* and *'Jhoom Jhoom Ke'*, turned Dilip into a tragedian—as per the actor's own admission. He was not happy with the tunes which were instrumental in creating the melancholic mood for him. But his misgivings were brushed aside. These songs have become legends. Similarly, Dilip objected to Lata Mangeshkar being the female singer, questioning how a girl from Maharashtra could ever sing in Urdu. Naushad again had his way. This was Lata's first film with Naushad. Lata's *'Uthaye Ja Unke Sitam'*, *'Tod Diya Dil*

Mera', '*Meri Ladli Ri Meri Ladli*' and others give a measure of the impact the singer had made and the faith that Naushad had in her.

Once Talat smoked in front of Naushad after recording his first song for him—'*Mera Jeewan Saathi Bichchad Gaya*' from *Babul* (1950). Talat in *Babul* was a huge success on Dilip Kumar. So popular the songs went on to become that Mehdi Hassan began climbing the ladder of success on the back of two songs (including Talat's '*Husnwalon Ko Na Dil Do*' from the same film) at a public performance in Karachi in 1957. But that did not matter. As a punishment, he was replaced by Rafi, on the same Dilip Kumar, in *Deedar* (1951). Naushad was a martinet in the music studio. His word was musical law.

In the later years, with the change of Naushad's fortunes, Lata stopped coming to his music room for rehearsals. In *Aadmi* (1968), Naushad (who had a very successful run with Talat) was arm-twisted by Manoj Kumar to take Mahendra Kapoor as his playback singer in the song '*Kaisi Haseen Aaj Baharon Ki Raat Hai*'. This is despite the fact that Talat had done the recording and the album had been released. So, the film had Mahendra Kapoor while the album had Talat.

With the advent of the 1960s, Naushad's sway lost a bit of steam. Films like *Leader* (1964), *Saaz Aur Awaaz* (1966), *Dil Diya Dard Liya* (1966) had outstanding songs. However, even those could not save them from sinking. This took their toll on Naushad's stature—slowly but surely. The latter half of the 1960s saw a change in the taste of listeners. Naushad bravely soldiered on and reinvented himself in *Ram Aur Shyam* (1967), *Saathi* (1968) and others. *Saathi* saw a complete makeover with Kersi Lord arranging the musical pieces. The result was totally unlike anything heard in a Naushad film till then.

In the 1970s, the face of film music changed completely. Naushad could not reconcile with modern times. He was considered outdated and out of style. Tunes composed to themes that defied logic and reality did not work. His musical arteries had hardened in the changed scenario. His music and films flopped, and he gradually faded away.

Naushad is no more. But old masters never die. The music lovers and connoisseurs still adore him. His music can never blur his image, even with the changing times. Like a diamond, a genius is forever.

I remember an incident in the mid-1960s very vividly. Shanti Mathur, the playback singer, had just finished singing Naushad's song *'Nanha Munna Rahi Hoon'* (*Son of India*, 1962) at my uncle's (music director Late Satish Bhatia) place. Every person in the room was teary-eyed. The sentiments it roused—the emotional fervour, the pride and hope, the love of country—are fresh in my mind even today. That this song still retains its original sheen came as a pleasant surprise when my daughter told me it was one of her favourite songs and that my grandson had also loved it and started learning it.

What better lyrics to pay one's salutations to the musical giant than this song of his from *Dil Diya Dard Liya* (1966):

"Phir teri kahani yaad aayi, Phir tera fasana yaad aaya
Phir aaj humari aankhon ko, Ek khwab purana yaad aaya."

20

The Maestro

Ghulam Ali

The various forms of *'lehar'* in a river or a lake or a sea or an ocean are finite. But Pakistani ghazal *ustad*, Ghulam Ali, can't be bogged down by such limitations. His throat can produce as many variants of *'lehar'* as time on the stage, and the audience permits. The *'lehar'* of his *'dil'* can roll on and on, never repeating. From a gentle ripple to a tsunami—he has them all in his musical armoury.

He was asked in an interview about his view of the Pakistani pop groups, and had replied, "Frankly, I am really bewildered at their style of singing. How can you sing a song by running and jumping around the stage? The stage is meant for performing, not for acrobatics."

Ironically, Ghulam Ali does exactly that. He may be sitting still, a musical emperor sitting cross-legged, with an indulgent smile and twinkling eyes, but his throat is effortlessly indulging in musical acrobatics; powerful, unwavering, aided by strong lungs; honed to perfection by decades of *riyaaz*. And his fans go ecstatic.

They find his style—no lengthy preamble by way of an *alaap*—hitting the ground running, cutting straight to the chase—scintillating, exciting, exhilarating.

They love the musical fireworks that the Pakistani maestro unleashes, they adore the way his notes jump from tree to tree. It's an adrenaline rush, and the audience emerges out of the concert with a heady feeling.

The *Ustad* recites the *shers* in his trademark manner without distorting the beauty of the poetry. He knows where to stop, and where to stress, so that the meaning comes across. Ghulam Ali's heavy, baritone voice has subtle variations, which can convey the entire gamut of emotions.

For his fans, he is a falcon, not a dove.

The cognoscenti has their own take on the matter.

He is a 'man of the masses', they claim. Acrobatics are fine, but there needs to be a gradual build-up by way of an *alaap*, without which there would be a feeling of unfulfillment in the minds of the discerning listeners.

The *alaap* is critical to any raag-based rendition, including a ghazal. It unfolds and adorns the raag. They further hold that his ghazals lack depth, poise and dignity. That they are short of aesthetics. Embellishments are of course integral to any rendition—be it *taandaari, sargams, murkees, harkats* or *khatkas*—but they need to be invoked moderately; else they will enervate the essence of the raag, though they may elevate the mood of the masses.

I saw an interview of Jagjit Singh where he mentioned that even though Ghulam Ali had mastered the *sur* and in terms of talent and grip, skill and virtuosity, was amongst the best of the best, his ghazals by and large lacked melody, and seemed to be 'uninspired' and 'ordinary'—save a few out of his large oeuvre.

This is the dilemma faced by any maestro—does one create and influence the taste of the audience, or does one cater to the public demand?

There is nothing wrong with either. And there is a vast audience that savours both the contemplative and the combustible. The choice to relish the ghazals of Mehdi Hasan and Ghulam Ali need not be either/or. If I want my heartstrings tugged, I play *'Gulon Mein Rang Bhare'* of Mehdi Hassan; when I want to my heart rate pumped up, I play *'Yeh Dil Yeh Paagal Dil Mera'* of Ghulam Ali.

Mehdi Hassan had the added advantage of having a huge treasure chest of film songs which he had 'ghazalized' (slowed the tempo, added semi-classical touches, introduced more stanzas)—which he sang when he wanted to become more accessible. He normally walked with the kings, but still retained the common touch.

Ghulam Ali also has done playback for Pakistani films. In fact, I heard him first time in 1973 with the song *'Mere Shauq Da Nai Aitbaar Tenu'* from the film *'Ek Thi Ladki'* (1973). It's an amazing song without any calisthenics. In any case, film songs don't allow that latitude. It's only when he does private ghazals that he smashes boundaries. The first ever song that I sang on stage was his—*'Baharon Ko Chaman Yaad Aa Gaya Hai'*.

At a private dinner of five persons at a Delhi farmhouse many years ago, I mentioned this fact to him. He insisted that I sing it. "But I have come to hear you, Sir," I protested. "How can I even dare to do such a thing before you?" But he wouldn't sing because the next day he had a public performance in Delhi and wanted to preserve his voice, but he kept insisting that I sing that same ghazal. With 'liquids' swirling inside me, I said "what the hell", closed my eyes, and inflicted on him the worst possible punishment!

Yet, though he talks with the crowds—that's his singing style—he still keeps his virtue. When singing in private soirees, amongst aficionados, Ghulam Ali's classical renditions put a smile on the faces of purists. It's not that he can't be tamed. Listen to his album *'Meraj-E-Ghazal'* with Asha Bhosle, specifically the ghazal *'Dayar-E-Dil Ki Raat Mein'*. As they say in musical parlance, he is completely *tayyar*, and ready for battle. If he has chosen a particular style that keeps his devoted audience screaming for more, so be it.

His solid foundation in classical music was laid from the age of 15 when he became a disciple of the legendary classical singer Bade Ghulam Ali Khan (after whom he is named). His training was provided mainly by Bade Ghulam Ali Khan's three brothers—Barqat Ali Khan, Mubarak Ali Khan, and Amanat Ali Khan.

That he is immensely popular in India and elsewhere, is a given. His songs have even made it to Hindi films.

I have seen several shows of his—both ticketed and private—since India opened its doors to him and other artists from across the border. Once in a while, the door to the country, sometimes to a city too, gets closed due to the politics of the day. But the love and passion for Ghulam Ali by the admiring legion of his followers never shuts down.

May God give Ghulam Ali, and his throat, many more years of good health and good music. The 'trapeze artist' still has many shows to do!

21

Singing for Their Supper

"Little Tommy Tucker sings for his supper, What shall we give him? White bread and butter."

Many musicians who made it big in Bollywood started out as advertisement jingle artists before their talent was recognized and they were given a movie break, like AR Rahman, Shilpa Rao, Kunal Ganjawala, Kailash Kher, Shaan, Amit Trivedi, Jagjit Singh, Chitra Singh, Shantanu Moitra, Ram Sampath, Sonu Nigam, Sona Mohapatra, KK, and Shankar Mahadevan. Jingles were, and are, a steppingstone for composing music or playback singing in the films. Of course, there are those who make it to Tinsel Town directly, without cutting their teeth extolling the virtues of soap or washing powder.

The playback singers of the 1950s and '60s did not have to follow that route. Jingles were unheard of in the 1950s and were few and far between in the 1960s. They were a novelty. All India Radio started commercials on Vividh Bharati only in 1967. Before that, the jingles would be full-fledged songs, and used to be recorded on 78/45 RPM discs by advertising companies and played at shops, markets, *mandis,* village squares, public gatherings, and marketing outreach programs. The records were usually manufactured by The Gramophone Company Limited, Dum Dum, for the advertisers.

But if *The Rolling Stones* could not avoid the fat wallets of the advertising world, and recorded '*Snap, Crackle, Beat!*' for Rice Krispies in 1964, then why should our own playback singers have been immune to the temptation?

All Indians who grew up in the 1950s and '60s remember the Murphy Radio, one of the earliest radio brands in Indian homes. And who does not remember its mascot—the Murphy Baby—a chubby toddler with its finger placed near its lips? The brand entered India around 1948 and was synonymous with the healthy and bonny baby featured in its advertisements. One of the most popular compliments given to beautiful, healthy children were calling them a 'Murphy baby'. Calendars and posters with the child's face were frequently hung in gynaecological clinics, maternity homes and shops.

In 2012, the 'Murphy Baby' phenomenon made a comeback and gained wide attention in the movie *Barfi*. The title song said it all: "*Barfi jab amma ji ki kokh mein tha soya, amma ne Murphy ka radio mangaya, Murphy munna jaisa lalla amma ka tha sapna.*"

Murphy was also closely associated with Hindi film music. It would organize the Metro-Murphy Singing Contest. In 1957, Mahendra Kapoor and Arati Mukherjee were the winners of the Metro-Murphy Singing Contest. And who were the judges? The crème de la crème of the music industry—Naushad, Anil Biswas, C Ramchandra, Vasant Desai, and Madan Mohan. Even singer Sudha Malhotra got her breakthrough with the Murphy Radio Singing Contest.

So, it was no surprise then that Murphy would purportedly rope in the top playback singer Mohammed Rafi to do their promotion. Murphy's famous advertising tagline was, "*Murphy ghar ghar ki rounak, Murphy ghar ghar ki shaan, Tarah tarah ke Murphy radio, la deten hain ghar mein jaan.*"

Yasmin Khalid Rafi, Rafi's daughter-in-law, in her book *Mohammed Rafi: My Abba—A Memoir* writes that she developed a love for film music and listened to it all day on the old Murphy radio while growing up in a small town of Madhya Pradesh.

Rafi also sang for Burmah Shell to promote kerosene oil: *"Ghar ghar mein muskaaye roshini, aur andhera haath maley, gaaon gaaon aur nagar nagar mein, Burmah Shell ka tel jaley."* The music was composed by Mukul Roy and lyrics were by S Athaiya.

Bata, which set up its shoe manufacturing factory in Batanagar, close to Calcutta, in 1934, had Hemant Kumar do their promotion by way of two songs in Bengali.

In 1964, Asha Bhosle sang for Himalaya Bouquet toilet and talcum powder of Hindustan Lever—'*Phool Ke Samman Hai*' penned by Jan Nisar Akhtar and composed by Ravi.

Earlier, in 1957, Hindustan Lever had Geeta Dutt sing for Rexona soap to music composed by Salil Choudhury and lyrics by Shailendra.

In fact, Salil wrote the lyrics and composed the music of several jingles—for Rexona soap, Lipton tea, Hamam soap, Cookme spices, Paludrine anti-malarial tablets and Dulal's Taal Mishri (Palm Sugar).

Salil also composed an informative song for the visitors to Calcutta cautioning them about the menace of pickpockets on the buses and streets. The song '*Kono Ak Pocketmaarer Kaahini Shonaai Shono*' was based on Salil's classic '*Kono Ak Gaanyer Bondhu*' and a 78 RPM record was released.

Salil also composed a piece of 12-second piano music for HMT watches.

Mukesh promoted a cigarette brand in the jingle '*Cigartton Mein Sabse Aala*'. He also sang a jingle for Gaay Chhap Dant Manjan.

Some of these commercials followed another route too—the songs that did not mention the product advertised directly but being based on the concerned subject with the announcer at the end mentioning the product.

Meena Mangeshkar sang for Geoffrey Manner's Gripe Mixture. This was a full-fledged lullaby *'Nindiya Ke Us Paar'* which could have been any film song. In the end, the announcer announced: *"Ma ki mamta ke saath lori ne janam liya, agar aisi lori ke baad bhi lalla chain se nahin sota, samajhiye usey Manner's Gripe Mixture ki zaroorat hai."*

Similarly, Sajjad Hussain, the composer of iconic songs such as Suraiya's *'Ye Kaisi Ajab Dastan Ho Gayi Hai'*, Lata Mangeshkar's favourite *'Ae Dilruba'* and Rafi's *'Phir Tumhari Yaad Aayi Ae Sanam'* (all from *Rustom Sohrab,* 1963) composed for Geoffrey Manner's Anacin. The lyrics for the song *'Meri Tanhaiyon Tum Hi'* (sung by Brij Varni) went: *"Meri tanhaiyon tum hi laga lo mujh ko seene se, ki main ghabra gaya hun, is tarah ro ro ke jeene se."* In the end it was announced, *"Yeh dard bhara geet aap ki khidmat mein Anacin banane waalon ne pesh kiya. Anacin ke chaar faaidey—dard door, zukham aur bukhar gaayab, isliye ghabrahat mein kami, tabiyat mein chain."*

These advertising discs are a collector's item—very few and highly priced. They need not be sung by well-known playback singers. They are available with old disc collectors, on rare discs sites, on eBay—available for a song. For example, a typical site hawking the disc of *'Surf—Jagmag Safed Aur Alishan'*.

Even the British Library lists some of these recordings. One such example is *'Kaisi Aisi Reet'* of Kafi Aspirin made by Bayer. The recording has been shown during the period 1935–55.

The era of such a fascinating slice of music and advertising history, where discs were used, and many of our classic playback singers lent their voice, is of course over now. But nostalgia has no end date!

22

The Classy Composer

Madan Mohan

Hindi film music is replete with What-Ifs, Maybes and Might-Have-Beens.

What if Madan Mohan had continued to serve in the Army? He had studied in Colonel Brown's Military High School, Dehradun, completed one year military training in 1943, and joined the Army during the Second World War as a Second Lieutenant. But it was not meant to be. He resigned after the War to pursue his love for music. The Army's loss was Hindi film music's gain—an immeasurable gain. The sensitivity and the fine sensibilities that marked his music was a far cry from the gore and violence of the battlefield. Madan returned to the war zone, albeit in reel life, in *Haqeeqat* (1964)—with stunning music including the best patriotic song ever composed (though not widely acknowledged) in *'Kar Chale Hum Fida'*; and *Hindustan Ki Kasam* (1973).

What if Madan has found success as a singer, and not gravitated towards composing. In 1947, he had recorded two ghazals, and in 1948, two more. In the same year, he sang a duet with Lata Mangeshkar under the baton of Ghulam Haider in *Shaheed*. There could not have been a better launchpad! But it was not meant to be, and Madan was destined to be behind the microphone, not in front. And that allowed the music lovers to be held in thrall by the sheer magic of his compositions.

What if Madan had succeeded as an actor? He had a striking personality, was fond of body building, had a robust physique. He wanted to try his luck as an actor. The fact that he was the son of Rai Bahadur Chunilal Kohli, co-founder of Filmistan Studios, may have had a role to play. But again, fate had other plans. His first film as a hero—*Parda*—got shelved after completing almost eight to nine reels of shooting and his only film foray was restricted to brief screen appearances in *Shaheed* (1948), *Ansoo* (1953) and *Munimji* (1954). And that allowed the yet-to-be-mined treasure trove to be brought to the surface, to the utter bliss of the discerning listeners.

What if Lata Mangeshkar had continued to have a misunderstanding with him, arising out of the handiwork of his ill-wishers (rich playboy), and not patched up with him? She had refused to sing for his first film *Aankhen* (1950) for this reason? When the reality dawned, Lata apologized to him. Just as well. Else, Hindi film music's once-in-an-era collaboration would not have seen the light of day. Interestingly, the first song that Madan sang, a duet with Lata—*'Pinjare Mein Bulbul Bole, Mera Nanha Sa Dil Dole'* (*Shaheed,* 1948) was picturized on a brother-sister pair. Who would have known that the song would prophesize the Madan-Lata relationship with Lata becoming the *rakhi* sister of her Madan *bhaiya*?

We are glad that fortune behaved in the manner it did!

Madan and Lata were made for each other. Without Lata's songs, Madan's true genius cannot be gauged (even though he composed some outstanding songs for other singers). Similarly, without Madan, Lata's oeuvre of musical gems would stand substantially diminished. Madan reserved the best tunes for her. Not that it didn't rankle other singers. Asha Bhosle (who rendered the spectacular *'Shok Nazar Ki Bijliyan'* (*Woh Kaun Thi,* 1964) and the frothy *'Jhumka Gira Re'* (*Mera Sayaa,* 1966) confronted Madan about it. Undeterred, Madan replied that Lata would always be his first choice.

But why Lata? The answer lay in Madan's compositional style. The words had to be sung in a manner to bring forth their beauty, their hidden meaning, their real intent. That required an emotional plunge into the deep waters of the music and the lyrics, to bring to the surface the pearls scattered on the sea floor. Madan was of the firm opinion that only Lata was capable of the deep dive.

Tunes, challenging ones, without sacrificing the melody, were crafted for Lata. She cleared them with full marks, with an appreciative nod of the maestro who never once doubted her ability to do so. What we got were songs that will remain eternal.

In the song *'Chhaayee Barkha Bahaar'* (*Chiraag*, 1969), Lata spreads out the word *'Chhaayee'* to bring out its exact meaning. Consider the three iconic unforgettable songs of *Woh Kaun Thi* (1964). Hear the way Lata renders *'Phir'* in *"Phir yeh haseen raat ho na ho"* (*'Lag Ja Gale'*); *'Kyoon'* in *"Aap kyoon roye"* (*'Jo Humne Dastan Apni Sunai'*); *'Rimjhim Rimjhim'* in *'Naina Barse Rimjhim Rimjhim'*—each in a unique way to elicit the import of the word and the emotion underlying it.

Madan was of the belief that Lata's voice was best suited for intense emotional songs. The loneliness in her persona lead to the intense emotions in her singing. The nuances in her songs were rendered with minute details and fine restraint.

Such a made-in-heaven collaboration could not have been possible without a personal chemistry between the two. Such was the respect and affection Lata had for Madan that, after his demise, his children were married by her—her name even appearing on the wedding card.

Not that other singers didn't sing outstanding songs of his—*'Phir Wohi Shaam'* by Talat Mehmood (*Jahan Ara*, 1964); *'Bhuli Hui Yaadon'* by Mukesh (*Sanjog*, 1961); *'Har Taraf Ab*

Yahi Afsaane Hain' by Manna De (*Hindustan Ki Kasam*, 1973); *'Simtee Si Sharmayee Si'* by Kishore Kumar (*Parwana*, 1971); *'Tum Jo Mil Gaye Ho'* by Mohammad Rafi (*Hanste Zakhm*, 1973); *'Aye Dil Mujhe Bataa De'* by Geeta Dutt (*Bhai-Bhai*, 1956); *'Shokh Nazar Ki Bijliyan'* by Asha Bhosle (*Woh Kaun Thi*, 1964), and many others. But Lata would always remain Madan's priority number one.

Madan remained a man of the classes. His compositions, encompassing pathos, nostalgia, romance, registered in your mind, then percolated to your heart. His tunes were an acquired taste. That's why they have no shelf life. Even his peppy, fluffy numbers mostly remained beyond the reach of the masses. Masses prefer casual, simple tunes—which can be sung under the shower—but they did not generally find a place in Madan's compositional style. His songs required intellect to appreciate the intricacies of the poetry and the melody. That was his limitation. But a self-imposed one.

That's why he was not a commercial success. If the man on the street cannot hum your song, you will remain confined to the drawing room. Your bank balance will forever remain modest. To his credit, Madan never compromised, and stuck to his core competency.

In his 25-year long career, out of his 95 films, only a handful became box office successes—*Bhai-Bhai* (1956), *Woh Kaun Thi* (1964), *Mera Saaya* (1966), *Heer Raanjha* (1970), *Laila Majnu* (1976). Films like *Jahan Ara* (1964) ran for only four days (No fault of Madan though—the film had superlative music, but the average listener probably did not agree).

Madan, while sticking to his style throughout his career, intelligently adapted to changing trends by changes in his tunes and orchestration, in a subtle way. So, whether it was Madan Mohan 2.0 or 3.0, it was always Madan Mohan! For example, hear the orchestration in the song *'Tum Jo Mil Gaye Ho'* (*Hanste Zakhm*, 1973)—in its modern approach, it excels in creativity and impact. Like a hurricane, it begins like a gentle breeze, gradually gathers momentum, followed by a short lull, then moves into full throttle. The melody and orchestral passages reflect the changing mood of the song—the plea of the lover, its acceptance, followed by the fever-pitched joyous celebration. A genius was at work, incorporating modern techniques to a time-tested compositional style.

Madan's proclivity towards the 'ghazal' genre manifested itself under the influence of his Lucknow days in 1946 where he worked as a Program Assistant in All India Radio, where he interacted with Begum Akhtar, Talat Mehmood and Barkat Ali.

Lata has stated that the way Madan could compose ghazals, no one else could. He was in a different class altogether. Composing a captivating melody with all the necessary ornamentations to highlight the ghazal's soul, was his forte. Each ghazal is a treasure and beyond measure.

Consider some of them—*'Hum Pyaar Mein Jalne Walon Ko'* (*Jailor*, 1958); *'Woh Chupp Rahein Toh Mere Dil Ke Daag Jalte Hain'* (*Jahan Ara*, 1964); *'Agar Mujhse Mohabbat Hai'* (*Aap Ki Parchhaiyan*, 1964); *'Yun Hasraton Ke Daag'*, *'Unko Yeh Shikayat Hai'* and *'Jaana Tha Humse Door'* (all three from *Adalat*, 1958).

His peers also had high regard for him. Naushad once remarked that Madan's two ghazals from *Anpadh* (1962)—*'Hain Isi Mein Pyaar Ki Abroo'* and *'Aap Ki Nazaron Nein Samjha'* were equal to all the songs he had composed in his life. A huge, unprecedented compliment from one maestro to another.

It was thus natural for Madan to be crowned, by listeners and peers, the Emperor of Ghazals. But this anointment also became his limitation. He got slotted and could not escape from the pigeon-hole.

Not that Madan Mohan only did ghazals. His other works with Lata are equally noteworthy—*'Doli Chadhate Hee Heer Nein Bain Kiye'* (*Heer Ranjha*, 1970); *'Main Toh Tum Sang Nain Milake'* (*Man-Mauji*, 1962); *'Woh Bhuli Daastaan'* (*Sanjog*, 1961); *'Meri Aankhon Se Koi Neend Liye Jaata Hai'* (*Pooja Ke Phool*, 1964); *'Jeeya Le Gayo Jee Mora Saawariya'* (*Anpadh*, 1962); *'Ja Re Badara Bairee Jaa'* (*Bahana*, 1960); *'Meri Veena Tum Bin Roye'* (*Dekh Kabira Roya*, 1957); *'Do Dil Toote Do Dil Haare'* (*Heer Ranjha*, 1970); *'Bairan Neend Na Aaye'* (*Chacha Zindabad*, 1959); *'Nainon Men Badara Chhaye'* (*Mera Saaya*, 1966) and several others underlying Madan Mohan's genius to craft a tune for any mood or situation. As the songs with Lata would reveal, he generally remained a serious composer for her.

Some songs of Madan have an interesting story to them.

While recording *'Aaj Sochaa Toh Aansoo Bhar Aaye'* (*Hanste Zakhm*, 1973), Lata was so moved that she broke down twice during her rendition. Eventually, Madan could only record the music track that day, Lata dubbing the next day.

The most surprising part was that Madan Mohan was not formally trained in music, yet he explored the vast variety of raags in his tunes, much to the admiration of the connoisseurs of Indian classical music. Reportedly, Bade Ghulam Ali was once singing a thumri in a *mehfil* when the song *'Kadar Jaane Na'* (*Bhai-Bhai*, 1956) wafted in from a radio close by. He immediately put his harp down and commented that this was perfect singing and that he won't sing any further.

An amusing incident took place while filming *'Naina Barse'* (*Woh Kaun Thi*, 1964). Lata was not available, so Madan recorded the song in his voice. It was a strange sight for the bystanders to see a petite Sadhna lip-synching to a male voice.

Yet, for all his mammoth abilities, he didn't win the Filmfare Award—the gold standard of popular appeal. The critical appeal came in the form of Sur Singar Samsad awards for *'Maine Rang Li Aaj Chunariya'* (*Dulhan Ek Raat Ki*, 1967), and *'Nainon Mein Badara Chhaye'* (*Mera Saaya*, 1966); and the National Award for *Dastak* (1970) mainly due to Lata's classical, and classy, trio—*'Baiyan Na Dharo'*, *'Maaee Ree Main Kaase Kahoon'*, and *'Hum Hain Mate-e-Koocha'*.

Madan also worked in All India Radio, Delhi, in 1947 where my maternal uncle Satish Bhatia also worked (he retired as Chief Producer, Light Music). They became close friends and Madan would always meet him whenever he came to Delhi. In one such meeting in 1962—a dinner at my uncle's place—he met Bhupinder, who was a guitarist under my uncle in AIR, Delhi. Madan requested him to sing and was impressed enough to invite him to Bombay to record *'Hoke Majboor'* (*Haqeeqat*, 1964) along with Rafi, Talat and Manna De. In 1975, Bhupinder would sing *'Dil Dhundta Hai'* (*Mausam*, 1975) under his baton.

By 1970s the musical tastes were changing. Madan was deeply hurt by the commercialization of music. He hit the bottle which would eventually lead to his death on 14th July 1975. The composer who thought he wasn't adequately appreciated, bizarrely found fame and recognition for his mediocre score in *Laila Majnu* in 1976. There was more to come. A treasure trove of hundreds of his unutilized tunes were discovered by his son. Some of these were released. A special mention needs to be made of the song *'Tere Baghair'*—an outstanding Rafi rendition. Yash Chopra utilized some unused tunes in *Veer-Zaara* (2004). Lata naturally lent her voice to the songs, arranged in a modern orchestration style by Madan's son Sanjeev Kohli which appealed, not only to Madan's fan base, but a new generation of listeners too. The album became the highest selling album of that year.

Madan was born on 25th June 1924 at Baghdad in Iraq. Madan may have left the world at the age of 51 (no age to die), but Madan the Composer can never die. He never blew his trumpet; he didn't have to. Very early in his career, Madan was aware of the timelessness of his legacy that he would leave behind when Lata echoed his self-belief in the song from *Baghi* (1953)— *'Hamare Baad Ab Mehfil Mein Afsaane Bayaan Honge/Baharein Humko Dhoondegi, Na Jaane Hum Kahaan Honge'.*

23

The Silken Singer

Talat Mehmood

'Hain Sabse Madhur Woh Geet Jinhein Hum Dard Ke Sur Mein Gaate Hain'.

Dev Anand sang this song on screen in *Patita* (1953). His playback singer was Talat Mahmood. Talat could well have been singing about most of his own songs.

His voice has been variously described as serene, melancholic, soulful, ultra-soft, romantic, majestic, hypnotic, poetic. But the two adjectives which truly capture the uniqueness of his voice are velvety and silken. Add to that his Lucknowi grace, his Urdu diction, his inflection, his *nazakat*, his intonation, his enunciation, his *soz*, and you have an aristocrat among singers. The vibrato in his voice, a gift of God, added that extra 'something' to his voice. Something beyond replication.

There have been many clones of Mohammad Rafi. There have been (fewer) clones of Mukesh. A large number of Bengalis, and many others, copy Kishore Kumar and Hemant Kumar (Hemant even had two soundalikes in the film industry when he was active—Subir Sen and Dwijen Mukherjee). But Talat? No chance. It just wasn't possible.

Having said that, there was a singer in Pakistan—Salim Raza—who did try to emulate Talat. One slice of history, not well known, is that Mehdi Hassan—the *Shehenshah* of ghazals—was a devotee of Talat and began climbing the ladder of success on the back of Talat's two songs. At a public performance in Karachi in 1957, he sang Talat's '*Ek Main Hoon Ek Meri Bekasi Ki Shaam Hai*' from *Tarana* (1951) composed by Anil Biswas and '*Husnwalon Ko Na Dil Do*' from *Babul* (1950) composed by Naushad. The crowd went ecstatic and thus began Mehdi Hassan's glorious career.

Another fact, again not widely known, is that Talat was very popular in Pakistan. He visited Pakistan and sang three songs for two Pakistani films, *Ghanghor Ghata* (1961) and *Chiragh Jalta Raha* (1962). The latter film was the launching pad of the legendary film actor Mohammad Ali. Talat also sang seven non-film songs including '*Khuda Woh Waqt Na Lae*' for which he was presented a shield by the Gramophone Company of Pakistan.

So how did Talat's own journey begin? His conservative Muslim background meant that singing was a big no-no. However, you cannot keep talent shackled. Despite his family objection, he opted for singing. He began learning music in Lucknow in the late 1930s. Having honed his talent, his first port of call was All India Radio, Lucknow in 1939 (when he was 16), where he began singing ghazals. HMV offered him his first disc in 1941. He then moved to Calcutta. In 1944 came the hit '*Tasveer Teri Dil Mera Behela Na Sakegi*'—a song that became hugely popular.

In 1949 he came to Bombay to sing for the Hindi film industry. His big break came with the song '*Ae Dil Mujhe Aisi Jagha Le Chal Jahan Koi Na Ho*' composed by Anil Biswas for *Arzoo* (1950). Talat had arrived! And, as is normally the case, his family belatedly welcomed his decision when he gained foothold and respect in the film industry.

Talat sang about 800 songs over four decades. Plus, he recorded about 200 non-film ghazals and geet. Not a long list. But each song is as classy as they come. What was Talat's contribution, besides of course the immense joy he provided his countless fans? He was the founder of the modern semi-classical as well as the non-classical ghazal. His influence upon other contemporary and succeeding ghazal singers has been profound. He transformed and re-energized the art and form of ghazal singing. His throat and his tongue were the ideal tools of the trade to popularize the genre. He conquered the souls of countless people throughout the globe—the cognoscenti, as also the man on the street. He was to the ghazal born!

Most songs, especially in the 1950–1970 period, can be identified by the way they have been tuned by their music composers. Each music director had a distinctive style which was stamped on the song. So, a song tuned by OP Nayyar, SD Burman, Madan Mohan, Roshan, Naushad and others could be clearly identified. Some people went even further and could identify a Shankar song from Jaikishan's. But this test failed with Talat's songs. His songs were HIS songs and the music directors had to leave their compositional style outside the recording studio. The songs had to be fitted to Talat's own genius. Here the singer demanded the bespoke suit, and his singing talent brooked no ready-to-wear apparel.

Who could have imagined OP Nayyar composing '*Pyar Par Bas Toh Nahin Hai*' from *Sone Ki Chidiya* (1958)? The song is not in the OP Nayyar style by any stretch of imagination. Incidentally, this film had Talat as a hero, but his film career was not a success. Or Ravi's '*Sab Kuchh Luta Ke Hosh Mein*' from *Ek Saal* (1957), or Khayyam's '*Shaam-e-Gham Ki Kasam*' from *Footpath* (1953), or Roshan's '*Main Dil Hun Ek Armaan Bhara*' from *Anhonee* (1952), or Shankar-Jaikishan's '*Tum Toh Dil Ke Taar Chhed Kar*' from *Roop Ki Rani Choron Ka Raja* (1961) (Talat also sang romantic songs occasionally), or SD Burman's '*Jaayen Toh Jaayen Kahaan*' from *Taxi Driver* (1954)—which incidentally fetched SD Burman his first Filmfare Award.

All these songs, and many more, are Talat's songs and not that of the composers, which is a rarity. Of course, this is just a generalization. Composers like Madan Mohan and Salil Chowdhury, who shared a special bonding with

Talat, are some exceptions whose style of composing was in complete unison with Talat's unique singing élan. Witness Talat's songs in *Jahanara* (1964)—*'Tere Aankh Ke Ansoo Pee Jaaoon'*, *'Main Teri Nazar Ka Suroor Hun'*, *'Phir Wohi Shaam Wohi Gham Wohi Tanhai Hai'*. Madan Mohan did not listen to the movie's writer-director who wanted Rafi. Madan wanted the film to be Talat's long-overdue comeback. His career had been floundering by then. And what winners they turned out to be, even though the film tanked. Salil's Talat oeuvre is full of gems including *'Itna Na Mujhse Tu Pyar Badha'*, and *'Aansoo Samajh Ke Kyun Mujhe Aankh Se Tumne Gira Diya'* from *Chhaya* (1961), and *'Raat Ne Kya Kya Khwaab Dikhaye'* from *Ek Gaaon Ki Kahaani* (1957).

One other interesting fact. I have referred above to *'Sab Kuchh Luta Ke Hosh Mein Aaye Toh Kya Kiya'*, *'Jaayen Toh Jaayen Kahaan'* and *'Tum Toh Dil Ke Taar Chhed Kar'*. Many may not know that Lata Mangeshkar has also sung these songs. And the list continues—*'Ai Mere Dil Kahin Aur Chal'* from the movie *Daag* (1952), *'Dil Matwala Lakh Sambhala'* from *Bewafa* (1952), *'Mera Qaraar Le Ja'* from *Ashiana* (1952).

So why is only the Talat version of these songs (called twin songs or tandem songs) fresh in public memory? The supreme quality of Talat's voice made singers nervous. Lata, in particular, dreaded singing not only duets with Talat because she felt that his rich and smooth voice would render hers dull in comparison, but also tandem songs which Talat had sung.

The 1960s saw a change in audience tastes. Ghazals and heart-rending ballads were not popular anymore. Talat continued to record songs, but less in number. His last soundtrack recording was in 1985. He went on highly successful concerts abroad including at the Royal Albert Hall in London and Madison Square Garden in New York, drawing packed houses of music lovers.

I attended one of his concerts in Delhi in the early 1980s. The bespectacled, soft-spoken voice that showed no signs of wear and tear, suit and tie, and his best of the best sung to his devotees packing the hall to the rafters. It was a magnificent *mehfil*, a top-drawer soiree.

As a person, Talat was soft-spoken and decent. Dilip Kumar, who teamed up with Talat for innumerable hits, termed Talat a perfect gentleman.

His goodness came at a cost. Raju Bharatan, the veteran film historian, mentioned an incident. On one TV show, while discussing Geeta Dutt, Asha Bhosle remarked, "*Unke saath koi ek* male singer *Mahmood-Mahmood kar ke tha* (A male singer called some Mehmood-Mehmood used to be with her)." This from Asha, who sang 51 duets with him during her 1951–1959 period of struggle, when she was suffering from the Lata-complex! Her non-acknowledgement of OP Nayyar, who gave her self-confidence, made her realize her self-worth, smoothened her rough edges, trained her, removed her from out of the shadow of her sister, is still understandable—there is a personal animus involved. But Talat? Forgetting his name? Forgetting his contribution? Not done!

In *Aadmi* (1968), even Naushad (who had a very successful run with Talat) was arm-twisted by Manoj Kumar to take Mahendra Kapoor as his playback singer in the song '*Kaisee Haseen Aaj Baharon Ki Raat Hai*', even though Talat had done the recording and the album had been released. So bizarrely, the film had Mahendra Kapoor, while the album had Talat. It is a pity that both Naushad and Dilip Kumar (the other hero) could not take a stand despite their most productive partnership with Talat in the earlier days.

Shockingly, Talat did not win a single Filmfare Award, though he was nominated just once for '*Jalte Hain Jiske Liye*' from *Sujata* (1959). But the government recognized his worth and awarded him the Padma Bhushan in 1992, in recognition of his artistic contributions in the spheres of cinematic and ghazal music.

As Talat so dulcetly put it in one of his iconic songs (amended suitably):

> *'Jalte Hain Jiske Liye, Hamari Aankhon Ke Diye, Dhoond Laye Hain Wohi, Geet Talat Hamare Liye, Gunguna Rahen Hain Yehi Geet Talat Hamare Liye'.*

24

One After the Other

Under the overarching banner of Hindi film songs, we have categories, genres, and facets. Some are rather obvious like 'club' songs, 'break-up' songs, or 'tandem' songs. Some have come to light with the advent of technology, such as songs with missing stanzas on vinyl records. However, there is one aspect which is not so obvious. You cannot know it in the audio format and many times, you may not even get to see it on YouTube. It only comes to light when you see the film. And since most of the films are old, only people on the wrong side of their 50s may recognize this peculiar feature—the feature of back-to-back songs in Hindi films when the second song follows the first one without a pause. Each song is different and finds a separate place in the album/cassette/CD. It just so happens that while you are still savouring the joy of the first ditty while watching the film, you get another one instantly.

Remember *Bobby* (1973)? How can one forget '*Na Chahoon Sona Chandi*'? Rishi Kapoor—oily-haired, young and innocent—dancing to the Goan folk song with a bottle-swigging, portly, Hitlerian-moustached Premnath, with Dimple Kapadia in a fisherwoman's dress demurely watching the proceedings. The moment the song gets over, '*Jhoot Bole Kauya Kaate*' begins, with Dimple joining in. The village square remains, the participants remain the same (the fisher-folk take over from the suited Goan Christians)—two songs in one setting! The first song with a Western beat, the second with a boisterous dholak. Two moods!

Now consider *Guide* (1965). Lata Mangeshkar's '*Mose Chhal Kiye Jaaye*' is immediately followed by Rafi's '*Kya Se*

Kya Ho Gaya Bewafa'. Both the songs are composed in Raag *Jhinjhoti.* Listen carefully and you will realize that they are the same tune but on a different scale. The songs may sound dissimilar, but they are not. The theme is the same. Lata's is that of anguish at '*Saiyan Beimaan*' and Rafi's also that of anguish at '*Kya Se Kya Ho Gaya*'. But the genius of SD Burman still created two moods from the same raag and same theme. Two songs, one raag, two moods.

In *Hare Rama Hare Krishna* (1971), '*Dum Maro Dum*' with its iconic opening guitar sequence sets the mood of the song—the *chillum*-smoking hippies swinging, raising the finger to society and singing "go-to-hell"! Zeenat Aman made a sensational entry in the film and the film industry with this song. The song finishes (only one stanza was used in the film. The song, however, has two), Dev Anand starts '*Dekho O Deewano*'. The brother needed to make an entry immediately to show his disapproval and request his sister (who doesn't yet know Dev is her brother) and her troupe to desist from escapism. No two songs in their theme and mood could be so diametrically opposite.

Then there is the well-known and the finest dream sequence in the Hindi film world from *Awara* (1951) involving two back-to-back songs: '*Tere Bina Aag Yeh Chandni*' and '*Ghar Aaya Mera Pardesi*'. The second follows the first with such seamlessness that one can be forgiven for thinking they are one single song. Here the mood shifts from plaintive to dread in the first song—"*Mujhko yeh narak na chahiye; mujhko phool, mujhko geet, mujhko preet chahiye; mujhko chahiye bahaar*", segueing to peace and calm in the second song which at the end again turns to dread. Two songs, same set, same dream sequence, same actors, three moods—mournful, anxious and tranquil.

There are many such examples.

As long back as in 1938, *Gramophone Singer* (composer Anil Biswas) had '*Kaahe Akela Dolat Baadal*' followed immediately by *'Ek Chhota Sa Mandir'*—both sung by Surendra.

Ram Rajya released in 1943—one of the two films Mahatma Gandhi ever saw—had such a pair (composed by Shankar Rao Vyas). These were *'Surya Dev Jagdish Tej Jinko'* and *'O Rani Maharani Itna Toh Karo Vichar'*. Its modern remake released in 1967 had four (yes FOUR!) back-to-back songs—*'Tha Andhera Chhaya Hua'*, *'Aaja Tujh Bin'*, *'Dar Lage Garje Badariya'*, and *'Hato Jao Mat Chhedo'*.

An interesting aside here: Vasant Desai, the music director, was chosen to receive the inaugural Dr Brihaspati Award (later known as Saraswati Award) but Naushad pointed out that two of the film songs were 'replicate' songs from the original *Ram Rajya*. It instead went to Naushad for the film *Palki*.

Nagin (1954) had two instances. Composer Hemant Kumar gave us *'Teri Yaad Mein'* and *'Oonchi Oonchi Dunya Ki Deewarein'*, and towards the end of the film *'Sun Rasiya'* and *'Mera Badli Mein Chhup Gaya Chand Re'*. Later, in *Nandini Durgesh* (1956), Hemant gave us *'Mat Maaro Shyaam Pichkari'* and *'Pyar Ke Rang Mein Saiyan'*.

Madan Mohan composed three absolute back-to-back classics that were filmed on three heroines who were pining for the men they thought had deserted them. One song, with three stanzas, each filmed on a different heroine would have done the trick. But then the Hindi film music would have been poorer by two songs. Nobody was complaining. *Dekh Kabira Roya* (1957) had these exceptional songs—*'Meri Veena Tum Bin Roye'*, *'Ashkon Se Teri Humne Tasweer Banayi Hai'* and *'Tu Pyaar Kare Ya Thukraye'*. Earlier, in *Madhosh* (1951), Madan Mohan had given us *'Dil Dhak Dhak'* and *'Nazron Ke Chaar Hote'*.

In *New Delhi* (1956), the evergreen catchy *'Nakhrewali'* composed by Shankar-Jaikishan leads to *'Zindagi Bahaar*

Hai'. *Naya Daur* (1957) had OP Nayyar transitioning from the easy rhythm of '*Dil Leke Daga Denge*' to the hot-blooded boisterousness of the patriotic '*Yeh Desh Hai Veer Jawanon Ka*'. *Chaudvin Ka Chand* (1960), whose title track fetched Rafi his first Filmfare Award, had '*Mera Yaar Bana Hai Dulha*' give way to '*Balam Se Milan Hoga*'. The composer for this was Ravi.

Nasir Hussain—the acclaimed producer-director—is rightfully regarded as the filmmaker who took such songs to a whole new level. In *Dil Deke Dekho* (1959)—the debut film of both music director Usha Khanna and actress Asha Parekh—Hussain had '*Megha Re*' composed in the traditional format, followed by a westernized '*Bade Hain Dil Ke Kale*'. Along with the feel, the look of the dancers also changed from Indian to western.

In *Yaadon Ki Baraat* (1973), he gave us '*Aap Ke Kamre Mein*' and '*Dil Mil Gaye*' that was composed by RD Burman. Then in *Hum Kisi Se Kam Nahin* (1977), we were treated to a dance sequence featuring '*Chand Mera Dil*', '*Aa Dil Kya*', '*Tum Kya Jano*' and '*Mil Gaya*'. Four songs, four singers (including composer RD Burman), four different melodies, four moods—yet each flowed into the succeeding song organically, without looking contrived.

In *Zamaane Ko Dikhana Hai* (1981), he slowed down and gave us just a pair—'*Bolo Bolo*' and '*Poochho Na Yaar Kya Hua*'.

So, what explains this phenomenon? Why back-to-back songs? The most obvious reason is that songs in Hindi films tell a story. What better way to transition from one emotional theme to another than to have a song immediately after another with a different mood so that the differentiation becomes obvious?

But there are other reasons as well. In *Pratigya* (1975), after belting out '*Main Jatt Yamla*', a drunk Dharmendra (drunk in love and alcohol) falls into the lake and moves on to a dream sequence '*Uth Neend Se Mirzia*'. Very normal for any person in his position! In *Mazdoor* (1983), a jilted Rati Agnihotri sings '*Tumhe Bhool Jaane Ka Haq*' to Raj Babbar at his wedding reception, which is followed immediately by '*Pehla Pehla Pyar*' sung by Padmini Kohlapuri at the honeymoon. This tactic works well to push the story along.

Sometimes, the mood remains the same in both the songs and could have been just one long song. But it would have been tedious to hear it on record or the radio. Also, such a long song could not have been accommodated on a 78-RPM disc. *Awara* (1951) is one such example ('*Tere Bina Aag Yeh Chandni*' and '*Ghar Aaya Mera Pardesi*'). It's essentially one song carved into two. Or take the case of dance competitions in Nasir Hussain films. Song after song is to be expected. Or sometimes, the film is overloaded with songs (like *Nagin*, 1954) and back-to-back is the solution.

The concept is almost non-existent now.

It was seen in *Ae Dil Hai Mushkil* (2016) where '*Cutiepie*' is immediately followed by '*Channa Mereya*'. Again, two moods. The formula still works. Ranbir could have been singing about this fascinating aspect of Hindi music of back-to-back songs, now been put out to pasture, when he sings this line from '*Channa Mereya*'—"*Mere zikr ka zubaan pey swaad rakhna*".

25

The Melodic Composer

Roshan

Hindi film music industry has many examples of artistes taking leave of our planet much before their song is complete. Mohammed Rafi passed away at the age of 56, Kishore Kumar at 58, Mukesh at 53, Geeta Dutt at 42. Shailendra expired at 43. Jaikishan died at 42 and Madan Mohan at 51.

Roshan took leave at age 50.

Like others, he too packed his short life with a musical legacy that's eternal. His oeuvre of classic gems is forever. His genius will be acknowledged in perpetuity. He composed for only 57 films, and only a handful of them proved to be chartbusters. But lack of commercial success did not come in the way of connoisseur's appreciation for his music.

Tulsidas' couplet—*'Manaa Tu Kaahe Na Dheer Dharat Ab/Dheer Dhare Sab Kaaraj Sudharat'* was transformed into *'Man Re Tu Kaahe Na Dheer Dhare/Woh Nirmohi Moh Na Jaane, Jinka Moh Kare'* in *Chitralekha* (1964), and the song was voted the best ever Hindi film song in a survey. Roshan was the music director.

When Lata Mangeshkar was to produce the musical *Bhairavi* in the mid-50s, she was spoilt for choice. From Naushad to Shankar-Jaikishan, each composer expected to win her vote. She chose Roshan. The film was, however, shelved. Mukesh took him for his home production *Malhar* (1951); as did Geeta Bali for her home production *Raag Rang* (1952) directed by her brother.

Roshan's brilliant career in the Hindi film industry, however, began with insecurity and self-doubt, notwithstanding the musical milieu he came from when he set foot in Bombay.

During his childhood at Gujranwala (Pakistan) where he was born, Roshan had little interest in his studies, but could play harmonium with ease. He quit his schooling early and went to Shahjahanpur (near Lucknow) where his father was in service. He learnt sarod from Ustad Allaudin Khan, and sarangi from Bundu Khan. He then studied at Marris College of Music, Lucknow (later known as Bhatkhande College of Hindustani Music). Roshan became a noted esraj player and came to Delhi to work at the All India Radio (AIR) as a staff artist for esraj as well as a music composer. He was rated highly by his colleagues at AIR and composed delightful songs. He worked in AIR for ten years.

A personal element here. My mother Usha Bhatia (staff singer) and her brother Late Satish Bhatia (who retired as Chief Producer, Light Music)—both with AIR, Delhi worked alongside Roshan and became close friends. Just before Roshan left for Bombay to pursue his musical dreams with his second wife Ira Moitra (who was his disciple and also worked as a singer with AIR), he stayed briefly at Husnlal's house (of Husnlal-Bhagatram) at Daryaganj, Delhi. My mother and uncle met Roshan and Ira Moitra on the eve of their departure. My mother would meet Ira Moitra more than three decades later in Bombay at a common friend's party where they would re-live their AIR days.

At Bombay, Roshan stayed in a garage of Husnlal. It was in this garage, where his first son Rakesh was born.

Roshan's first film *Neki Aur Badi* (1949) (before that he assisted Khurshid Anwar in *Singaar*) was offered to him by its maker Kidar Sharma—recognizing Roshan's hidden talent—by replacing Snehal Bhatkar. When the film proved a failure, a dejected Roshan cried before Kidar Sharma that he wanted to commit suicide. After patiently listening to Roshan, Kidar Sharma told Roshan that he had no objection.

He asked whether he would like to be drowned in Haji Ali or in Versova. However, he assured him that if he deferred his decision, he could give him another chance in his next film *Bawre Nain* (1950).

Roshan agreed. But there was more to come.

One day, a film distributer came to Kidar Sharma's office, when Roshan was also present. He offered to pay a staggering sum of money on the condition that Roshan be replaced by Husnlal-Bhagatram in *Bawre Nain*.

Roshan immediately went to the adjacent room and started weeping. Kidar Sharma followed him. Roshan requested Kidar Sharma to replace him, and to make money in the process. Kidar Sharma went back to the distributor and refused.

Once during the recording of *'Kahaan Tak Hum Uthaaye Gham'* (*Arzoo*, 1950), Anil Biswas heard Roshan sobbing behind him. When asked the reason, Roshan said he was not fit to be a composer and would never be able to compose such tunes. Anil Biswas slapped him hard to make Roshan come to his senses. He asked him how he would survive in the industry with such an attitude and told him to fight and have confidence in his ability. Incidentally, Anil Biswas had slapped Mukesh too during Mukesh's debut song in *Pehli Nazar* (1945). It worked for both.

Later in life, Anil Biswas would compare Roshan's music to pure honey dropping from a honeycomb.

The music lovers are grateful to Kidar Sharma for the faith he reposed in Roshan's capability, as well as integrity exhibited by him in saying no to money. *Bawre Nain* is where Roshan's journey began in our hearts and mind. *'Khayalon Mein Kisi Ke Is Tarah Aya Nahin Karte'* by Mukesh and Geeta Roy, and Mukesh's *'Teri Duniya Mein Dil Lagta Nahin'*, were two of the stand-out songs which are popular to date.

In *Malhar* (1951), Roshan composed some alluring melodies including *'Bade Armanon Se Rakha Hai Sanam Teri Kasam'* by Mukesh and Lata. *Nau Bahar* (1952) had *'Ae Ri Mein Toh Prem Diwani Mora Dard Na Jaane Koye'*. *Anhonee* (1952) had the delightful Talat Mehmood number *'Main Dil Hun Ik Armaan Bhara'*. In *Aji Bas Shukriya* (1958), Lata sang—*'Saari Saari Raat Teri Yaad Sataye'*.

In the '50s, Roshan's compositional style was soft and subtle, while being melodious. His orchestration was low-key, yet through distinctive use of Indian musical instruments, he enhanced the mood-building quality of the song. The style was however connoisseur oriented. It was internalized. So, if there were some hits, there were more misses.

Roshan realized the limitation. Lack of commercial success made him re-orient his musical strategy. In the '60s, the music became more externalized, more mainstream. The orchestral arrangements became more Westernized, more forceful. But at its core, his music always retained its originality and rich melodic overtones.

Though he used all the singers very effectively, Lata's contribution to his body of work was immense. She sang as many solos as Rafi, Asha and Mukesh put together. Unlike other composers who made Lata sing at high pitch, Roshan explored the amazing depth of her voice at lower octaves.

Lata believed in and supported Roshan. She stepped into object to Roshan being replaced by OP Nayyar in *Mehbooba* (1954), an issue she escalated to the Cine Artistes' Association. Eventually, Roshan shared credit with OP Nayyar in the film. Roshan never forgot how Lata had stood by him.

It was in the '60s that Roshan bloomed. The Roshan that the common listener knows emerged in this period.

Roshan took off in 1960 itself with *Barsaat Ki Raat*. The movie became a big hit because of its music. It had not one, not two, but three qawwalis including undisputedly the best ever composed for a Hindi film— *'Naa Toh Karwan Ki Talash Hai'*—sung by Manna Dey, Mohammed Rafi, Asha Bhosle, Sudha Malhotra, and SD Batish—its captivating rhythm, lyrics, instrumentation keeping the listeners enthralled. The 12-minute long qawwali took 24 hours to record and became the stuff of cinematic legend. This magnificent qawwali saw Roshan use a variety of musical instruments, including the rhythmic hand clapping in a way that sped up the tempo until the crescendo. That was one of the hallmarks of Roshan's music—the perfect use of instrumentation.

The other qawwalis were—*'Nigha e Naaz Ke Maron Ka Haal'*—sung by Shanker Shambhu, Asha Bhosle, and Sudha Malhotra; and *'Jee Chahta Hai Choom Loon'*—sung by Balbir, Asha, Sudha Malhotra and Bande Hasan. In addition, there were other fascinating melodies, which made the film a perfect musical hit—*'Zindagi Bhar Nahin Bhoolegi, Woh Barsaat Ki Raat'*—sung by Lata and Rafi; and *'Maine Shaayad Tumhein, Pelhe Bhi Kahin Dekha Hai'* by Rafi. Then there was the classical title music—*'Garjat Barsat Saawan Ayo Re'*—sung by Kamal Barot and Suman Kalyanpur. Earlier, in *Malhar* (1951), Roshan had used the same traditional *bandish* in *Goud Malhar*—*'Garjat Barsat Bheejat Aayilo'* sung by Lata.

In *Aarti* (1962), there was Lata's *'Kabhi to Milegi, Kahin Toh Milegi'*; Rafi's *'Ab Kya Misaal Doon'*; and the Lata/Rafi duet *'Tere Bin Sajan Lage Na Jiya'*.

Dil Hi Toh Hai (1963) was another splendid musical treat. Manna Dey sang one of his epic classical songs—*'Laagaa Chunri Mein Daag, Chhupaaun Kaise'*. Roshan composed a lush, complex melody, its intricate notes complementing Manna Dey's vocal acrobatics. Then there was Mukesh's—*'Tum Agar Mujhko Na Chaho Toh Koi Baat Nahin'*. Besides, there was a qawwali sung by Asha—*'Nigahein Milane Ko Jee Chahta Hai'* and another by Manna Dey and Asha—*'Parda Uthe Salaam Ho Jaye'*.

Roshan's grip over the qawwali genre was unparalleled and no other composer came close to him. Roshan was a master in knowing when to let music take a back seat—sometimes to the voice, sometimes to the lyrics. He understood when to keep his music in the foreground and when to let his music recede. Roshan's music was as unassuming as he himself, never placing itself centre stage, nor slipping into nondescript anonymity, but complementing the voices just so.

Roshan's deep love and understanding for Urdu poetry and literature ensured that his songs always resonated with rich, expressive lyrics. Sahir Ludhianvi and Majrooh Sultanpuri were his go-to lyricists.

The film *Taj Mahal* (1963) was another landmark in Roshan's career. Consider the songs—*'Jo Waada Kiya Woh Nibhana Padega'* (Rafi/Lata); *'Zulm e Ulfat Pe Hamein Log'* (Lata); *'Jo Baat Tujh Mein Hai Teri Tasveer Mein Nahin'* (Rafi); and a qawwali—*'Chandi Ka Badan Sone Ki Nazar'* (Lata, Rafi, Manna Dey and Meena Kapoor). The maestro was conferred the Filmfare Award for the music of this film.

Kidar Sharma produced yet another version of the film *Chitralekha* in 1964 based on the novel of Hindi laureate Bhagwati Charan Verma. The earlier *Chitralekha* was produced by him in 1941 and music was composed by Ustad Jhande Khan. The songs became very popular including *'Tum Jao Jao Bhagwan Bane'*.

This time, Kidar Sharma selected Roshan. Roshan did not disappoint and repaid the trust reposed by his mentor, and then some. The music was enthralling. Just two examples—*'Sansaar Se Bhage Phirtey Ho'* and *'Ae Ri Jane Na Doongi'*. I have already referred to *'Man Re Tu Kaahe Na Dheer Dhare'* earlier.

Dooj Ka Chaand (1964), *Bheegi Raat* (1965), *Nai Umar Ki Nai Fasal* (1966), *Dadi Maa* (1966) were some other films with superlative music.

Mamta (1966) was a significant film in Roshan's musical journey. Lata sang some stirring classics *'Rahein Na Rahein Hum'*; *'Rehte The Kabhi Unke Dil Mein'*; *'Sakal Ban Magan Pawan Chalat'*; and *'Vikal Mora Manwa Un Bin Haye'*. Then there was the poignant duet of Hemant and Lata *'Chhupa Lo Yun Dil Mein Pyar Mera, Ke Jaise Mandir Mein Lau Diye Ki'* which never fails to move the listener. Roshan's music was soft, sublime, and evoked a love that was pure, sacred, devotional.

In *Bahu Begum* (1967), there was *'Pad Gaye Jhoole Sawan Rut Aayee Re'* sung by Lata and Asha and Rafi's *'Ham Intzaar Karenge Tera Qayamat Tak'*.

In *Noor Jehan* (1967), Suman Kalyanpur sang *'Sharabee Sharabee'*, and Lata *'Raat Ki Mehfil Sunee Sunee'*.

All songs listed are representative of the essential sweetness of Roshan's tunes based on Indian classical and folk music, whose fragrance continued to stay with the listener long after the song was over.

Roshan died on 16th November 1967. His death was dramatic. At a party, while he was enjoying his drink, he slumped in the chair of a massive heart attack. He died instantly. His last film *Anokhi Raat* was in making. The film had memorable songs including Mukesh's philosophy of life *'O Re Taal Mile Nadi Ke Jal Mein, Nadi Mile Sagar Mein, Sagar Mile Kaun Se Jal Mein, Koi Jane Na'*. Lata's song *'Mehlon Ka Raja Mila'* was yet to be recorded. His wife Ira Moitra arranged the recording.

Roshan's evergreen song best describes his permanent abode in our hearts: "*Rahen Na Rahen Hum, Mehka Karenge, Banke Kali Banke Bahaar, Bagh-e-Wafa Mein.*"

26

The Classical Titan

Manna Dey

Mohammed Rafi, THE singer, had this say about Manna Dey: "You listen to my songs, I listen only to Manna Dey's songs." Bharat Ratna Lata Mangeshkar was a Dey fan. It is, therefore, a mystery why this singing giant remained throughout his career as an 'also-ran'.

That he was a classical titan is acknowledged. That he was an indomitable performer is a given. That he enriched the Hindi film music's musical vocabulary is accepted. His vocal artistry and virtuosity are recognized. Why, therefore, did he not sit in the first row? Why was he always consigned to the second place? Why did Talat Mehmood, Rafi, Kishore Kumar and Mukesh always remain ahead of him?

He was unsurpassed in classical compositions. Except for Rafi and Talat (to some extent), the other two did not count. Consider some of his songs in the classical genre: '*Poochho Na Kaise Maine Rain Bitayee*' from *Meri Surat Teri Aankhen* (1963), '*Kaun Aaya Mere Man Ke Duare*' from *Dekh Kabira Roya* (1957), '*Tum Bin Jeevan Kaisa Jeevan*' from *Bawarchi* (1972), '*Jhanak Jhanak Toree Baaje Payaliya*' from *Mere Huzoor* (1968), '*Re Man Sur Mein Ga*' from *Lal Patthar* (1971), '*Phool Gendva Na Maaro*' from *Dooj Ka Chand* (1964), '*Sur Na Saje Kyaa Gaoon Main*' and '*Bhay Bhanjana Vandana Sun Hamari*' from *Basant Bahar* (1956), '*Laaga Chunri Mein Daag*' from *Dil Hi To Hai* (1963), '*Aayo Kahhan Se Ghanshyam*' from *Buddha Mil Gaya* (1971), and so many others. In the Qawwali of all Qawwalis—'*Na Toh Karvaan Ki Talaash Hai*' from *Barsaat Ki Raat* (1960)—only this genius, with his inimitable *paltaas* and *sargams*, and total command of the *Sufiana* journey from the worldly to the spiritual, could have pulled off this Roshan/Sahir masterpiece—Rafi took charge of the second half when the solid foundation had already been laid.

And who else could have taken on Pandit Bhimsen Joshi in *'Ketaki Gulaab Ki'* from *Basant Bahaar* (1956)? Though understandably Manna Dey was apprehensive of having to square up against the classical stalwart, the fact is that even Pandit Bhimsen Joshi was no less anxious, given Manna Dey's absolute mastery over classical singing and technique in Hindi film songs, as opposed to concert singing where Pandit Bhimsen Joshi would ply his trade. Manna Dey's singing was superlative, and he took this delight in Raag *Basant* to even greater heights.

Manna Dey was also simply outstanding in sentimental/introspective/philosophical songs. His *'Kasme Vaade Pyar Wafa Sab'* from *Upkar* (1967) was so soulfully done that even Lata wondered how he emoted so well. And to think that this song was being offered to Kishore Kumar earlier! It was Kishore Kumar who said that only Manna Dey could invest the song with the emotions that were needed. And what exceptional feelings he endowed the song with! His other songs in this category include *'Tu Pyar Ka Saagar Hai'* from *Seema* (1955), *'Ai Mere Pyare Watan'* from *Kabuliwala* (1961), *'Jeevan Se Lambe Hain Bandhu'* from *Aashirwad* (1968), *'Zindagi Kaisi Hai Paheli'* from *Anand* (1971), *'Tujhe Suraj Kahun Ya Chanda'* from *Ek Phool Do Mali* (1969), *'Yaari Hai Imaan Mera'* from *Zanjeer* (1973), *'Nadiya Chale'* from *Safar* (1970), *'Yehi Paigham Hamara'* from *Paigham* (1959), and others.

But no professional singer can live by these genres only. These are niche genres. They may edify the soul, stimulate the intellect, and appeal to the finer senses. But that is it. For a commercial Hindi film singer, these cannot be the bread and butter. At best, they are a great dessert.

To survive successfully, the staple has to be songs that entertain—romantic songs, fun songs, dance songs, upbeat songs. In general, mainstream songs that occupy the middle ground, which are easy listening, not demanding, not taxing, but commercial 'normal' songs. And it helps significantly if the singer becomes the ghost voice of a big star. That is what Rafi, Kishore and Mukesh became. How did Manna Dey fare here? Not very well, I am afraid. But that was not his fault entirely.

Manna Dey became the voice of Raj Kapoor because Mukesh had signed a contract forbidding him to sing in another film till his film *Mashuqa* (1953) in which he was acting with Suraiya was completed. *Shree 420* (1955) was in production and Mukesh had already sung a few songs. Manna Dey got the opportunity to sing the rest of the songs: '*Dil Ka Haal Sune Dil Wala*', '*Pyaar Hua Iqraar Hua*' and '*Mud Mud Ke Na Dekh*'. This new voice of Raj Kapoor was taken to an ultra-romantic height in *Chori Chori* (1956) with '*Aaja Sanam Madhur Chandni*', '*Yeh Raat Bheegi Bheegi*' and '*Jahaan Main Jaati Hun*'. But then, Mukesh got back, and Manna Dey was shown the door. After such winsome songs, it was tragic. Manna Dey would, 15 years later, again do playback for Raj Kapoor with '*Ae Bhai Zara Dekh Ke Chalo*' in *Mera Naam Joker* (1971) and win the Filmfare Best Singer Award for it.

So that was a short-lived though highly successful pairing. With Shammi Kapoor, he tellingly sang as his voice in *Ujala* (1959): '*Jhoomta Mausam Mast Maheena*', '*Ab Kahaan Jaaye Hum*', '*Chham Chham Lo Suno Chham Chham*' and '*Suraj Zara Aa Pass Aa*'. But it was not meant to be. Rafi became Shammi Kapoor's ghost voice.

Of course, Manna Dey sang some delightful songs in the commercial entertainment space like '*Chale Ja Rahein Hain*' from *Kinare Kinare* (1963), '*O Meri Zohra Jabeen*' from *Waqt* (1965), '*Aao Twist Karein*' from *Bhoot Bangla* (1965), '*Dil Ki Girah Khol*' from *Raat Aur Din* (1967), '*Soch Ke Yeh Gagan Jhoome*'—the delightful duet with Lata in *Jyoti* (1969), '*Phir*

Kahin Koi Phool Khila' from *Anubhav* (1971), *'Abhi to Haath Mein'* from *Seeta Aur Geeta*(1972), *'Har Taraf Ab Yehi Afsane Hain'* from *Hindustan Ki Kasam* (1973), *'Dharti Kahe'* from *Do Bigha Zameen* (1953), *'Tu Chuppi Hai Kahaan'* from *Navrang* (1959), *'Muskara Laadle'* from *Zindagi* (1964), *'Tum Gagan Ke Chandrama'* from *Sati Savitri* (1964), *'Chalat Musafir'* from *Teesri Kasam* (1966), *'Ram Krishna Hari'* from *Chanda Aur Bijli* (1969), *'Na Maangun Sona Chandi'* from *Bobby* (1973), and others.

One iconic song that pitted Manna Dey against Rafi, Talat and Bhupendra (making his debut) was *'Hoke Majboor Mujhe Usne Bhulaya Hoga'* in *Haqeeqat* (1964). Each singer had an exclusive *antara* to showcase his interpretation. All the singers were outstanding, and Manna Dey left the unique impress that defined him.

But even in this main course, except for a few upbeat and romantic songs, songs were still suffused with seriousness. It was, for the most part, a sombre listening, provoking reflection and not necessarily pleasure. The classical underpinning was always present—sometimes overtly, sometimes just lurking under the surface. The smiles, the clapping and dancing which a robust *'Zohra Jabeen'* would elicit were largely missing in most songs. Songs like *'Yeh Dosti Hum Nahin Chhodenge'* in *Sholay* (1975)—an eternal male-bonding song—were few and far between. A song is successful if it can be hummed by non-singers. How many are there in Manna Dey's repertoire? You figure.

Even though Manna Dey sang over 4,000 songs in all languages, including non-film songs, his success rate in the mainstream space remained limited. Why was this so?

SD Burman never considered him to be hero-playback material. Many other music directors also thought his voice was not 'commercial' and that it was dry and characterless. There was no attractiveness to it. That he was only good for particular kind of songs, and not for the run of the mill songs that were the mainstay of Hindi films. Some believed that he had pronunciation and enunciation problems in Hindi. He was too well entrenched in the classical mould to open out—a problem commonly associated with classical singers. Many composers would expect him to stick to plain and simple singing without any reconnaissance into the classical territory. Manna Dey was too good for his own good. He knew too much. Many music directors would have an inferiority complex around him. Once a singer is set in his ways, he cannot change his stripes.

But the biggest tragedy was that since singing was Manna Dey's profession, and his success was confined to the classical and sentimental/introspective/philosophical genre, with only limited success in the mainstream space, he was exploited by composers to sing for comedians. He had no choice—singing was what brought food to the table. Even SD Burman, whose '*Upar Gagan Vishal*' from *Mashaal* (1950) set both SD Burman and Manna Dey on an upward trajectory, used him for Mehmood in '*Pyar Ki Aag Mein*' in *Ziddi* (1964) and '*Kisne Chilman Se Maara*' on Johnny Walker in *Baat Ek Raat Ki* (1962). Roshan made him sing for Mehmood in '*Laagee Manvaa Ke Beech*' in *Chitralekha* (1964), Laxmikant-Pyarelal made him sing '*O Meri Maina Tu Manle Mera Kehna*' on Mehmood in *Pyar Kiye Ja* (1966), and Chitragupt had him sing '*Jodi Hamari Jamega Kaise Jani*' in *Aulad* (1968), again on Mehmood. Not that Rafi did not sing for Mehmood or Johnny Walker. But the composers did not change their compositional style for such songs. If one did not know any better '*Ajhun Na Aaye Balma*' from *Saanj Aur Savera* (1964) could never have passed off as a song picturized on Mehmood. It is only when one watches it does one wince at the picturization of such a fine classical duet. Similarly, OP Nayyar kept his signature style similar for both Guru Dutt and Johnny Walker in the films. But the songs composed for Manna Dey clearly show the 'village idiot' or the 'court jester' style. It was clearly risqué singing and sounded double-edged on screen. Just hear the buffoonery in SD Burman's *'Banao Batiyan Hato Kahe Ko Jhooti'* in *Manzil* (1960). When a classical maestro sings *'Meri Bhains Ko Danda Kyun Mara'* from *Pagla Kahin Ka* (1970) composed by Shankar-Jaikishan, the music directors largely responsible for his classical oeuvre, it is easy to imagine his helplessness and frustration. Ironically, in these comic songs, Manna Dey sounded boisterous and freewheeling.

'Ek Chatur Naar'—the famous duel between Manna Dey and Kishore Kumar in *Padosan* (1968) was in a different league though. Manna Dey was not at all happy to be losing to Kishore—even in the film—in this classical stand-off. But in reality, he genuinely feared Kishore. Not because Kishore was classically superior to him—not even close. But Kishore had a unique and unaffected style of singing which tended to overshadow the subtleties of classical music. The average listener would any day prefer an uninhibited, unconstrained natural style than a tight, nuanced, rule-bound, intricate style. Singing with abandon, and not caution is what most listeners prefer.

This duel is emblematic of why Manna Dey lost out to the other singers.

Manna Dey, with Asha Bhosle, sang the title song of V Shantaram's *Boond Jo Man Gayi Moti* (1967) whose music was composed by my maternal uncle, the late Satish Bhatia. I pointed out this fact to him when he was the Chief Guest at a music program where I was one of the singers. He of course remembered and gave his blessings. Unlike most other participants, I just could not summon the requisite courage to sing his songs and doing even a fraction of justice to them. His songs are his songs—only the most accomplished singers can sing them with the same intensity, the same élan as he could.

The government recognized his immense contribution to music by awarding him the Dadasaheb Phalke Award, Padma Shri, and Padma Bhushan. Incidentally, Padma Bhushan, from amongst Manna Dey's peers, has only been given to Talat. Rafi has only been awarded the Padma Shri and no Padma Awards for Kishore Kumar and Mukesh. Critical acclaim versus popular acclaim—that is the eternal conundrum.

His autobiography *Memories Come Alive: An Autobiography* is replete with his humility, his underestimation of his own true worth, his self-effacement and his acknowledgement that the other singers were better than him. But we do not have to agree with his self-assessment. For a vast legion of music aficionados and common listeners, his songs have provided not just joy but also solace, appealed to both the heart and the mind. His lines from the *Basant Bahaar* (1956) song describe his artistry the best—'*Sangeet Man Ko Pankh Lagaye, Geeton Se Rhimjhim Ras Barsaaye, Swar Ki Sadhna Parmeshwar Ki*'.

27

Singing on the Hustings

During the 1960s and 1970s, the Family Planning Program in India was being promoted in a large way, and communication was a vital component for its success. The Directorate of Advertising and Visual Publicity (DAVP) and the Films Division were tasked with its propagation.

The *'Lal Tikon'* (red triangle) logo—one of the icons of the program—was ubiquitous; as was the other icon—an illustration of a small happy family comprising a man, a woman, and their son and daughter. Growing up in that era, I remember them vividly—staring at us from hoardings, posters, paintings on walls, newspapers, everywhere.

But what drove home the program's national significance to me, as well as millions of others, was hearing Mohammad Rafi—the singer whom I and the nation worshiped—give the program his musical approbation (along with Asha Bhosle) in his inimitable style:

"Hum Na Sochenge Apne Bachhon Ki Toh Sochega Kaun,
Sukh Ka Raaz Hai Bus Do Bachhe, Sukh Ki Nishani Lal Tikon
Lal Tikon, Lal Tikon, Lal Tikon"

The Family Planning Association of India roped in Rafi to sing *'Main Albela Hindustani'* and Mubarak Begum for *'Chand Ki Nagariya Se'* to promote family planning.

The Five-Year Plan also received Rafi's singing endorsement (in duet with Lata Mangeshkar, no less):

"Kehdo Yeh Gaaon Ke Jaat Ko
Aur Shehar Ke Gentleman Ko
Kaamyab Hum Karke Rahenge
Paanch Saal Ke Plan Ko"

All over the world, and especially in India where music is an abiding partner in every Indian's journey from womb to tomb, music is the most efficacious medium to engage masses for political and social change.

It helps to increase awareness and brings to light critical issues which other methods may fail to do.

It is, therefore, no surprise that political parties consider this method an integral 'must-have' in their political campaigning. Their programs and promises and achievements, through well-known singers, reach out to the masses more potently than the best orators and advertisements in their arsenal.

Besides endorsing the government schemes, Rafi was also roped in by the Congress to support it during elections:

"Watan Ke Naam Ke Liye
Gareeb Awaam Ke Liye
Yeh Waqt Ki Pukar Hai Ki
Congress Ko Vote Do"

There was another election song Mohammad Rafi lent his voice to:

"Congress Ko Vote Dein
Do Bailon Ki Jodi Wala
Congress Ka Amitt Nishan
Jiske Peechhe Bhara Pada
Azaadi Ka Itihaas Mahaan"

How could Mukesh be left out? He sang '*Congress Vijay Ho*'.

All the songs sung by the venerable singers were original in tune and lyrics.

Rafi's magic, however, did not work in 2014. Biswajit, the well-known actor, stood for elections from New Delhi constituency as a Trinamool Congress candidate, essentially to tap into the large Bengali population living in Chittaranjan Park. Every day, an auto rickshaw would make several rounds of the area, blaring Biswajit's hits from a loudspeaker.

It was great to hear Rafi's '*Pukarta Chala Hun Main*' (*Mere Sanam*, 1965), '*Humdum Mere Maan Bhi Jaao* '(both from *Mere Sanam*, 1965) '*Nazar Na Lag Jaaye*' (*Night In London*, 1967), and other songs. Even Hemant Kumar couldn't work his magic with songs such as '*Beqaraar Karke Humme Yun Na Jaayiye*' (*Bees Saal Baad*, 1962). Mahendra Kapoor never had a chance with '*Laakhon Hai Yahan Dilwale*' (*Kismat*, 1968). While the older generation may still have felt nostalgic, the younger generation felt no resonance. Defeat may have reminded Biswajit of his well-known song '*April Fool Banaya, Toh Unko Gussa Aaya*' (*April Fool*, 1964).

The election music landscape has undergone a massive change in quantity and quality now. With a multiplicity of parties, aggressive and divisive elections, a plethora of singers and studios, technology and its ability to churn out songs overnight, the 'Election Song' has turned into an institution of its own. It's everywhere. There is no hiding from it. It's on every platform, at every rally and procession.

Consider the case of the popular Haryanvi singer-dancer Sapna Choudhary who is a mega star in rural areas, where her stage shows attract mammoth crowds. Her videos go viral, attracting fans beyond Haryana.

Though Choudhary is a Haryanvi singer, she has a broader appeal in rural north India, especially within the Jat community who dominate dozens of parliamentary constituencies in Rajasthan, Delhi and western Uttar Pradesh, apart from Haryana. That's why both the Congress and the BJP were desperate to have her in their corner. She joined the latter in 2019. She sings her own hit songs at rallies. Incidentally, she even campaigned for an independent candidate against the BJP candidate in the Haryana assembly elections in 2019 till the red-faced party dissuaded her.

Then there are popular songs whose lyrics are changed to highlight the political party's achievements, or to decry the Opposition.

In Kerala, the song '*Kasturi*' had rattled the ruling UDF during the 2016 Assembly Elections. The song had targeted the report of the Kasturirangan Panel on the Western Ghats. The song would blare out from every nook and cranny of the state, and adversely impacted the UDF. In a remarkable show of professionalism, the same songwriter (KAM Kareem) also penned a song on the murder of TP Chandrasekhar by the Left for the UDF.

But why parodies? Why not original songs? New songs do not attract listeners as much as familiar music does—wittily rewritten to deliver sarcasm, invective and poll promises.

But on the national level, things begin to change. Many original songs enter the fray. Consider the anthem '*Saugandh Mujhe Iss Mitti Ki*' of the BJP, sung by Sukhwinder Singh, penned by Prasoon Joshi, and composed by Aadesh Shrivastava.

The same song, but dedicated to the soldiers and the nation, has been sung by Lata too (she does mention Prime Minister Modi in her preamble); the music has been composed by Mayuresh Pai.

In the earlier elections, AR Rahman's Oscar-winning '*Jai Ho*' was used by the Congress in in its election campaigns with different variants—each having its own lyrics. Instead of being original, the party decided to rely on a well-known tune.

In 2017, Alka Yagnik and Sonu Nigam sang a song on Prime Minister Modi—'*Son of India*', written by Bindeshwar Pathak, Founder of the Sulabh Sanitation Movement.

Kailash Kher has been very active and has sung across party lines. He did a song for AAP. Later, in 2017, he did a song for BJP—'*UP Ke Mann Ki Baat Karein*'. Kher even sang '*Swachh Bharat Ka Irada Hai*' at the Modi government's two-year celebrations. He also sang '*Vote Do*', not affiliated to any party, exhorting people to exercise their franchise.

When Shankar Mahadevan came out with *'Breathless'* in 1998, who would have imagined that the same tune and concept would be recreated two decades later in a new avatar—'*Non-Stop India*'—highlighting the various schemes of the Modi government.

Udit Narayan sang '*Modi Aanewala Hai*' in 2014. He also sang for the BJP in 2016—'*Chal Kamal Ke Saath*'.

And there are many more. This is just a brief glimpse of the sheer size and vibrancy of the 'institution' that is the 'Election Song'.

Can any article on the 'Election Song' be complete without a mention of Kishore Kumar? During the Emergency, Kishore was banned by the Ministry of Information & Broadcasting on All India Radio, and Doordarshan. His crime—refusal to participate in a public event organized by the Indian Youth Congress.

When the Emergency was revoked in 1977 and the Congress shown the door, Kishore exacted his revenge in the only way he knew best—through his music. In the film *Nasbandi* (1978), he sang a song '*Gandhi Tere Desh Mein*', decrying the state of the nation with this opening salvo:

"Janata Ki Awaaz Hai Yeh
Sun Le O Bapu Gandhi
Yeh Kaisa Hahakaar Desh Mein
Yeh Kaisi Aag Ki Aandhi"

(a clever reference to the movie of the same name which was banned during the Emergency).

In the last stanza, Kishore highlights the contribution of the leaders in overthrowing the Congress government:

"Saare Desh Par Zulm o Sitam Ke Ghor Andhere Jab Chhaye
Tab Prakash Ki Kirnay Lekar Jai Prakash Aage Aaye
Vijay Laxmi Pandit Ne Janata Ka Manobal Badha Diya
Raj Narayan Ne Na-Mumkin, Mumkin Karke Dikha Diya
Mazhab Se Kam Nahi Mulk, Bole Jama Masjid Ke Imam
Prajatantra Ko Nav Jeevan Dene Aaye Jagjivan Ram
George Fernandez Tod Ke Aaye Ilzaamon Ki Zanjeeren
Shri Morarji Ke Aane Se Chamak Uthi Phir Taqdeeren
Charan Singh Aur Chandrasekhar Ne Logon Ke Dilon Ko Jeeta
Vaapas Le Aayi Janata Apni Aazadi Ki Sita
Atal Bihari, Advani, Nana Ne Kiya Uddhar
Gandhi Tere Naam Ki Ab Hogi Jayjayakar"

However, the 'Election Song' can only do so much. Eventually it's not the song that is going to bail out the respective political parties, but their performance. As the song from *Roti* (1974) puts it:

"Ye Jo Public Hai Sab Jaanti Hai
Aji Andar Kya Hai, Aji Baahar Kya Hai
Ye Sab Kuchh Pehchanti Hai"

28

A Rare Composer

Jaidev

Hindi music composers belong to three categories. This can be best illustrated by considering the musical journey of the song from point A to point B.

The first category—to which most composers belong—involves a straightforward journey, without twists and turns, easy to bear, passengers languorously slouched, no thinking involved.

The second category involves a journey with gentle undulations, a slip road here, a detour there, sometimes on the fringe of the forest, sometimes at the edge of the beach. Here the passenger sits upright, mind alert, soaking in the wondrous sights, feeling exhilarated.

Then there is the third category—to which a very miniscule number truly belong. This involves a journey with sharp ascents and descents, perilous hair-pin bends, off-road driving, jumping headlong into forests and deserts. Here the passenger goes through a maelstrom of emotions. There is shock and awe. But very few passengers gradually settle down and are amazed at the kaleidoscopic ride. They get hooked. They get addicted. They cannot get enough. The remaining passengers prefer not to undertake the journey again.

Jaidev belonged to the third category. He was unwilling or unable to switch to other categories. 'Niche' does not even begin to define him.

Being niche has its advantages. You are an independent operator, not a slave to public taste. There is no compromise in your art. Your creation is an honest reflection of your soul. You remain true to your musical instincts. There is no pandering, only self-indulgence. You are the toast of the cognoscenti. Singers love the challenge you throw at them. Negotiating your labyrinthine melodies gives them a professional satisfaction of the highest order and affirms their self-worth.

But it also has disadvantages.

You end up living in a shabby one room rented house. The only company you have is a bottle of liquor. You drink water from a mud pot and sleep on the floor. When you die, the only asset you can call your own is your harmonium. You may be the only music composer from Hindi films to have won the National Award thrice (*Reshma Aur Shera*, 1971; *Gaman*, 1975; *Ankahee*, 1985) and Sur Singar Samsad Awards four times, but you die under-appreciated, unsung.

Born in Nairobi on 3rd August 1918, Jaidev spent most of his childhood in his maternal aunt's place in Ludhiana. He fell in love with films and decided to become an actor and ran away to Bombay at 15. He was unsuccessful and came back but, undeterred, he ran off again. He was hired by Wadia Movietones for small time roles in mythological films and Fearless Nadia stunt movies (such as *Hunterwali*, 1935; *Miss Frontier Mail*, 1936). Having realized that his acting career was going nowhere, he enrolled in 1943 in Almora's Music Centre run by Ustad Ali Akbar Khan and Pt. Ravi Shankar. But the Centre soon shut shop.

Later, Jaidev started accompanying Ali Akbar Khan in his sarod recitals. When Ustad Ali Akbar Khan was signed as a composer in Chetan Anand's films under the Navketan Films banner, Jaidev followed him into the film industry.

Ustad Ali Akbar Khan composed music for Chetan Anand's *Aandhiyan* (1952) and *Humsafar* (1953) where Jaidev assisted him. Both the films and their music flopped, and Ustad Ali Akbar Khan called it a day. Jaidev stayed on and started assisting Navketan Films' new composer SD Burman—*Taxi Driver, Munimji, House No. 44, Kala Pani, Sujata, Laajwanti, Insaan Jaag Utha,* and others.

In 1955, he got his first break in *Joru Ka Bhai*. He would do some 40 odd films in next three decades—an abysmal number for any genius.

Right from the get-go Jaidev revealed to the world his composition style. The song from his first film *'Subah Ka Intezar Kaun Kare'* was a dreamy, melodious number, very different from your 'normal' Hindi song; an extraordinary song that showcased his exceptional artistry.

It was a forerunner of what was to come from his baton till his death.

So, what was a typical Jaidev song? It was not a commercial concoction; it did not earn an instant applause. It was not a hummable fun and dance number. It was serious, intricate, layered; inspired by Hindustani classical and folk music. It wove a rich tapestry of musical and lyrical nuances. There was a subtle variation of pace and mood. It was difficult to appreciate on the first listening; but it grew on you, wrapping you in its complexity: raag-based structure, leisurely pacing, soothing orchestration, sensitive lyrics and myriad musical variations.

The song was cerebral—it appealed to the intellectual mind. The connoisseurs would give a thumbs up to his different, original musical approach. But the common man was not wooed. Because of his unwillingness or inability to compose simple songs with catchy lyrics and crowd-pleasing tunes, his music seldom tasted commercial success. He forever remained an intellectual composer. Producers considered him an excellent composer but only fit for small budget films.

In a materialistic world, with no time to stand and stare, no time to invest in emotional enrichment, such a classically oriented composer was doomed to become an anachronism.

His music offered ample scope for the singer to show off the *gayaki ang*. His tunes were fabulously detailed with striking ornamentations. Lata and Jaidev's association produced some precious gems. Lata's singing was the perfect platform to display Jaidev's dazzling skills.

Not that he did not have outstanding songs with other singers. He created memorable classics in different voices: Rafi—*'Kabhi Khud Pe Kabhi Haalaat Pe Rona Aaya'* (*Hum Dono*, 1961); Mukesh—*'Jab Gham-e-Ishq Sataataa Hai'* (*Kinare Kinare*, 1963); Talat—*'Dekh Li Teri Khudaaee'* (*Kinare Kinare*, 1963); Manna Dey—*'Pyaas Thi Phir Bhi Takaazaa Na Kiya'* (*Alingan*, 1974); Kishore Kumar—*'Yeh Wohi Geet Hai'* (*Maan Jaaiye*, 1972); Yesudas— *'Chand Akela Jaye Sakhi Re'* (*Alaap*, 1977); Bhupinder—*'Ek Akela Is Shahar Mein'* (*Gharaonda*, 1977); Suresh Wadkar—*'Seene Mein Jalan'* (*Gaman*, 1984); Asha Bhosle—*'Maang Mein Bhar Ley Rang Sakhi Re'* (*Mujhe Jeene Do*, 1963); Chhaya Ganguly—*'Aap Ki Yaad Aati Rahi Raat Bhar'* (*Gaman*, 1984); Runa Laila— *'Tumhe Ho Na Ho'* (*Gharaonda*, 1977); Hariharan—*'Ajeeb Saaneha Mujh Par'* (*Gaman*, 1984). Non-film compositions like Manna Dey's *Madhushala* (of Harivansh Rai Bachchan) and Asha Bhosle's *'Ghazal, Geet, Bhajan'* were an unforgettable treat.

The 1950s produced tragic, melancholic beauties like *'Har Aas Ashqbaar Hai, Har Saans Beqaraar Hai'* (*Kinare Kinare*, 1957) with its slow waltz rhythm, intricate use of clarinet and organ.

His music in *Hum Dono* (1961) became very popular. While *'Main Zindagi Ka Saath'*, *'Kabhi Khud Pe Kabhi Haalaat Pe'*, and *'Abhi Na Jao Chhod Kar'* became a listener's delight, two Lata bhajans stood apart with imaginative tunes and immaculate renditions. *'Allah Tero Naam, Ishwar Tero*

Naam'—based on Raag *Goud Sarang* seemed a simple melody but was indeed a complex song. It was close to Lata's heart, and she chose it in the 1982 program *'Mortal Men, Immortal Melodies'*. The merging with and separation of the chorus from Lata's voice was fascinating. The other bhajan *'Prabhu Tero Naam'* had such musical and emotional intensity, such intricacy that this Raag *Dhaani* based bhajan left one spellbound.

'Raat Bhi Hai Kuchh Bheegi Bheegi' (*Mujhe Jeene Do*, 1963) was an offbeat *mujra* song with pace and passion. The chorus usage—*"Chham-chham, chham-chham"* showed Jaidev's mastery over this aspect.

In *'Mohe Na Yun Ghoor-Ghoor Ke Dekho, Najar Lag Jaayegi'*, he let go of his reservation and composed a full-on playful fun number which was pacy, folksy, flirtatious, robust and rustic which Lata sang with full abandon.

Besides these two films, he did not receive any box-office approval in the 1960s.

In *Reshma Aur Shera* (1971), Jaidev composed his pièce de résistance—*'Tu Chanda Main Chandni'*—probably the most complex song ever composed in the annals of Hindi film music. The song was like an exquisite painting; painted with striking colours of emotion and enticing textures of melody. Lata's vocals were tested to the full, and she delivered. No other song had ever portrayed the amazing range of his complex creativity in such sparkling fashion. Unpredictable changes in the song's mood, pace and notes could only have been conceived by a genius.

A singer is a complete singer only if she can render this enigma of a song with complete fidelity. This song is near non-negotiable.

Another song from the film *'Ik Meethi Si Chubhan'* was a romantic song par excellence.

The film failed but Jaidev got the National Award.

Jaidev did compose catchy tunes once in a blue moon.

'Yeh Dil Aur Unki Nigaahon Ke Saaye' (*Prem Parbat*, 1973) was Jaidev's response to the critics accusing him of not having the ability for composing popular tunes. However, even here he could not help himself, and despite its ostensible accessibility, it had enough nuances to make the connoisseurs swoon.

Other prominent songs in this era were *'O Mitwaa Badra Chhaye Re'*—one of Lata's finest semi classical romantic songs, and *'Yeh Wohi Geet Hai'* (both from *Maan Jaaiye*, 1972); *'Pyaas Thi Phir Bhi Takaazaa Na Kiya'* (*Alingan*, 1974); *'Zindagi Cigarette Ka Dhuan'* (*Faslaa*, 1974); *'Kaahe Manawa Naache Re'*, and *'Chand Akela Jaye Sakhi Re'* (both from *Alaap*, 1977); *'Tumhein Dekhti Hun* (*Tumhare Liye*, 1978); *'Ek Akela Is Shahar Mein'*, and *'Tumhe Ho Na Ho'* (both from *Gharaonda*, 1977); *'Seene Mein Jalan'*, and *'Aap Ki Yaad Aati Rahi Raat Bhar'* (both from *Gaman*, 1984); *'Jag Ko Sulana'* (*Jumbish*, 1986).

My mother—then Usha Bhatia and her brother late Satish Bhatia (both working in All India Radio, Delhi in the '50s—my mother as singer, and uncle as music composer) knew Jaidev very well when he was based in Delhi before he left for Bombay. It was Jaidev who insisted that my mother pursue a college degree after school and it was he who filled up her college admission form. Her BA degree from Delhi University is thanks to him.

I too was fortunate to have met Jaidev. To commemorate India's victory in the 1971 War, Lata gave a public performance at Ramlila Maidan, Delhi in 1972. She sang *'Sarfaroshi Ki Tamanna'*, and *'Satyamev Jayate'* composed by Jaidev. A day earlier, Lata along with Usha, Hridayanath and Jaidev, visited my uncle for tea where I had the ultimate pleasure of meeting all of them.

Jaidev composed *'Main Zindagi Ka Saath Nibhata Chala Gaya, Har Fiqr Ko Dhuen Mein Udata Chala Gaya'* (*Hum

Dono, 1961). More than a decade later, he would return to the theme of 'zindagi' being *'Cigarette Ka Dhuan'* (*Faslaa,* 1974). A line from the latter song would hopefully be how history would view him—*"tere paaon ko chumengi, parbat ki sab chotiyan"*.

29

The Queen of Melody

Malika-e-Tarranum Noor Jehan

From Allah Wasai to Baby Noor Jehan, to Madam Noor Jehan, and eventually earning the title of *Malika-e-Tarannum* (Queen of Melody) in a country which is literally spoilt for riches in the female singing department, is the musical road Noor Jehan traversed. A temperamental character who rushed through life at breakneck speed, she led a glamorous life complete with torrid liaisons with co-stars, marriages to film personalities and relationships with Pakistani Presidents. The journey began much before Partition. Had she not crossed over in 1947, she would have continued to sing in India. How that would have panned out in terms of the musical landscape that developed in the Hindi film industry since Independence is anybody's guess. But the fact is that she did migrate and continued to weave her magic in Pakistan.

She was born in Kasur, Punjab on 21st September 1926. When she was barely five years old, her mother noticed her interest and potential for singing. Noor Jehan was sent for classical training to the best *ustad* there was—Bade Ghulam Ali Khan. After her training was over, she began singing in Lahore—usually in the live song-and-dance performances prior to film screenings. She then moved to Calcutta along with her family to join the film industry. It was at this stage that she came to be known as Baby Noor Jehan. She acted in several Punjabi films, all made in Calcutta. At this stage, however, she was too young to be taken seriously by the Calcutta film industry and was overshadowed by greats like Mukhtar Begum and Kajjanbai.

She then moved back to Lahore in 1938. The renowned music director Ghulam Haider composed some songs for her which became popular. Her first film role as an adult was opposite Pran in *Khandaan* (1942). Its success led to her shifting base to Bombay with her future husband, director Shaukat Hussain Rizvi (whom she would marry in 1943). From 1945 to 1947, she became one of the biggest film actresses with films like *Badi Maa* (1945), *Zeenat* (1945), *Gaon Ki Gori* (1945), *Anmol Ghadi* (1946) and *Jugnu* (1947). Her sensuous face backed by stunning singing made her a rage.

She put her classical training to full effect, infusing her singing with emotional modulations and lyrical expressions. Her competitors—Suraiya and Kanan Bala—stood no chance.

Anmol Ghadi was directed by Mehboob Khan starring Surendra, Suraiya and Noor Jehan (both rivals). The film was tailor-made for singing stars, and Noor Jehan exploited this fully. The film was a musical hit and still remembered for its music by Naushad, with hits like '*Aawaaz De Kahaan Hai*', '*Jawaan Hai Mohabbat Haseen Hai Zamana*' and '*Mere Bachpan Ke Saathi Mujhe Bhool Na Jaana*'. The film became the highest-grossing film at the Indian box office in 1946.

'*Aawaaz De Kahaan Hai*' is inextricably linked to Noor Jehan's brief tenure in India and defines her musically in the Indian consciousness. When she visited Bombay in 1982, she sang this song. She was royalty when she left; she was royalty when she came back 35 years later. The introduction she received from Dilip Kumar, the adulation she received from her fans, stood testimony to it.

After Partition, Noor Jehan moved to Pakistan. Her first film there was *Chan Wey* (1951) which was directed by her and her husband. Then one film came after another.

One film deserves mention—*Koel* (1959)—for its outstanding songs. The film is regarded as one of the all-time great films to come out of Pakistan and was a huge success at the box office. *Koel* was also Noor Jehan's last big, successful film as an actress and her last but one film as a leading lady. One standout song was '*Dil Ka Diya Jalaya*'. The timbre and control with which Noor Jehan essayed the song was simply amazing. There were other great solos too by her in the film.

But the song that encapsulates Noor Jehan as a singer, and especially later in her career, as a performer, is '*Mehki Fizayen*'.

Her smouldering looks, her quivering lips, her bewitching eyes, her come-hither invitation was mind-blowing. Her coquettishness, her *adaa*, was in full display in the song.

She would use these elements later in life as a performer on stage and in television studios. She would be flirtatious, playful. She was masterful in exhibiting charisma and had a riveting presence. This persona was backed by an extraordinarily full-throated but soft velvety voice which hit the high notes with felicity without losing the *sur* or power. It was as clear and innocent as a mountain brook. Lata Mangeshkar reportedly commented that Noor Jehan's vocal range allowed her to sing as low and as high as she wanted, the quality of her voice always remaining the same.

She divorced Rizvi and married Ejaz Durrani—a film actor, in 1959 (it would end in divorce too in 1970). He pressured her to give up acting. Her last film as an actress/singer was *Mirza Ghalib* (1961). Thereafter, it was only to be playback singing. Three decades of acting finally came to an end.

And what a start she got. Legendary poet Faiz Ahmed Faiz's nazm '*Mujh Se Pehli Si Mohabbat Mere Mehboob Na Maang*' appeared as a song in the film *Qaidi* (1962).

Noor Jehan composed and sang the song in the film. Reportedly, she composed it spontaneously in a gathering that was celebrating Faiz's release from prison (where he was sent for his Communist views). Everyone including Faiz liked it so much that Faiz remarked, "*Aaj se yeh nazm meri nahin rahi, Noor Jehan ki ho gayi hai*". Seven years later, this *nazm* would inspire Majrooh Sultanpuri's '*Teri Aankhon Ke Siwa*' in the film *Chirag* (1969).

Noor Jehan had a long and illustrious playback career fetching her several awards along the way. No title can compete with the honorific *Malika-e-Tarannum* that she received from the Government. I saw a very moving tribute paid by the *Shahenshah-e-Ghazal* Mehdi Hassan to Noor Jehan, about how he came from a classical tradition and could succeed in the playback film industry due to the breathing techniques and throw of words and other advice given to him by her, much to her embarrassment.

The one song that she will always be identified with her is the evergreen, much copied and extremely popular '*Sanu Nehar Wale Pul Te Bulla Ke*' from *Dukh Sajana De* (1973).

Noor Jehan, like some other singers from her country, became better with age. Like aged wine and malt, the years added depth, richness, and more emoting prowess to her voice. The voice became rounded, mature, and rooted in *theraav* or calmness. It was redolent of experience, of decades of queenship. But the bedrock was always an abiding innocence-infused voice. She may have become voluptuous, but she could still be childlike.

The singing became more assured. She re-recorded all her old hits with a modern feel and instruments and the result was astounding. An old song, a great one when it was first released, became even more brilliant in the re-recording. She sang all such re-worked songs on Pakistan TV and the entire catalogue captures the greatness of not only the singer but the performer as well. Her shimmering sarees, her dazzling personality, her gestures, her accessing her molten sexuality and shooting it at the audience through her eyes and lips, her pout, her fluttering eyelashes, her lustrous eyes were a treat to watch. She may have become a dowager, but her magnetism had got bigger.

Noor Jehan was the first female star of Indian cinema and laid the foundation of playback singing. She inspired a generation of singers including Lata Mangeshkar, before singlehandedly kick-starting music in Pakistan and inspiring subsequent generations there.

Although she's no more, her larger-than-life persona remains intact. Between our two countries, she is a shared heritage who shall always be loved and revered. And even though she may not hear our *"awaaz"*, her *duniya* of a formidable legacy will always remain *"jawaan"*.

30

The Rebel with a Cause

Sahir Ludhianvi

Film lyricists have generally been, and still are, second class citizens in the film music pecking order. Everyone knows the names of singers, most know the music directors, but most lyricists, save a few, remain in the shadows. The awe and respect are missing.

There have been a few though who have walked shoulder to shoulder with music directors like Shailendra. But there has only been one who was ranked above them all.

Shailendra wrote on truisms without recourse to sermonizing. These were delivered gently with kid gloves. But only one person managed to take off these gloves and punch the listeners right in the face with unvarnished truth. He caught them by the scruff of their neck and held the mirror of society to them. He made them wince at the harsh truths, and forced them to reflect, to acknowledge, to act.

He lifted the carpet and threw the dust underneath at them. He was uncompromising and unafraid; he had integrity and he had talent—unimaginable amounts of it.

Sahir Ludhianvi was born Abdul Hayee to a decadent zamindar; his mother Sardar Begum being the eleventh wife out of twelve. His dissolute ways forced her to leave her husband with Abdul. But litigation and physical threats deprived Abdul of a happy childhood. The father's wanton ways, the ill-treatment of his mother, and the uncertainty of those years remained bitter memories.

'Duniya Ne Tajurbaat-o-Havaadis Ke Shakl Mein, Jo Kuchh Mujhe Diya Hai, Lauta Raha Hoon Main.'

Brave is the man who can bare his soul to the world and draw from his experiences to express himself. The memories of his childhood were funnelled to his writing. Poetry became a matter of cathartic release for him. He placed his mother on a high pedestal. If his poems and songs in later years eloquently expressed the plight of women, this was due to the challenges she faced.

In *'Jinhe Naaz Hai Hind Par'* (*Pyaasa*, 1957) he wrote on the plight of women in the *'badnaam bazaar'* in a hard-hitting way—*"Yahaan peer bhi aa chukey hain, jawaan bhi/Tan-o-mand bete bhi, abbaa miyan bhi/Yeh biwi bhi hai aur behen bhi aur maa bhi/Jinhe naaz hai Hind par woh kahaan hain"*.

In *Sadhana* (1958), he wrote: *"Aurat Ney Janam Diya Mardon Ko, Mardon Ne Usey Bazaar Diya/Jab Jee Chaahaa Kuchlaa Maslaa, Jab Jee Chaahaa Dutkaar Diya."*

In *Trishul* (1978), he did something totally unexpected. Opposing the traditional view that a mother's duty is to offer shelter to her young son, in *'Tu Mere Saath Rahega Munne'* he wrote: *"Main tujhe raham ke saaye mein na palne doongi/Zindagaani ki kadi dhoop mein jalney doongi/Taaki tap-tap ke tu faulad baney/Maa ki aulad baney."*

Sahir would take a different angle, would think on a tangent, and make one introspect and marvel at his novel way of viewing things.

The other major influence on Sahir was that of the Progressive Writers Movement (PWM). He subscribed to PWM's view that literature could not exist in isolation, as art for art's sake. It was to be used to bring about a social change. As a result of his childhood experiences, which nurtured a distaste for zamindars and capitalism, his interest in communism, and involvement in student politics in college, he was naturally drawn to the PWM. Unlike traditional Urdu poetry, which was centred on *husn*, *saaqi* and *ulfat*, progressive writers wrote on the *mazdoor*, the *muflis* and the *jamhoor*.

Sahir's initial forays, because of his college romances, were directed at love. Ultimately, he began to raise crucial questions about the world around him. Love for the beloved transformed into love for the entire world. In *Didi* (1959), he wrote:

> *"Zindagi sirf mohabbat nahin kuchh aur bhi hai*
> *Zulf-o-rukhsar ki jannat nahin kuchh aur bhi hai*
> *Bhookh aur pyaas ki maari hui is duniya mein*
> *Ishq hi ek haqeeqat nahin kuchh aur bhi hai*
> *Tum agar aankh churao to yeh haq hai tumko*
> *Maine tumse hi nahin sabse mohabbat ki hai."*

If his poems and lyrics had a bitter tenor to them, it was because he was overwhelmed by the circumstances around him. It was this rare sensitivity towards the plight of the exploited sections that formed the cornerstone of his poetry. In his much-acclaimed poem '*Talkhiyan*', he powerfully spoke of the structures of exploitation and their agents like the capitalist, the usurer, the priest, and others.

While he critiqued the nation, and was cynical of politics, he never lost faith in the collective power of people. He urged the masses to bear the injustices a little longer while giving them hope of the arrival of a better tomorrow. In *Phir Subah Hogi* (1958), he wrote:

> *"In kaali sadiyon ke sar se, jab raat ka aanchal dhalkega*
> *Jab dukh ke baadal pighlenge, jab sukh ka sagar chhalkega*
> *Jab ambar jhoom ke nachega, jab dharati naghmein gayegi*
> *Woh subah kabhi toh aayegi."*

One other example of Sahir jettisoning the conventional approach was seen in his poem 'Taj Mahal'. Instead of seeing the monument as an ode to love, Sahir decried the vanity of an emperor in using the wealth at his disposal to create a structure that would forever mock the love of ordinary people. A shorter version of this poem was used as a song in the film *Ghazal* (1964)—*'Mere Mehboob Kahin Aur Mila Kar Mujhse'*: *"Ik shahanshah ne daulat ka sahara lekar/Hum gareebon ki mohabbat ka udaayaa hai mazaak/Mere mehboob kahin aur mila kar mujhse."*

When he joined the film industry, the producers were not willing to risk a poet doing a lyricist's job; they were apprehensive about introducing a literary element in a medium that otherwise catered to the masses. They were mistaken and his songs became hugely popular. He proved that film songs and good poetry were not contradictory. He gave film songs an intellectual quotient. His verses never lacked in virtuosity or depth. They had unmatched poetic quality, aesthetic finesse, refined language, and beautiful imagery. His words went beyond film situations and became larger statements regarding life and humanity.

Consider these stanzas from the song *'Main Zindagi Ka Saath'* from *Hum Dono* (1961)—*"Barbadiyon ka sog manana fizool tha/Barbadiyon ka jhashan manata chala gaya"; "Jo mil gaya usi ko muqaddar samajh liya/Jo kho gaya main usko bhulata chala gaya"; "Gham aur khushi mein fark na mehsoos ho jahaan/Main dil ko us muqaam pey lata chala gaya"*. The song goes way beyond the context of the film and becomes a philosophy of life.

Sahir wrote on a variety of themes—romance, despair, cabaret, freewheeling ditties, agony, human relationships, philosophy, catharsis, existential questions. They had a strong visual aspect to them. He took recourse to nature's beauty for romantic themes, synthesizing nature with love and using nature's breath-taking splendour to draw a parallel with the emotions one experiences in love.

In *Humraaz* (1967), he wrote: *"Shabnam key moti, phoolon pey bikhrey/Dono ki aas faley/Neele gagan ke taley, dharti ka pyaar paley"*. In *Jaal* (1952), in the song *'Yeh Raat Yeh Chandni Phir*

Kahaan' he wrote, *"Pedon ki shakhon pey soyee soyee chandni/ Tere khayalon mein khoyee khoyee chandni/Aur thodi der mein thak ke laut jayegi/Raat yeh bahaar ki phir kabhi na aayegi/Do ek pal aur hai yeh samaa/Sun ja dil ki daastaan."*

One of the most intriguing aspects of Sahir's life was his relationship with Amrita Pritam—already married. Their relationship was defined largely by silence. She was deeply in love with him. When Sahir's alleged affair with singer Sudha Malhotra came to light, a distraught Amrita wrote some of the most despondent poetry during that period. She separated from her husband and lived the rest of her 40-odd years with Imroz. Sudha got married and that was the end of her supposed liaison with Sahir. Sahir's failure to convert his relationships was his unwillingness to share himself with anybody else except his mother.

However, these romantic relationships yielded classic songs such as *'Jaane Woh Kaise Log Thay Jinke, Pyaar Ko Pyaar Mila'* (*Pyaasa*, 1957) and the ultimate break-up song from *Gumrah* (1963)—*'Chalo Ek Baar Phir Se, Ajnabi Ban Jaayen Hum Dono'* (published as a poem *'Khubsoorat Modh'* earlier in *'Talkhiyan'*). He articulated everlasting romance in *'Jo Waada Kiya Woh Nibhana Padega'* (*Taj Mahal*, 1963) and took a gentle jibe at cold-hearted women in *'Jeevan Ke Safar Mein Rahi'* with—*"Jo inki nazar se khele/dukh paaye, mussibat jheley/ phirtey hain yeh sab albele/dil lekey mukar jaane ko"* (*Munimji*, 1955).

Sahir believed in the present, in the now— *'Aage Bhi Jaaney Na Tu, Peechhe Bhi Jaaney Na Tu/Jo Bhi Hai Bas Yahi Ik Pal Hai'* (*Waqt*, 1965); *'Zindagi Hasney Gaane Ke Liye Hain Pal Do Pal/Ise Khona Nahin, Kho Ke Rona Nahin'* (*Zameer*, 1975).

Sahir had a multi-faceted view of India. On the one hand, he lamented the decadence—*'Yeh Duniya Agar Mil Bhi Jaaye Toh Kya Hai'* (*Pyaasa*, 1957) and *'Cheen-o-Arab Hamara/Rehne Ko Ghar Nahin Hai/Hindustan Hamara'*—a satirical take on Iqbal's poems (*Phir Subah Hogi*, 1958). But he was also a patriot—*'Yeh Desh Hai Veer Jawaano Ka'* (*Naya Daur*, 1957), and showed optimism about the future of the country in *'Jaagega Insaan Zamana Dekhega'* (*Aadmi Aur Insaan*, 1969).

Sahir was an atheist. Having seen the communal riots in 1947, he scorned the custodians of religion in *'Tu Hindu Banega Na Mussalmaan Banega/Insaan Ki Aulad Hai Insaan Banega'* (*Dhool Ka Phool*, 1959) and *'Sansar Se Bhagey Phirtey Ho/Bhagwan Ko Tum Kya Paogey'* (*Chitralekha*, 1964). He even scoffed at the Creator—*'Aasmaan Pey Hai Khuda, Aur Zameen Pey Hum/Aaj Kal Woh Is Taraf Dekhta Hai Kum'* (*Phir Subah Hogi*, 1958). Yet, that did not impact his song writing skills when religious fervour was called for *'Allah Tero Naam, Ishwar Tero Naam' (Hum Dono, 1961); 'Hey Rom Rom Mein Basney Waaley Ram'* (*Neel Kamal*, 1968).

There is timelessness in Sahir's songs. His work and its relevance are eternal. His songs have no shelf life. This song from *Kabhi Kabhie* (1976) beautifully captures the eternal poet:

> *"Main Pal Do Pal Ka Shaayar Hoon, Har Ek Pal Meri Kahaani Hai,*
> *Har Ek Pal Meri Hasti Hai, Har Ek Pal Meri Jawaani Hai."*

With Ravi at his residence.

With Usha Khanna at her residence.

With Mahendra Kapoor at a Tax Event.

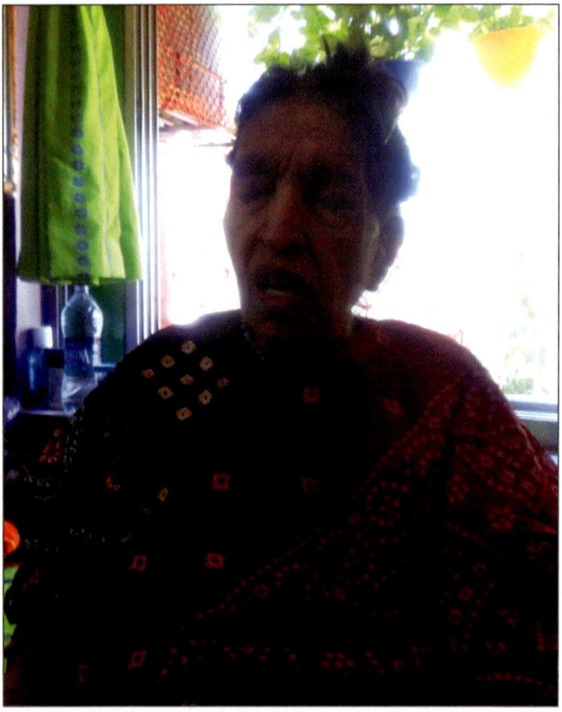

With Mubarak Begum at her residence.

With Ghulam Ali on the eve of his concert in Delhi.

OP Nayyar on the harmonium at our residence in Mumbai.

STAR ROMANTIC MUSIC MAESTRO OF THE CENTURY
THE LEGENDARY

O.P. NAYYAR

Photo by Sateesh Panikar

With love and affections to dear Ajay Mankotia, O.P. Nayyar 6.9.2000.

Researched, Compiled and Edited By
VISHWAS NERURKAR

Assisted By
BISHWANATH CHATTERJEE

Signed message of OP Nayyar to me.

With Khayyam at his residence.

31

A Tale of Sad Neglect

Mubarak Begum

Mubarak Begum, who lived on the fringes of the Hindi film music industry, died in penury.

When I met her in her one-room flat in Mumbai's suburb Jogeshwari, she was lying on a cot, clearly unwell. The flat was brimming with relatives including a daughter struck by Parkinson's.

She got up and sat on the cot, arthritis-ridden legs dangling down, and spoke to me at length about her journey in the playback industry.

She then delighted me with snippets of her well-known songs. Her voice was frail and tremulous. Yet, at her old age, and without any *riyaaz*, she was still in *swar*.

I presented her with a small financial tribute and came back greatly saddened. This was a serious talent that just withered away because of lack of opportunity on account of cut-throat competition that our film industry is known for.

Though she rendered some immortal songs, her oeuvre was defined largely by *mujra* numbers and B-grade film songs. One of the best devotional songs that I have heard is *'Devta Tum Ho Mera Sahara'* from Kamal Amrohi's *Daera* released in 1953.

Mubarak's mellifluous voice took it to a different level. Though it was technically a duet, Mohammed Rafi only played a supporting role though by then he was a big name.

In fact, Mubarak is on record acknowledging Rafi's respect for his co-singers, so much so that he lowered his pitch in this song when Mubarak couldn't match his original pitch.

Jamal Sen, the music director, used Mubarak in the other songs from this film as well.

Her selection to sing playback in *Daera* was serendipitous. With other singers not available, Mubarak was taken to meet Kamal Amrohi who was busy with a recording and asked his representative to take a decision. Her voice was approved.

The film unfortunately was not a success and didn't do much for her career.

Who can forget Mubarak in the evergreen duet with Rafi—*'Mujhko Apne Gale Laga Lo'* from *Humrahi* (1963)? It is one of the most romantic songs in Hindi films. But Mubarak may never have sung this iconic song when it was released. She recorded the song as a filler, to be dubbed by Lata Mangeshkar later. Music director Jaikishan waited till the last minute for Lata to show up, but she never did. So, Mubarak was retained. Rafi also played a part in persuading Jaikishan to retain Mubarak to encourage her.

In the film *Teesri Kasam* (1966), people remember Waheeda Rahman's famous dance numbers, sung by Lata and Asha Bhosle. But the real *nautanki* style *'Hai Mohabbat Bahut'* was sung by Mubarak for Waheeda. The typical *nautanki*-style singing and Waheeda's unrestrained dancing made this a memorable song.

Similarly, *'Be-Murrawat, Be-Wafa, Begana-e-Dil Aap Hain'* from the 1964 film *Sushila,* sung under the banner of C Arjun, became very popular.

She even sang a few songs for Pakistani films during her visit to Pakistan in the late 1950s. These included songs in *Raaz* and *Bada Aadmi* and a duet with the Pakistani great Ahmed Rushdi.

She sang an incredibly beautiful duet with Talat Mahmood—'*Kuch Ajnabi Se Aap Hain Kuch Ajnabi Se Hum*' from *Shagun* (1964) under Khayyam.

'*Woh Na Ayenge Palat Kar Unhe Lakh Hum Bulayen*' from *Devdas* (1955) under SD Burman occupies an iconic place in Mubarak's career. The other *mujra* song that became a big hit was from *Madhumati* (1958) under Salil Chaudhury—'*Hum Haal-e-Dil Sunayenge*'.

But one song that stood head and shoulders above her entire repertoire and defined her was '*Kabhi Tanhaiyon Mein Yun Hamari Yaad Ayegi*' from *Hamari Yaad Ayegi* (1961), with music by Snehal Bhatkar. The song became an anthem of lovesick souls.

Here again lady luck played a huge role. Lata was to record this song but was busy with a V Shantaram recording. Kidar Sharma, the well-known director, could not accept this unprofessional attitude and replaced Lata with Mubarak.

Mubarak was also a prolific singer of private ghazals and *naats*.

Mubarak was very bitter with the way her life turned out to be. The sadness about what could have been informed her every word, her every gesture when she spoke to me.

She deserved much more...much, much more. She has moved on to a better place.

32

The Imperious Queen

Iqbal Bano

The creative arts affect human beings in multifarious ways. But music, amongst them, has the most intimate connect with the individual and society. The 'song' in particular rests on top of the musical pyramid. While the combination of lyrics, composition, and singing play a vital role in weaving the wizardry, it is the singer who delivers the final product to the listeners.

The product, however top-drawer, will remain unheralded in the hands of an unexceptional singer. Among other things, the song can entertain, it can edify, it can move nations, and it can transport one to perfect peace and happiness, a state of bliss and ecstasy. Some singers in India have ticked these boxes.

Across the border, there have been such singers too. In particular, their music has been bestowed by 'good fortune' and 'prosperity' (meaning 'Iqbal' in Urdu) by the presence of one singer who has redefined the meaning of excellence in her chosen craft—Iqbal Bano.

Born in Delhi in 1935, with her childhood spent in Rohtak, she is, like some others from Pakistani music industry, a shared legacy of both countries. Though her oeuvre is considerable, just a few of her songs are enough to anoint her as the supreme practitioner of ghazals, *nazms* and thumris.

From a young age, she developed love for music and was coached in classical music by Ustad Chaand Khan, a maestro of the Delhi gharana. During her teens, he recommended her to the All India Radio, Delhi, where she started singing her first songs.

Bano's family migrated to Pakistan in 1952. That same year, at age 17, she married a *zamindar*. Farsightedly, though unusually for a man of his background, he facilitated her passion for music; most women artists of the day didn't enjoy that kind of freedom, which is why this is worth mentioning.

Iqbal Bano and her husband settled in Multan. She soon attained star status as a playback singer for many popular films such as such as *Gumnaam* (1954), *Qatil* (1955), *Inteqam* (1955), *Sarfarosh* (1956), *Ishq-i-Laila* (1957) and *Nagin* (1959). She also appeared regularly on Radio Pakistan for classical performances and, in 1957, her debut public concert at Lahore Arts Council (a city she would later return to) was a massive success, and her live concerts started attracting large crowds.

Her stellar *nazm* needs to be mentioned at this stage—*'Ulfat Ki Nayi Manzil Ko Chala, Tu Bahein Daal Ke Bahon Mein'* from the film *Qatil* (1955). The song was composed by Master Inayat Husain and written by Qateel Shifai. The song was about betrayal, and the composition needed to be simple. A complex melody line would have detracted from the issues being addressed in the song. And so, it was.

The film song, even though top class, reached its iconic status many decades later when Bano had reached middle age and was performing live concerts.

Like some of her peers, such as Noor Jehan, she had a thin, reedy, shrill voice in the initial years of playback singing. Decades later, this voice, like Noor Jehan's, would become full-bodied, rich, luxuriant, with *thaharav*, brimming with self-assurance and experience.

That is when this song realized its destiny. Bano took charge and invested the song with pathos, indignation, accusation and hurt.

The embellishments that she introduced imbued the song with these emotions. When she sang, one could sense her heart furrowed with perfidy, and feel the blood that oozed out of her pained voice. Bano took the song to another level!

Another Inayat Husain beauty also deserves a mention—*'Payal Mein Geet Hain Chham Chham Ke'* from *Gumnaam* (1954), written by Saifuddin Saif. In this case too, Bano, enriched it beyond all limits in her later years.

Another song which deserves heaps of accolades is *'Daagh-e-Dil Humko Yaad Aane Lage'* (1975), written by Baqi Siddiqui, and composed by Master Manzoor, which she sang for Pakistan Television.

By now, her voice, like aged wine, had acquired depth and sweetness. Both the creators did an outstanding job, but Bano, as was her wont, took this song of despair and heartbreak much further. She used the echo effect with such finesse and facility that her melancholia came cutting through the cold winter night of desolation like a knife.

Other than Urdu, her repertoire of ghazals in Farsi was impressive and she was highly regarded in both Iran and Afghanistan.

Before 1979 she was often invited to the Jashn-e-Kabul, the annual cultural festival of Kabul. She was awarded the Tamgha-i-Imtiaz (Pride of Performance) in 1974.

It was sheer bliss to watch her live performances. With the brilliance of her voice and total command over musical movements, emphasizing a word or executing a *taan* with her graceful hand movements, making the songs come alive, made the experience mesmerizing.

In due course she generated more and more public appeal and, from 1981, began singing the poems of Faiz Ahmad Faiz. (He died on 20th November 1984.) Bano greatly admired the poet, who after winning the Lenin Prize, had to seek refuge abroad. She imbued his revolutionary poetry with fervour and immediacy. Faiz's poetry was banned by the military government of General Zia ul-Haq who had seized power in 1977.

Undeterred, Bano brought his poetry to the illiterate but poetry-loving masses and made them politically and socially aware.

But Faiz also wrote romantic poetry. Iqbal Bano's rendering of Faiz's *'Dasht-e-Tanhai Mein, Aye Jaan-e-Jahan, Larzan Hai'* needs to be highlighted. Never was a romantic *nazm* so touchingly written—and in the hands of Bano, it became something else.

So deep and lasting the bond between the singer and Faiz's poetry became that Faiz's daughter Salima Hashmi reportedly stated that Bano would always have a special place in the hearts and minds of her family and was like a member of their family.

Which brings us to the song—*'Hum Dekhenge'*—which will forever be linked to her. A song of protest, a song of revolution, a song of change; a song of the people, by the people, for the people; a song of democracy, of freedom, justice, and equality. A song sung at every protest in the sub-continent. A call for action, the gripping anthem became the battle cry of the downtrodden. Bano had a huge role in it.

In 1978, a year after the oppressive martial law was imposed, Faiz wrote the poem *'Hum Dekhen Ge, Lazim Hai Ke Hum Bhi Dekhen Ge'*, critical of the authoritarian ruler, which Bano boldly and defiantly sang, in her powerful and passionate voice, before a crowd of 50,000 at Lahore's Alhamra Arts Council on 13th February 1986, rousing them.

She wore a black sari. Both the sari and Faiz were banned at the time.

The poem used innuendo and traditional Islamic imagery to attack Zia's dictatorship and expressing a conviction that one day the oppressed will become the rulers of their own destiny.

While there is no video of Bano's performance, audio recordings give an idea of the power of her rendition and the effect it had on the assembled crowd.

As 'punishment', she was barred from all officially sponsored concerts and was not permitted to appear on television. Her songs were banished from the airwaves. This drastic action on the part of the authorities served only to increase her popularity. Bano attracted a cult following, and her message and voice are still heard to this day as a symbol for revolution. Bano, by popularizing the poem by her impassioned rendition and singing it at every opportunity, became the face of the song.

In India too, the poem had become a symbol of protest—be it Jantar Mantar, India Gate, against Dow Chemicals in Bhopal, anti-nuclear stir at Jaitapur, at women's marches. It was also sung in the anti-CAA-NRC protests.

Bano performed in India a few times—including as part of the Indo-Pakistan cultural exchange program in 1989. The enthusiastic reception she got here underlined her immense popularity here as well.

Iqbal Bano died on 21st April 2009. On her 12th death anniversary, Urdu poet Mahmood Rampuri's couplet seems very apt—*'Maut Uski Hai Kare Jiska Zamana Afsos, Yun Toh Duniya Mein Sabhi Aaye Hain Marne Ke Liye'.*

Iqbal Bano will continue to enthral her listeners through her outstanding music and musicianship.

33

No Partition in Film Songs

The Hindi film playback singing landscape has changed over the years.

There are many strands in this change—technology, item songs, multiple music directors in the same film, explosion in the number of singers, lack of any significant differentiation amongst singers (as it existed between Rafi, Kishore, Mukesh, Talat, Manna De, Hemant, Mahendra Kapoor), limited longevity of songs and singers.

But what stands out is the sheer number of songs being sung by Pakistani singers. Their songs are very popular.

Witness three Pakistani singers being nominated for the 2017 Filmfare Awards—Best Playback Singer (Male) Atif Aslam for '*Tere Sang Yara*' (*Rustom*) and Rahat Fateh Ali Khan for '*Jag Ghoomeya*' (*Sultan*), and Qurat-ul-Ain Balouch for the Best Playback Singer (Female) for '*Kari Kari*' (*Pink*).

They, as well as other singers like Shafqat Amanat Ali and Ali Zafar have been belting out hits after hits.

Pakistani singers have been singing in Bollywood for about five decades now.

However, their presence had been more intermittent than sustained, as it is presently.

The trend started with Runa Laila in the early '70s after the Bangladesh War.

Though technically she was a Bangladeshi when she visited India, she had been a front-ranking singer in Pakistan, having won two Nigar Award trophies for Best Female Playback Singer.

She brought in exotica and the unknown quotient not hitherto heard in Hindi film music.

Mehdi Hassan sang the theme song *'Aas Ka Jhoota Bandhan'* of *Mrig Trishna* (1975). He also sang *'Main Aatma'* in the unreleased film *Dhun* (1991).

Ghulam Ali came visiting in the early '80s for concerts. He did not do any playback save the concert-favourite *'Chupke Chupke'* in *Nikaah* in 1982 (Pakistani actress-singer Salma Agha also did playback in the film) and *'Yeh Dil Paagal Dil Mera'* in *Maati Maange Khoon* (1984).

In fact, Salma was nominated for Filmfare Best Female Singer for three songs of *Nikaah*, eventually winning for *'Dil Ke Armaan'*.

In the same year, Nazia Hassan, another Pakistani singer, was nominated for her song *'Boom Boom'* from the movie *Star*.

Nazia had earlier won the Filmfare Award for *'Aap Jaisa Koi'* from *Qurbani* (1980).

Who can forget Reshma's passionate anthem for unrequited love *'Lambi Judai'* from *Hero* (1983)? She sang in a few films thereafter.

Nusrat Fateh Ali Khan took the country by storm in a bizarre manner—through an unabashed copy of his ecstatically spiritual *'Dum Mast Qalandar Mast Mast'* by Viju Shah in the form of *'Tu Cheez Badi Hai Mast Mast'* from *Mohra* (1994).

Khayyam had first introduced Khan in *Nakhuda* 13 years earlier, in a qawwali, but it largely went unnoticed. Khan got the stature his genius deserved only in *Mohra*.

He composed as well as sang for some films (Lata and Asha have also sung under his baton).

Is the cross-border exchange one-sided? What is not well known is that Indian singers have also been hopping across the border to record in Lollywood (Lahore being the centre of the Pakistani film industry).

In fact, our artists have gone across right from the '50s and '60s, when the movement from the other side was non-existent. It dried up thereafter, but again picked up in the last two decades.

In sheer numbers, Pakistani singers in Bollywood presently outnumber the reciprocal traffic, but that is because of the numerical mismatch in the number of films made in the two countries with Bollywood far outnumbering Lollywood.

It started with Indian playback singer Geeta Dutt who sang two songs in *Miss 1956* (1956)—*'Ik Baat Sunati Hun'* and *'Mohabbat Karle Kisi Pey Marlay'* with music by GA Chishti. The film was directed by Roop K Shorey, and the heroine was Meena Shorey. However, though the 78 RPM records were issued, before the movie was released, the producers changed their minds and had these songs sung by Munawwar Sultana and Zubeda Begum.

Mubarak Begum sang four songs for *Raaz* in 1959 including a duet with Ahmed Rushdi and a club song *'Patli Kamar Mori Tirchhi Nazar'*.

She sang one song for *Bada Aadmi* in 1957 (again a duet with Ahmed Rushdi).

Hemant Kumar sang *'Raat Suhani Hai'* in *Humsafar* (1960). Reportedly, he sang at least one more song.

Talat Mehmood visited Pakistan and sang three songs for two Pakistani films, *Ghanghor Ghata* (1961) and *Chiragh Jalta Raha* (1962).

The latter film was the launching pad of the legendary film actor Mohammad Ali.

Talat also sang seven non-film songs including *'Khuda Woh Waqt Na Lae'* for which he was presented a shield by the Gramophone Company of Pakistan.

Asha Bhosle sang in *Yehudi ki Ladki* (1963).

There was a lull after that.

In 1995, Asha Bhosle sung two duets (with Adnan Sami)—*'Zara Dholki Bajao Gorio'* and *'Kya Hai, Yeh Uljhan Kya Hai'* in the Pakistani movie *Sargam*. She sang in *Mausam* (1999). Reportedly, she has sung thirteen songs in all.

Tere Pyar Mein, which was released in December 2000, had songs by Hema Sardesai, Kavita Krishnamurthy, Sonu Nigam and Jaspinder Narula.

Interestingly, credits were not given to the singers to avoid controversy.

Fictitious names were used. The same happened with *Ghar Kab Aao Gay* released that year.

Yeh Dil Aapka Hua released in 2002 had songs sung by Kumar Sanu, Sonu Nigam and Kavita Krishnamurthy.

It was the first film which openly credited the name of Indian singers. *Koi Tujh Sa Kahaan* (2005) had songs by Udit Narayan, Alka Yagnik, Shreya Ghoshal and Abhijeet (who ironically has condemned Bollywood filmmakers for working with Pakistani artists).

Mohabbattan Sachiyan (2008) had Sonu Nigam, Shreya Ghoshal, Sunidhi Chauhan and Richa Sharma.

In *Khule Aasman Ke Neechay* (2008), all the songs were by Indian singers (Sonu Nigam and Alka Yagnik) and acclaimed Indian poet Nida Fazli was the lyricist.

In *Mein Ek Din Laut Kay Aaoonga* (2007), songs were sung by Asha Bhosle, Sunidhi Chauhan and Alka Yagnik.

Devdas (A Classic Love Story) (2010) had songs by Asha, Kavita Krishnamurthy, Shreya Ghoshal, Sonu Nigam, and Alka Yagnik.

In *Love Mein Ghum* (2011), few songs were sung by Shreya Ghoshal, Shaan, Sunidhi Chauhan and Kailash Kher.

In *Main Hoon Shahid Afridi* (2013), one song was by an Indian singer Neeti Wagh.

In *System* (2014), nearly all songs were in the voices of Indian singers. The music director was Shailesh Suvarna, an Indian.

In *Bin Roye* (2015), few of the film songs were in the voices of Indian singers like Rekha Bharadwaj, Ankit Tiwari and Harshdeep Kaur.

Jawani Phir Nahi Ani (2015) had a song by Mika Singh. Armaan Malik and Shreya Ghoshal sang in *Janaan* (2016). Salim and Sulaiman were among the music directors.

The list is not exhaustive.

An average Pakistani's knowledge and love for Hindi film music knows no bounds. This has existed from the Partition till the present day.

Hindi film songs are as integral to the aural landscape in Pakistan as they are in India.

But it is not reciprocal.

The Pakistani film songs of the Golden Period of the '50s and '60s (yes, there existed a Golden Period there too) that an average Indian heard were those which were sung by visiting Pakistani playback artistes.

Even here the exposure was limited because the repertoire of most visiting artistes (Mehdi Hassan, Ghulam Ali, Iqbal Bano, Farida Khanum, and others) was heavily tilted in favour of non-film songs.

Out of his vast formidable chest of songs, Mehdi Hassan only sang a smattering of film songs like '*Ranjish Hi Sahi*', '*Rafta Rafta*', '*Pyar Bhare Do Sharmiley Nain*', '*Mujhe Tum Nazar Se Gira Toh Rahe Ho*', '*Ab Ke Hum Bichhde*', and few others. Even these film songs he 'ghazalised'—slowed the tempo, added stanzas, introduced embellishments, changed the melody in'*Ab Ke Hum Bichhde*'.

I have heard Pakistani film songs since I was young and the joy of listening to Mehdi Hassan, Ahmed Rushdi,

Mujeeb Alam, Masood Rana, Noor Jahan, Mala, and others is no less than listening to our own.

However, there is an evergrowing awareness amongst the Indians of music (mainly non-films) from across the border these days. Coke Studio, Pakistan is very popular in India. The show's success across both sides of the divide underscores how common musical cultures can thrive and be appreciated in spite of the vicissitudes of political relations between the two countries.

Talent lies on both sides of the border and cross-pollination can only enrich our shared heritage.

34

Poor Man's Lata

Usha Mangeshkar

I was preparing for my UPSC exams one evening in early 1981 in my room (I was staying with my uncle those days), when I heard a man shout excitedly from the square below (these were government quarters)—"*Mata chadh gayi, Mata chadh gayi*". In no time, I could hear people assembling outside and my own aunt rushed out. Curious, I stepped out to the first-floor balcony to see what the fuss was all about. A throng had collected outside the house below and people were jostling to get inside through the door. This required a closer examination, and I too went down. There was a stampede which I had to negotiate to eventually get inside.

What I saw in the drawing-room held me in thrall, as it did the others sitting with folded hands (which I found odd but whose mystery would shortly get resolved). The lady of the house, our neighbour, always in a cervical collar for spondylitis, was collar-free and was moving her head in a circular motion, with hair flying all over the map, eyes closed. The motion picked up momentum and soon became frenzied. I wondered how this was even possible medically.

In the midst of all this surreal drama, my attention veered towards the loud song blaring from a huge speaker. Of course, what I was hearing was nothing unknown. The entire country knew it. It was played in temples, *pandals, satsangs, bhajan mandlis* and *bhandaras*. It was being played all over the nation since 1975.

The singer was Usha Mangeshkar. The song was '*Main Toh Aarti Utarun Re*' from the film *Jai Santoshi Maa* (1975).

The film made history when it was released. A small-budget film, its filmmaker could not afford the reigning singers' fees to sing the famous bhajans penned by Kavi Pradeep. Usha was roped in instead (that would be her misfortune—a poor filmmaker's Lata). It remains her most popular work. In the film's remake in 2006, she was retained for the same songs. She is irreplaceable. In retrospect, getting Usha to sing was a masterstroke. Her voice is what works in large religious gatherings—demanding attention from all devotees, right down to the back row.

Usha is the youngest sister among the sisters—Lata Mangeshkar, Meera Khadikar and Asha Bhosle, and elder to her music-director brother Hridaynath Mangeshkar. With Lata and Asha as sisters, how could anyone succeed? How could one break through the clutter? When even Asha remained overshadowed for so many years and finally came into her own with OP Nayyar, what chance did Usha have? Very tough. Not that she was not trained—she had formal training under Ustad Amanat Ali Khan and Ustad Aman Ali Khan. But in the virtuosity department, she remained behind Lata and Asha. Her voice sounded somewhat like Lata's. Listen to '*Ankhon Mein Surma Daal*' from *Rani Roopmati* (1957).

Then how did she sound different from Lata in the *Jai Santoshi Maa* bhajan?

Till the film came along, the similarity with Lata made her career unremarkable. It was bound to happen. If Lata had not stopped singing with Rafi over the royalty dispute, Suman Kalyanpur would have been nowhere, so similar she was to Lata. When you have the best, why go to the second-best, even if she is the sister.

There is a school of thought that opinines that had she not been a Mangeshkar, she may have fared much better. The constant comparison that inevitably takes place when siblings are involved would have been absent and perhaps given her more self-confidence. But given her superficial similarity to Lata, any self-assurance would not have mattered. In fact, being a sibling helped her. Her repertoire consists of many duets, most of which are with her sisters. Most of these are dance numbers. But, if occasionally the heroine was a part of the song, her sister would sing for the heroine.

With other singers, she occasionally got an opportunity to sing duets for the main lead, but for low-budget films. For big banners, her contribution was always a duet or two for the side heroine, and not the main lead. She even had trios and quadruples with other singers.

Her most famous Hindi film duet is '*Aplam Chaplam Chaplai Re*' from the movie *Azad* (1955) with Lata. The song triggered more offers for such dance numbers.

Her other well-known duet is '*O Albele Panchhi*' from *Devdas* (1955) with Asha. '*Tum Ko Piya Dil Diya*' from *Shikari* (1963) was another duet with Lata Mangeshkar that was the most celebrated song from the movie and still maintains its popularity. Both the sister-singers got equal parts in the song.

'*O Meri Maina*' from *Pyar Kiye Ja* (1966) with Manna Dey was a comic song that she sang for the third female lead. In this song, one could discern a change taking place in her voice quality. A full-throated song was where she and Lata were as different as chalk and cheese. Her voice developed an edge and became piercing and shrill and naturally loud. Lata could keep the softness, but with Usha in such songs, the softness went out of the window. This voice timbre would later stand her in good stead in *Jai Santoshi Maa* and some other films. This is the voice that most people remember her by.

Her other notable duet with Asha was '*Chhuk Chhuk Chak Chak*' from *Rafoo Chakkar* (1975) that was filmed with Rishi Kapoor and Paintal dressed as women. No marks for guessing whose voice Usha was. Again, she exhibited her new voice.

'*Shaam Rangeen Hui Hai*' from *Kanoon Aur Mujrim* (1981) with Suresh Wadkar was a delightful duet coming at a time when music had touched rock bottom. C Arjun, the music director, who also was the music director in *Jai Santoshi Maa*, used her softer side and produced this gem. She could sound dulcet if the song allowed it.

Usha did perform solo too. The numbers though far and few, were memorable. For instance, her first Hindi film song—'*Bhabhi Aayi Bhabhi Aayi*' from *Subah Ka Tara* (1954)—was filmed on a child.

While it was a great start for Usha, she could not make a mark in A-grade films. She began accepting songs from B-grade movies and got typecast for those films. Very occasionally she would get a chance for subsidiary songs in A-grade movies. Another solo number in which the innocence in her voice was evident was '*Chachi Akad Gayi*' from *Panchayat* (1958). This song was again filmed on a child.

Her voice was not limited to bhajans. '*Yeh Na Thi Hamari Qismat*' from *Main Nashe Main Hoon* (1958) was a Mirza Ghalib ghazal that she has rendered wonderfully.

Music director Chitragupt offered some songs to her over the years, mainly for B-grade movies and mythological movies. One among those delightful numbers was '*Thandi Hawaon Kali Ghataon*' from *Zimbo Comes to Town* (1960). '*Lage Nahi Mora Jiya*' from *Banarasi Thug* (1962) was another delightful solo. However, this is not to be confused for the

Lata classic with the same title from *Ghunghat* (1960). The depth of emotions could be discerned *'Mere Mehboob Sun'* from *Bhootnath* (1963). She had an opportunity to sing for main lead, Mala Sinha, in *'Yeh Aaj Kal Ke Ladke'* from *Dillagi* (1966). Alas, such opportunities were rare.

In *'Sanjh Bhayi, Jhanjh Bhed Jiyara Ke'* from *Sapna* (1969), she had to sing a semi-classical song, composed by Jaidev. Remember, it was not simple to negotiate Jaidev. However, Usha did it well and this is where her training showed through.

Another music director who saw her potential and trusted her with excellent numbers was SD Burman. For instance, *'Mero Toh Giridhar Gopal'* from *Phagun* (1973) is when Usha sang the Meera bhajan for Waheeda Rehman.

One song that brought her massive fame was *'Mungda Mungda'* from *Inkaar* (1977) composed by Rajesh Roshan, which took on a life of its own. It was picturized on Helen.

Usha helped lyricist Majrooh Sultanpuri with Marathi words for the song. She had sung for Rajesh Roshan earlier—a duet with Asha in the super hit film *Julie* (1975) and sang for his other films like *Khatta Meetha* (1978) and *Hamari Bahu Alka* (1982).

Unfortunately, her lot did not improve much even after some blockbuster hits. In comparison, her Marathi songs, both film and non-film were immensely popular. She sang in other languages too, like Bengali, Gujarati, Kannada, Bhojpuri and Nepali.

She has had formal training in dance before she joined films. She paints as well. Her singing talent did not reach its full potential, not for lack of trying but because fate dealt a hand where she was born in the first family of Hindi film music, with sisters who would rule the airwaves for several decades. But she did carve out a niche, however modest.

Being nominated for Filmfare Awards thrice is no mean feat. She was nominated for *'Main Toh Aarti'* from *Jai Santoshi Maa* (1976), *'Mungda'* from *Inkaar* (1978) and *'Humse Nazar Toh Milao'* from *Ikraar* (1980).

In the aftermath of India's victory over Bangladesh, Lata Mangeshkar gave a public performance at Ramlila Maidan, Delhi in 1972. She sang *'Sarfaroshi Ki Tamanna'* and *'Jayate Jayate Jayate'* composed by Jaidev. A day earlier, Lata along with Usha, Hridayanath and Jaidev, visited my uncle—late Satish Bhatia—music director, for tea where I had the pleasure of meeting all of them. Who would have known then that nine years later, Usha would once again visit the same colony again, this time as the voice of a goddess!

Going back to the story where we started, after a few minutes of the fevered rotation of the head, the purpose of the congregation became clear when the question-answer session began. People would ask questions, and the lady would give short replies in a voice that was not hers. Some of these questions were very personal, but nobody minded. Such a phenomenon did not happen often. Make the most of it. I too, at the prodding of my aunt, asked whether I would clear the exam. *"Mehnat ka phal meetha hota hai,"* is the answer I got.

With the blessings of Goddess Santoshi Maa, the bhajan and the voice behind it will defy age and remain timeless.

35

Malika-e-Ghazal

Farida Khanum

Sometimes a creation becomes bigger than its creator. In this case, two creators—Sohail Rana and Fayyaz Hashmi. Sohail Rana is the Pakistani film music director par excellence, composer of Mehdi Hassan's inarguably best Pakistani film song—'*Mujhe Tum Nazar Se*', and one of Ahmed Rushdi's finest—'*Haan Isi Mod Par*', both songs from *Doraha* (1967). Fayyaz Hashmi is the well-known Pakistani film lyricist whose very first song—'*Sab Din Ek Samaan Nahi Tha*'—in 1941 launched Talat Mehmood.

And then there is the singer who initially presented the creation to the world—Habib Wali Mohammad. This MBA from Syracuse University, New York, was based in Bombay and hailed from the family of an industrialist. While he eventually migrated to Pakistan in 1957, he was well-known in India, having recorded '*Lagta Nahin Hai Ji Mera*' under the music direction of Saraswati Devi (India's first female music director). The ghazal became very popular since it was broadcast on Radio Ceylon. However, it was Rafi who brought the ghazal into the national consciousness.

A similar fate befell Habib Wali Mohammad regarding this song. The song would forever be linked to only one person who came to the party later. But that is the destiny of some songs. Their new interpreter turns the original creation into an 'institution' and gets indelibly associated with it. The original creators and singer can only take a backseat and watch their creation being majestically moved to the universal stage by the sheer genius of the cover singer.

Farida Khanum. The song that her name conjures is *'Aaj Jaane Ki Zidd Na Karo'* from the film *Badal Aur Bijli* (1973).

No two live versions will be exact copies. It all boils down to the audience, the mood, the setting, the musicians, the emotions. The introduction and placement of the musical ornamentations—*kan-swar, meend, gamak, khatka, andolan* and *murki* may vary from performance to performance. The emotions invested, the throw of the honey-sweetened rich voice, the style of delivery, the lyrical flourishes, the *adaa*, a hint sometimes of coquettishness even while dealing with yearning and anguish, the coil of the lips, the twinkle in the eyes, the poise, the gestures—each rendition is new. That is why it remains fresh and timeless. It is a *nazm* beyond compare, and with Farida Khanum helming it, it attains divinity.

She has an inner muse which constantly inspires her every time she sings it.

She does not require musicians for this song. Unplugged, the song is even more beautiful, haunting and seductive. Musicians just detract from the intensity of feeling imbuing not only every word but the silence between the words too.

But it will be very unfair to treat Farida Khanum as a one-song-wonder. She is more. Much more.

She was born in the fall of 1929 in Calcutta. Her family moved from Amritsar to Lahore in Pakistan when she was 18 years old. She followed in the footsteps of her famous elder sister—singer Mukhtar Begum. Under the tutelage of the renowned Ustad Ashiq Ali Khan of Patiala Gharana, she learnt khayal, thumri and dadra.

In one of her interviews, she has stated that she would have been a classical singer had she not migrated. In Pakistan, the classical singers were so good that she would not have been able to match the extremely talented *ustads*.

She was always interested in poetry and decided to shift to the semi-classical genre, rather than struggle in a difficult field. She was, of course, being modest.

She gave her first public concert in 1950 at the young age of 21 and then joined Radio Pakistan, where she gained recognition for herself. She became a well-known singer when President Ayub Khan invited her to a public recital in the 1960s.

After that she tasted massive success. Her outstanding songs are too many to count. To name a few, *'Woh Ishq Jo Humse Rooth Gaya'*, *'Maine Pairon Mein Payal Toh Bandhi Nahin'*, *'Raat Jo Tum Ne Deep Bujhaye'* and *'Woh Mujh Se Hue Ham Kalam'*.

All these decades, she has been sitting atop the pedestal of love and affection showered on her by her vast legion of fans. Every song bears her unique identity and soul. The Queen of Ghazal's songs are redolent with emotion and virtuosity. Her contribution to the genre has been immense. This is borne out by not only her sell-out records and stage shows, but also the awards she has been bestowed with—the Pride of Performance Award in 1970 (Pakistan), Hilal-i-Imtiaz in 2005 (the second-highest civilian award in Pakistan) and the Hafiz Ali Khan Award in 2005 (India).

She has visited India often. Her fans are on both sides of the border. I was very fortunate to see her perform live in New Delhi. The Siri Fort Auditorium was packed to the rafters. The concert was pure magic. She mesmerized the audience, had them in raptures and applauding endlessly, asking for more. The diva sang one soulful ghazal after another. She would elegantly acknowledge every applause with an *aadab* and a kiss of her hands. She was truly majestic. Her performance was overwhelming, her aura graceful. And yes, she did sing *'Aaj Jaane Ki Zidd Na Karo'*, which was the highlight of the show. "One can lie with words, not music," she said.

In 2015, at the age of 86, she sang this *nazm* in Coke Studio (Pakistan) Season 8.

In March 2020, she rendered yet another *nazm* during an Instagram live session with musicians Vishal and Rekha Bhardwaj.

It was natural that this iconic song, this eternal love ballad, would be re-sung by many artists. Asha Bhosle sang it in her album *Asha Bhosle: Love Supreme* (2006).

The song was used as background music in a scene in *Monsoon Wedding* (2001). It was recreated by Pritam and featured in *Ae Dil Hai Mushkil* (2016) in the voice of Shilpa Rao. And the list goes on.

This veteran singer will continue to live in our hearts. The thrall that she held us all in, and continues to hold, will never diminish. Her immense legacy '*yunhi pehlu mein baithe rahegi*'.

36

Public Display of Angst

In the '50s and '60s what did the Indian man do when his ladylove rejected him? He would reason with her; maybe plead with her; or perhaps even threaten her. Or he would see her viewpoint and accept it gracefully; he might even become her friend. Of course, he would get hurt. He would either take it on the chin, or hit the bar, dive into depression, or withdraw from society. But eventually, things would become normal, and he would move on in life.

But in that era the Indian film hero did one thing more—which you and I did not get to. He would attend her engagement or wedding ceremony, or any social function where guests and her new beau were in attendance, sit at the piano, and sing out his anguish, his disappointment, his ire, his frustration. He would be wry; his words would reek of *double entendre*. He would remind her of their love. But he would also assure her that he bore her no ill-will and would quietly exit from her life. He would wish her a happy future with the partner she had chosen. All very dignified, no violent outburst. All this drama would ensure that the lady's special day was wrecked. A final musical good riddance!

This PDA, or the Public Display of Angst, had attained the stature of a genre in the Hindi film music. Some memorable songs in the '50s and '60s belong to this category.

One of the earliest such song was *'Jhoom Jhoom Ke Nacho Aaj, Gao Khushi Ke Geet'* from *Andaz* (1949) sung on screen by Dilip Kumar. This Naushad–Majrooh classic had Mukesh doing playback duty and as was his wont, he packed the song with pathos (in fact, all the four songs of Dilip, as well as one unreleased song were sung by Mukesh). Dilip, who loved Nargis, was devastated to know that she only treated him as a friend and was engaged to Raj Kapoor. On the piano, before a large gathering of the glitterati, with Cuckoo doing her dance routine, he expressed his pain (*"Kisi ko dil ka dard mila hai, kisi ko man ka meet"*). Nargis squirmed uncomfortably while Raj Kapoor looked quizzically at her.

Who can forget Dev Anand poignantly pointing out to Asha Parekh that *"Quaid mangi thi, rihai toh nahin mangi thi"* in *Jab Pyar Kisi Se Hota Hai* (1961)? The song *'Teri Zulfon Se Judai Toh Nahin Mangi Thi'* was a classic Shankar-Jaikishan/ Hasrat Jaipuri creation, sung feelingly by Rafi when he was at the peak of his career in the early '60s. Pran, in a suit and a hat, was the third angle in this song, very happy with the turn of events.

Then there was *'Rang Aur Noor Ki Baraat Kise Pesh Karoon'* from *Ghazal* (1964) sung by Sunil Dutt, in the voice of Rafi. His lady love Meena Kumari, upstairs with other ladies, was getting ready for the wedding ceremony while Rehman, pleased as punch, was sitting downstairs with the men and the maulvi. Sunil, in his graceful style, launched into a lament (*"Main un apnon mein hun jo aaj se begaane hain"*).

A teary Meena, hands clutching her throat, left no one in doubt about her predicament. At the end, the song rose dramatically to a crescendo, with Meena matching the drama by rushing to her bedroom and falling on the bed. The Madan Mohan-Sahir combination gave us two more memorable ghazals from the same film with *'Ishq Ki Garmiye Jazbaat'* and *'Naghma o Sher Ki Saugat'* with the same refrain—*"kise pesh karoon"*.

'Dil Jo Na Kehe Saka' was the gold standard in this genre. From *Bheegi Raat* (1965), Rafi belted out this emotion-packed humdinger of a song from the word go (*"Chaliye mubaarak jashn dosti kaa, daaman to thaamaa aap ne kisi kaa"*).

The action took place in Nainital. Pradeep Kumar gulped down wine to a high-octave prelude, then got down to business while Meena Kumari could only watch mournfully and Ashok Kumar act uncomfortably dignified. He was not a villain here, just a wrong man at the wrong time, in the wrong circumstance. Majrooh penned the lyrics, and the sensational music composed by the maestro Roshan.

And just so that everybody in the surrounding hills knew the fragile state of his mind, Pradeep kept the energy on high-octane. The echo from the hills was audible in the song. The most dramatic moment in the song came towards the end when Pradeep looked up to see Meena gone and was stunned into silence while the music continued. A few bars later, he joined in and completed the song. A real treat!

Manoj Kumar sang '*Naseeb Mein Jiske Jo Likha Tha*' to Asha Parekh in a restaurant in *Do Badan* (1966). He let her know that "*Kisi ke hisse mein pyas aayi, kisi ke hisse mein jaam aaya*". Pran played the third person in the equation. The lyrics, which won Shakeel Badayuni the Filmfare nomination, were beautifully composed by Ravi (also nominated) and sung by Rafi.

Milan (1967) had Sunil Dutt sing to Nutan on her wedding day—'*Mubarak Ho Tumko Sama Yeh Suhana*', while Deven Verma smiled idiotically. Mukesh soulfully acknowledged—"*Koi cheez apni hui hai paraai, kisi se milan hai kisi se judaai*" in this Laxmikant-Pyarelal/Anand Bakshi beauty.

The same year saw the release of *Patthar Ke Sanam* in which Manoj Kumar sang the title song to his love interest Waheeda Rehman. He rebuked her ("*Badi bhool hui, arrey humne yeh kya samjha, yeh kya jaana*") while Mumtaz, who wanted to marry Manoj, relished Waheeda's discomfiture. Rafi yet again scored in this Laxmikant-Pyarelal/Majrooh song.

Who doesn't remember Shammi Kapoor's '*Dil Ke Jharoke Mein Tujh Ko Bitha Ke*' from *Brahmachari* (1968)? The ambience of the pain of parting created by Shankar-Jaikishan's Filmfare-winning music (the orchestration, the humming, the piano, the saxophone), Hasrat's lyrics, and the dancing ensemble was truly sensational.

Rajshree and Pran were at the receiving end of Shammi's plaintive "*Meri mohabbat ko thukra de chahe, main koi tujhse na shikva karoonga*". Rafi magnificent outpouring of grief secured him the Filmfare Award.

Everyone is familiar with the song '*Tum Bin Jauun Kahan*' from *Pyar Ka Mausam* (1969). Both the Rafi and Kishore versions of this RD Burman/Majrooh gem became very popular. However, there was one more version—a sad one—sung by Rafi. Shashi Kapoor was humiliated by Asha Parekh's father and mockingly asked to sing a song. Shashi sat at the piano and defiantly began, "*Meri nazar mein sirf tum ho, ke aur mujhko pata nahin hai; tumhari mehfil se uth raha hoon, magar rasta kuch nahin hai*". Then he started to sing the song.

In the same year there was '*Chandi Ki Deewar Na Todi*' sung by Mukesh and picturized on Jeetendra in *Vishwas* (1969). The object of his opprobrium ("*Kal tak jisne kasme khaaeen, dukh me sath nibhane ki, aj voh apne sukh ki khatir, ho gai ik begane ki*") was Aparna Sen while, unusually, the villain Manmohan played the piano. This Kalyanji-Ananadji/Gulsham Bawra song became very popular with rejected lovers, just as '*Meri Bheegi Bheegi Si Palkon Mein*' (*Anamika*) became four years later.

'*Tu Auron Ki Kyun Ho Gayi*' from *Ek Baar Muskaraa Do* (1972) was an aberration to the songs described earlier. OP Nayyar was a maverick, and his iconoclastic leanings were evident in the song. The lyrics penned by Indeevar—"*Tu hamari thi, jaan se pyaari thi, tere liye maine, duniya sanwari thi*"—lent themselves to a sad sombre song. But OP Nayyar injected the song with high testosterone and gave it an energetic beat. The beauty of the song lay in this very incongruity. Deb Mukherji hammed his way through with accusatory looks and gestures, while Tanuja looked shell-shocked. No subtlety, no oblique references; total bluntness.

And the list goes on—'*Mere Dushman Tu Meri Dosti Ko Tarse*' from *Aaye Din Bahaar Ke* (1966); '*Waqt Karta Jo Wafa*' from *Dil Ne Pukara* (1967); '*Yeh Shama Toh Jali Roshni Ke Liye*' from *Aaya Sawan Jhoom Ke* (1969); '*Mere Naseeb Mein Ai Dost*' from *Do Raaste* (1970); '*Khush Rahe Tu Sada*' from *Khilona* (1970); '*Teri Galiyon Mein Na Rakhein Ge Kadam*' from *Hawas* (1974); '*Kya Hua Tera Vada*' from *Hum Kisise Kam Nahin* (1977); '*O Saathi Re*' from *Muqaddar Ka Sikandar* (1978), and many others. The template has changed over time, but the basic concept remains the same—public declaration of hurt.

It was not only the Hindi hero who felt wronged. Women also went through the same emotions and chose the public forum to air them. The most memorable example was '*Ajeeb Dastan Hai Yeh, Kahan Shuru Kahan Khatam*' from *Dil Apna Aur Preet Parai* (1960) where Meena Kumari let Raj Kumar, sitting with Nadira, have it—"*Mubaarakein tumhe ke tum kisi ke noor ho gaye, kisi ke itne paas ho ke sab se door ho gaye.*" Also, '*Dushman Na Kare Dost Ne Woh Kaam Kiya Hai*' from *Aakhir Kyon* (1985).

Our neighbours also exhibited their pain in public in the same manner. There were some remarkable songs in this category: '*Jab Koi Pyaar Se Bulayega*' (*Zindagi Kitni Haseen Hai*, 1969), '*Ab Ke Hum Bichhde*' (*Angarey*, 1972), '*Tumhe Dekhoon Tumhare Chahane Walon Ki Mehfil Mein*' (*Piya Milan Ki Aas*, 1968), and '*Main Khushi Se Kyon Na Gaoon*' (*Lori*, 1966), and others.

From 1980s onwards, the magic of this genre waned off. Songs were few and far between. '*Aur Is Dil Mein Kya*

Rakha Hai' from *Imaandaar* (1987), '*Mubarak Ho Tumko Yeh Shaadi'* from *Haan Maine Bhi Pyaar Kiya Hai* (2002) were some examples.

They failed to generate the aura and the drama of the '50s and '60s. In '*Acchha Sila Diya Tune Mere Pyaar Ka'* from *Bewafa Sanam* (1993), Krishan Kumar killed Shilpa Shirodkar at her wedding. This would have been bad form in the '60s, but times were changing.

With more exposure; more information; unfettered inter-mingling; social networking; multiple partners; a more pragmatic approach to life, the present generation is chilled out and such a public display in films appears antediluvian. The genre now exists in the fond memories of the earlier generations. This is the day and age of "*Mere saiyan ji se aaj maine breakup kar liya*", with the hero good-naturedly wondering "*Humko bin bataaye tune yeh kab kar liya?*" ('*The Breakup Song'* from *Ae Dil Hai Mushkil*, 2016).

37

Pushing Boundaries

One song that gave me immense joy, when I was nine years old, was the title song of *Love in Tokyo* (1966). The song was a feel-good, bubbly, and energetic but the icing on the cake was Mohammad Rafi belting out *'Jaaapaaaan, Love In Tokyo'*. The accent was Indian, Japan pronounced as it is in Hindi, but it didn't matter.

English words in a Hindi song? That made the song a cut above the rest; cool, groovy, exotic. This was an attempt at westernization and reflected the gradual transformation of spoken Hindi. That year, another Rafi song, the ebullient *'Suno Suno Miss Chatterji, Mere Dil Ka Matter Ji'* (*Baharen Phir Bhi Aayengi*, 1966) also made waves.

A year later, in 1967, came *An Evening in Paris* with its title song *'Dekho, Dekho, Dekho, Dekho, Dekho, An Evening In Paris'*; *Night in London* with *'O My Love, Nazar Na Lag Jaye'*; and *Farz* with *'Happy Birthday to You'*. These songs were great fun, never mind Rafi's Punjabi diction when singing in English.

Earlier, Rafi had done something similar with *'April Fool Banaya'* (*April Fool*, 1964) with Saira Banu screaming "Yuuuuu....." and Rafi responding with "Very Good". Then there was *'Baar Baar Dekho'* (*Chinatown*, 1962) with the punchline *'Tally Ho'* but sung as *"Taali Ho"* and written as such in the song lyrics.

Why an English huntsman's cry to the hounds on sighting a fox came to be incorporated into the song by Majrooh Sultanpuri is something I didn't understand then, and don't till date. But Majrooh had also written *'C.A.T. Cat Mane Billi'* in *Dilli Ka Thug* (1958)—sung by Kishore Kumar and Asha Bhosle. Maybe it was just a random phrase put in as a refrain. But no one complained, and the song became very popular, hinged largely on the imaginative insertion of *'Tally Ho'*.

There was Rafi's *'Pyar Ho Toh Kehdo Yes, Pyar Nahin Toh Kehdo No'* (again by Majrooh) from *Dil Deke Dekho* (1959). What a peppy, effervescent song it was with such an imaginative English-laced ultimatum! And *'All Line Clear'* by Rafi/Johnny Walker in *Chori Chori* (1956)—'clear' pronounced as *'kil-year'*. The bagpipes were added for authenticity.

And even though *Kaagaz Ke Phool* had serious, philosophical, sombre songs, it had Rafi doing playback for Johnny Walker in—*'Hum Tum Jise Kehta Hai Shaadi, You Know Hai Poora Barbaadi, Jo Tum Lalchaoge Piche Pachtaoge, Mind You Jayegi Azaadi'*.

Rafi wasn't the only singer doing the Hinglish songs. There were others too. But he seemed to have a predominant share.

It was natural for Rafi to progress to full-fledged English songs, even though he was not fluent in English. It is believed that he cut an entire album in English though only two songs survive and are known. Not a bad feat for a singer who struggled with English. The music was given by Shankar-Jaikishen and lyrics by Harindranath Chattopadhyaya; they had approached Rafi with the prospect of doing the English album.

The two songs were *'Although We Hail from Different Lands'* based on the tune of *'Baharon Phool Barsao' (Suraj,* 1966), and *'The She I Love'* based on the tune of *'Hum Kale Hain Toh Kya Hua'* (*Gumnaam,* 1965). Harindranath coached Rafi with the English lyrics. Rafi was very happy with the outcome and presented Harindranath with all his albums. However, Harindranath did not accept the gift and asked

Rafi that he sing *'Chahunga Main Tujhe Saanhj Savere' (Dosti,* 1964*)* for him. Rafi took his harmonium to Harindranath's house and did the needful.

The refrain of *'Although We Hail From Different Lands'* is Lennon-esque—*"Although We Hail From Different Lands, We Share One Earth And Sky And Sun, Remember Friends, The World Is One". 'The She I Love'* begins with *"The She I Love Is A Beautiful, Beautiful Dream Come True, I Love Her, Love Her, Love Her, Love Her, So Will You".*

Though these English songs pale in comparison to the absolute supremacy he exercised over Hindi songs, Rafi never backed down and made a valiant effort to overcome his fears and come out of his comfort zone. In the biography *Mohammed Rafi: Golden Voice of the Silver Screen,* Sujata Dev writes about how the unlettered singer would politely turn down requests for autographs.

As his fame grew, "he began practicing his signature diligently and when Ammi (mother) enquired why he was wasting reams of paper, he told her that he did not want to deprive his fans and so was learning to sign his name in English," Rafi's son, Shahid, told Dev. "Soon he began signing autographs in English and enjoyed doing so. It came as a great compliment for all his efforts when a journalist mentioned that he had the best signature in the industry."

Singing in English gave Rafi the courage to sing in other foreign languages during his tours abroad.

In India, he had already sung *'Rasa Sayang Re'* from the movie *Singapore* (1960). The words and tune of the opening line was adapted from a popular folk tune of Malaysia/ Indonesia. During his tour to Mauritius, he sang in Creole—*'Mo Le Coeur Toujours Soif Zot L'amour Camarade'* (My heart will always be thirsty for your love, my friends), based on the tune of *'Ehsaan Mere Dil Pe Tumhara Hai Doston'* (*Gaban,* 1966).

He sang in Dutch—*'Ik Zal Jou Nooit Vergeten Al Zal Ik In India Zijn'* (I will never forget you, although I will be in India) based on *'Baharon Phool Barsao'* (*Suraj*, 1966). In Surinam, he sang in the local language—*'Aai Aai Ya, Milobi Sararang Sukoo Sukoo'*, based on *'Aai Aai Ya Sukoo Sukoo'* (*Junglee*, 1961). In Sri Lanka, he sang a song in Sinhalese based on *'Ramaiya Vastavaiya'* (*Shree 420*, 1955). He sang in Persian—*'Aye Taaza Gul'* (O fresh flower), with Afghani singer Zheela.

He has also sung in Arabic—*'Haeeyuli Sultaan Qaboos Hibaadal Maimunhun'*. In fact, Rafi had the unique distinction of giving the *azaan* at the Kaaba in Mecca in the early '70s. Masood Rana, the well-known Pakistani playback singer was with Rafi and recorded the *azaan*. Rana declared that this was the greatest treasure of his life.

Rafi was an outstanding singer and a good human being, who was always experimenting, pushing boundaries, exploring new frontiers. He wasn't afraid of failure and had faith and confidence in his own abilities and hard work. He never left his listeners down. Going back to Rafi's poser from *Dil Deke Dekho* (1959)—*'Pyar Ho to Kehdo Yes'*, the reply can only be a resounding 'yes'.

38

Singing in the Club

In the early 1980s, a colleague of mine (a promotee officer on the verge of retirement) found out that I was a member of a well-known erstwhile British club in Lutyens' Delhi and expressed a desire to spend an evening there. We went one Saturday.

The music band's equipment was already ready on the stage at the corner of the main bar. The place was packed, and my guest smiled in approval. Shortly, the band walked in, in black tuxedos and bow ties, took stage and started the proceedings.

A lady crooner took the mic. English music of the 1960s was the fare. Again, my guest nodded approvingly. Gradually, couples—mostly elderly—took the floor for waltz and foxtrot. My guest by now was tight as an owl and clapping with the beat.

After about half an hour, his enthusiasm had visibly ebbed and, leaning across, he asked when ladies in skirts would come in and start dancing. I was dumbstruck!

Clearly, he was still stuck in the time warp of the 1950s and 1960s when a 'club song' featured frequently in Hindi films. In fact, it had acquired a genre of its own. Like some others, this institution has also fallen by the wayside, yielding place to other forms.

How does one define a 'club song'? How is it different from a cabaret? Since I have no primer to fall back on, I venture to answer by my experience of having watched the famous and memorable 'club songs' and gleaning their essential characteristics from such viewing.

The venue used to be a public place, not residence, which was normally a club or restaurant. It could even be a gambling den or a bar. The patrons, in evening dinner dress, were seated at dining tables and food and drinks service continued during the performance. Smoking was the norm.

A full-fledged music band of Anglo-Indians used to ply their trade on a stage; tuxedoed, playing western instruments—trumpets, clarinets, saxophones, drums, guitars; sometimes even a double bass. There could also be just a single instrument played by the singer—but that was an aberration.

The singer could be male or female. Usually, there was a retinue of dancers accompanying the singer. In the 1950s and 1960s, most of these dancers were Anglo-Indians, usually wearing skirts. That image had been etched in the mind of my guest, and millions of others.

The basic purpose of the 'club song' was entertainment, not titillation. That's what differentiated the two genres. Cabaret dancers were scantily clad and aggressive in their dance movements. Club dancers, if female, would be demure, clad in silk or satin gown.

So how did it start? The country had recently won independence. The ways and habits of the British, as reflected in their eating, drinking and entertainment habits in 'whites-mostly' clubs in cities, cantonments, railway townships and plantations, and tony restaurants, were imbibed by the upper crust Indians.

The musicians in the bands were Anglo-Indians, and later, Goans. The music was waltz, rock 'n' roll, calypso, Latino. For example, in Calcutta, restaurants such as Trincas, Blue Fox, Mocambo and Moulin Rouge used to have live bands; dinner jackets were mandatory and only the *crème de la crème* dined here.

The depiction of this culture in films was a natural progression. Of course, the songs were in Hindi and a poetic license was taken in the depiction. But the inspiration clearly originated from such clubs and restaurants.

Cuckoo and Helen, both Anglo-Indians, were the main dancers of this genre in films. Though the traditional Indian dance forms also featured once in a while, it would take several years for such dance forms to get firmly entrenched in Hindi films. Till then, the 'club songs' were the major entertainment feature of Hindi films in the 1950s and 1960s.

Naturally, all such songs are too many to enumerate. I will only highlight some landmark songs.

The first such song was '*Patli Kamar Hai, Tirchhi Nazar Hai*' from Raj Kapoor's *Barsaat* (1949). A young, suave and rakish Prem Nath sang the song and danced with Cuckoo. This was the first film of Shankar-Jaikishan. All the songs were massive hits.

The song that really started the trend of 'club songs' was '*Tadbeer Se Bigdi Hui*' from *Baazi* (1951). The song was sung with such vivacity and sensuousness by Geeta Dutt, matched on the screen by Geeta Bali's oomph and coquettishness to a dejected Dev Anand in a gambling den, that it became a huge hit.

The song changed Geeta Dutt's image as a singer of weepy songs and bhajans and showcased her talent to be much more versatile. Sahir Ludhianvi, who had penned this ghazal, had expected SD Burman to compose it in the style of a ghazal—a soulful, philosophical ditty.

He was aghast when it was composed as a 'club song'—the western lilt provided by the Spanish guitar and fast tempo providing an upbeat ambience. Sahir would have walked out of the film had not Geeta smoothed his ruffled feathers. And the rest is history!

Even Anil Biswas, the doyen of Hindi film music, who dexterously walked the tightrope between classical and popular music, composed '*Dil Chura Loon*' in *Faraar* (1955), both the Geetas yet again stamping their class.

Fast forward to *Howrah Bridge* (1958). It had not one, not two, but three 'club songs', composed by the inimitable OP Nayyar—another composer responsible for giving Geeta Dutt a makeover. Geeta did not disappoint and once again exhibited her mettle in this genre in '*Mera Naam Chin Chin Chu*', singing with gay abandon.

The Hawaiian guitar prelude, the fast-paced clapping, the idiosyncratic nonsense lyrics, the catchy tagline: *"Hello Mister, How Do You Do?"* and Helen's exuberant dancing (this was her first film as a full-fledged dancer) was guaranteed to make the song a superhit. So much so that it was used in *Salaam Bombay* (1988). In *Ghulam* (1998), Aamir Khan sang the first line of the song.

Then there was '*Aayeye Meherbaan*' sung by Asha. This song, which gave Asha her first distinctive image, and portrayed with come-hither sensuousness by Madhubala, had given the song an iconic status.

And finally, '*Dekh Ke Teri Nazar*'. Madhubala, in the voice of Asha, performed on a ship during a voyage from Rangoon to Calcutta, with Ashok Kumar in attendance. The opening bongos and the western melody of the piano accordion have made this one of the most memorable preludes. As was the style of OP Nayyar, all the songs had western rhythms in the *mukhda* and dholak in the antara.

1959 was an important year for 'club songs'. Among the musical gems of *Anari* was the song *'1956, 1957, 1958, 1959'*. Another film *Love Marriage* in the same year had *'Teen Kanashtar Peet Peet Kar'*. Dev Anand, after listening to the rock 'n' roll music for a few minutes, couldn't stand it anymore. He climbed on the stage where the band was playing, stopped the music, and after taking an *alaap* started—*"Teen*

Kanashtar Peet Peet Ke Galaah Phaad Kar Chillanaa, Yaar Mere Mat Buraa Maan, Ye Gaanaa Hai Na Bajaana Hai".

His lady love Mala Sinha, attired in a saree and wearing a bindi, looked on approvingly. He was being very prescient because a decade later, the 'club songs' would almost become extinct in films. But for now, they were still the flavour of the season. *Dil Deke Dekho* (1959)—Asha Parekh's and composer Usha Khanna's debut film and Shammi Kapoor's makeover film—had the perennial favourite *'Dil Deke Dekho'*.

A year later came *Ek Phool Char Kante* (1960). It had two 'club songs'. The music was by Shankar-Jaikishan. The first one was called *'Beautiful Baby Of Broadway'* sung by Iqbal Singh. It was a revolutionary song in its singing and picturization. It was a Sardar impersonating Elvis—rock 'n' roll, twists, shakes, you name it. Very infectious and never heard or seen before.

Interestingly, the song was originally recorded as *'Bombshell Baby of Bombay'* and filmed as such. However, the film got in trouble with the censors over the word 'Bombshell'. The lyrics had to be changed to *'Beautiful Baby of Broadway'*.

The song on the record still had 'Bombshell' though the film song had 'Beautiful'. Sunil Dutt also had a 'club song' *'O Meri Baby Doll'* in the same film. Even though he did a vigorous job of it, it paled in comparison to what Iqbal Singh did.

1961 saw RD Burman's inaugural film—Mehmood's *Chhote Nawab*. RD showed his class right from the word go and came up with outstanding music including the 'club song' *'Matwali Aankhon Wale'*.

Chinatown (1962) had two such songs— *'Yamma, Yamma, Yamma'*, and the evergreen *'Bar Bar Dekho'* with the very un-Chinese tagline—'Tally Ho'. *Tere Ghar Ke Saamne* (1963) had *'Dil Ki Manzil'*.

1965 was a landmark year for this genre. Four 'club songs' ruled the radio waves. Mehmood's *Bhoot Bangla* had the explosive *'Aao Twist Karein'* which took the nation by storm. The song, based on Chubby Checker's *'Let's Twist Again'*, immortalized the twist in Hindi films.

The other three songs all featured Ted Lyons & His Cubs as the music band.

Gumnaam had a very popular and mesmerizing 'club song'—*'Jaan Pehchan Ho'*. The look and feel of the song were so full of life that it was impossible to sit still and listen to it. The guitaring was top class and while it remained western in form, the Indian moorings were evident. A fantastic fusion it was that catapulted it to the western shores. It featured in the 2003 Hollywood film *Ghost World* as a backdrop to the opening credits. And who can forget the brilliant Heineken Beer Commercial—*The Date*—anchored on this song?

The other song was from *Janwar*—*'Dekho Ab Toh Kisko Nahin Hai Khabar'*. Inspired by the Beatles' *'I Want To Hold Your Hand'*, the song was performed with gusto by Shammi Kapoor and Rajshree, with the energetic band dressed up as the Beatles, mop tops and all.

The fourth was an instrumental piece from *Mere Sanam* where the band played while Oscar made moves (dancing and otherwise) on Asha Parekh. The same film had *'Humdum Mere Maan Bhi Jao'*, a song with *Punjabiyat* written all over it but restrained in its robustness by western dance rhythms.

And then came *Teesri Manzil* in 1966. With Shammi Kapoor playing the role of a hotel band drummer Rocky, there had to be 'club songs'. And what a fantastic job RD Burman did. He took the format to its zenith. *'Aaja Aaja'* and *'O Haseena Zulfon Wali'* were chart-toppers bringing the nation to the dance floor.

Raat Aur Din (1967) had *'Dil Ki Giraah Khol Do'* by Nargis (her last film) and Feroz Khan.

By the 1970s, the number of restaurants serving live entertainment diminished. The nature of music had also changed. Anglo-Indian bands found their influence waning. Films moved on to disco music.

Later would come 're-mixed songs' and 'item songs'. The 'club song' was yielding place gradually to the new order. There was a brief revival with *'Kaisi Paheli Zindagani'*—performed to perfection by the sultry Rekha in *Parineeta* (2005). But that was expected since the film had the 1960s look and the song was a throwback to the restaurants in Calcutta of that era. Similarly, *Bombay Velvet* (2015) set in the '60s, had three 'club songs'—*'Mohabbat Buri Bimari'*, *'Sylvia'* and *'Dhadaam Dhadaam'*.

While some clubs still manfully plod on with western bands even these days on weekly dance nights, big events, like the New Year's Eve Night, invariably need to have Hindi film dance numbers belted out by DJs. Trincas, the iconic institution on Park Street in Kolkata, used to have a tuxedoed band playing English classics till mid-2000s.

It used to be the high point of my frequent visits to Calcutta. Then, suddenly, the band changed its repertoire to Hindi. It had a new singer and the discomfort on the face of the 60-years plus band members was clearly visible. Their innings was over. But the place was packed to the rafters and the appreciative crowd couldn't get enough.

'Club songs' did yeoman service in providing entertainment in the 1950s and 1960s but now reside, not on the floor, but in fond memories of that generation!

39

Lost Verses

The songs that you hear in your early years, when memories are just beginning to form, stay with you forever. From the age of four till seven (till 1964), I was in Calcutta, and heard amazing songs on radio and the 45-RPM records that my parents played on the record-changer.

Aarti, Gumrah, Sangam, Asli Naqli, Bandini, Aayi Milan Ki Bela, Aaj Aur Kal, Taj Mahal, Tere Ghar Ke Saamne are some of the films whose songs are forever etched in my consciousness. I knew the words, the prelude and interludes, the embellishments, every nook and cranny. One song that stood out was *'Teri Pyaari Pyaari Soorat Ko'* (*Sasural*, 1961) The tune was catchy; the theme was original (later, Hasrat Jaipuri would use a similar concept in *'Is Rang Badalti Duniya Mein'* in *Rajkumar*, 1964); it had the catch line *'chashm-e-bad door'* (whose meaning my parents had to explain)—later, when one heard Hasrat more extensively, one realized that such catch phrases were his forte. The song was easy to sing; and the prelude and interludes were straightforward and melodic (which was expected of Shankar-Jaikishan). The two stanzas conveyed the essence of the hero's concern for his lady-love, delivering it in such a beautiful way!

Imagine, therefore, my shock when I discovered the third stanza. I approached it with mixed feelings: shock that someone I knew so well had a hidden side all along; anger at being deprived of the full song all these years; curious as to how the stanza would fit into the overall scheme of things (would it add value? would it be an interloper insinuating itself into a much-loved national icon? after all, after *'kisi ki nazar'*, *'meri nazar'*, *'mausam ki nazar'*, and *'khud ki nazar'*, who else was left to give *nazar*?); thrilled at the prospect of getting acquainted with a new facet of the song's personality; and trepidation as to whether it would comfortably roll off my tongue, now that it had come out of the closet and would demand to be sung with equal respect and fervour.

Mystery solved. Rajendra Kumar was cautioning B Saroja Devi—*'Nikla Na Karo Tum Raahon Par, Zarron Ki Nazar Na Lage'*.

This is not the only song.

Some songs that the radio/record listening nation had taken for granted had this unknown side. Of course, they were available in their musical fullness in the movies. If I had seen *Sasural* (1961), the missing stanza wouldn't have been missing for me. But the main source of the songs those days—the radio and gramophone records—did not have them.

It is thanks to YouTube that film song clips are now available, which has led to the discovery of these rare treasures.

The old songs whose lost stanzas have come out are being looked at with fresh interest, and music aficionados are coming to terms with how the songs now sound in their entirety.

Here are more examples from some of the most recognizable and adored songs:

The list is very long. Songs like *'Sau Saal Pehle'* (*Jab Pyaar Kisi Se Hota Hai*, 1961), *'Ai Gulbadan'* (*Professor*, 1962), *'Tujhe Jeevan Ki Dor Se'* (*Asli Naqli*, 1962), *'Tu Kahaan Yeh Bataa'* and *'Dil Ka Bhanwar Kare Pukar'* (*Tere Ghar Ke Saamne*, 1963), *'Jhoom Jhoom Dhalti Raat'* (*Kohraa*, 1964), *'Khwab Ho Tum Ya'* (*Teen Devian*, 1965), *'Jhumka Gira Re'* and *'Tu Jahaan Jahaan Chalega'* (*Mera Saaya*, 1966), *'Pal Bhar Ke Liye Koi'* (*Johny Mera Naam*, 1970), it goes on and on.

Not only had the stanzas been deleted, but, in many instances, they had been abridged. So, while the song *'Jungle*

Mein Mor Naacha' in the film *Madhumati* (1958) had the second stanza repeated (like the first one), in the audio, it did not happen. Before one could fully savour Shailendra's *'Kisi Ko Harey Harey Note Ka Nasha Hai, Kisi Ko Suit, Boot, Coat Ka Nasha Hai'*, the stanza reached its concluding line.

I once had an embarrassing moment with the accompanying music band while singing *'Tu Mere Saamne Hai'* from *Suhagan* (1964). I had practised on a longer version of the stanza (where the first part is repeated). The band had practised on the shorter version. They were professionals and immediately took corrective action on stage.

Even the prelude and interludes were not immune from the heartless editing that sometimes happened to shorten the song.

So, why did it happen? Alas, the reasons lie in the finite amount of recording that was possible on a record. No such restrictions applied in the movie. The producers, music directors and recording companies didn't relish the idea of the operation, but a record could contain only so much. The challenge was to delete or abridge the stanzas/music in a manner which was not jarring and maintained the integrity of the song. And in this respect, a stellar job had been done all these decades.

Then there are stanzas that were written, but not recorded. They are missing from the film as well as from the audio. *'Ek Haseen Shaam Ko'* from *Dulhan Ek Raat Ki* (1967), had one such stanza, which was included in the lyrics booklet that was part of the album.

> *"Sochta Hoon Ab Sunadoon, Kya Nazar Ka Faisla Hai,*
> *Mere Dil Ne Ek Saathi, Zindagi Ka Chun Liya Hai,*
> *Jiske Kadmon Mein Dil Ka Thikana Ho Gaya."*

The stanza fitted the meter of the both the tunes that Madan Mohan composed for the song's two stanzas.

Does the abridgement still happen?

With new technology, where there is no limitation on the length of the song in the audio format, it normally shouldn't happen. But it has happened in the recent past. The title track of '*Ae Dil Hai Mushkil*' (2016) had a stanza missing. Lyricist Amitabh Bhattacharya explained it away because of technical reasons. But he wished it had been retained. However, such songs are rare. Here's how it was written:

"Tere Liye Hoon Main/Bas Ek Haadsa
Mere Wajood Ki/Hai Tu Hi Dastaan
Jis Jagah Tu Mujhe/Thi Chhod Ke Gayi
Hoon Aaj Bhi Usi/Doraahe Pe Khada
Meri Zindagi Hai/Wahin Pe Thami
Meri Har Kami K/Hai Tu Laazmi
Main Jee Sakoon Tabhi/Tu Ho Sake Jo Haasil
Tere Bina Guzaara/Ae Dil Hai Mushkil"

Thanks to the new technology and social media, the fabulous treasures from inside Aladdin's magic cave are seeing the light day. Just as an encore lifts the spirit of the audience at the end of a particularly satisfying play, the missing stanzas and music do exactly that.

Now to memorize and practise them!

40

Gandhi and Film Music

Every person in the room was teary-eyed. Shanti Mathur, the playback singer, had just finished singing her song *'Nanha Munna Rahi Hoon'* (*Son of India*, 1962) at my uncle—the late music director Satish Bhatia's place. The sentiments it roused, the emotional fervour, the pride and hope, the love of country are still fresh in my mind even after all these years. That this song still retains its original sheen came as a pleasant surprise when my daughter told me it was one of her favourite songs.

What about songs on Gandhi? Do they inspire and motivate people? What was Gandhi's influence on the music industry? *'Bande Mein Tha Dum, Vande Mataram'* sung by Sonu Nigam, Shreya Ghoshal and Pranab Biswas, and its film—*Lage Raho Munna Bhai* (2006)—brought back Gandhi, firmly into mainstream cinema and national consciousness. The attention to Gandhi's theories revived an interest in Gandhism under the term *Gandhigiri*.

This song was, however, not the only one to be based on the life and teachings of Gandhi. One such instance was a private song released in 1948, a few months after Gandhi's assassination—*'Suno Suno Ae Duniya Waalon Bapu Ki Ye Amar Kahani'*.

Gandhi's death came as a jolt to the film industry as well. As a mark of tribute, this song was conceived. It required the composing genius of Husnlal-Bhagatram, the lyrical brilliance of Rajendra Krishan and the soulful appeal of a young Rafi to make people rededicate themselves to Gandhi's ideals. Days leading up to and following Independence had seen horrific violence that killed millions and Gandhi himself. The song underscored the futility of the madness which had convulsed the nation.

The lyrics recounted Gandhi's life from his education in London, his work in South Africa, to the independence and social movements in India. In the last verse, the music slowed dramatically and Rafi recounted Gandhi's last day, singing *"ahimsa ke seene par himsa ne goli barsayi"*.

On Independence Day, 1948, Rafi was invited to sing this song at Nehru's house. The song had such an effect on Nehru that tears rolled down his cheeks! The song reportedly sold a million copies in the first month of its release. Two years later, Nehru invited Rafi to sing *'Lehrao Tiranga Lehrao'* on India's first Republic Day.

The next song was *'De Di Humen Azadi Bina Khadg Bina Dhal, Sabarmati Ke Sant Tune Kar Diya Kamaal'* from *Jagriti* (1954). The song was written by Kavi Pradeep, composed by Hemant Kumar and sung by Asha Bhosle. Mourning the tragic loss, Pradeep reaffirmed the greatness of Gandhi. *Jagriti* was a children's movie replete with high ideals. All the songs were full of patriotic fervour and have remained classics till date.

Interestingly, *Jagriti* as well as all its songs were copied by the Pakistani film *Bedari* released three years later in 1957. This song became *'Aye Quaid-e-Azam Tera Ehsan Hai Ehsan'*. The other songs were *'Hum Laye Hain Toofan Se Kashti Nikal Ke'*, *'Aao Bachon Sair Karain Tum Ko Pakistan Ki'*, and *'Chalo Chalen Ma'*. Child actor Ratan Kumar (Nazir Rizvi) was the common link. After *Boot Polish* (1954) and *Jagriti*, he moved to Pakistan, where he played the same role in *Bedari*.

Then there was *'Mere Bapu Se Ye Kehna'* from *Matlabi Duniya* (1961) sung by Talat Mehmood. With disillusionment having set in, Mehmood sang to Gandhi that his country still wept over his loss—*"Mere Bapu se yeh kehna, ki tumhara desh rota hai, tumhari kalpnao ka, yahan par khun hota hai"*.

Finally, a song from the movie *Bharat Ke Shaheed* (1972)—*'Mohandas Karamchand Gandhi Param Pujari Ahinsa Ke'*—sung by Mahendra Kapoor and composed by Prem Dhawan. The song traced Gandhi's history and ended with: *"San bayaalis me gunja inka naara, chhodo Hindustan aakhir sach ki jeet huyee, aur chal diye gore inglistan."*

Interestingly, there were two songs composed on lyrics penned by Gandhi. One was *'Namrata Ke Samrat'*. Sardar Patel's daughter Maniben had written to Gandhi asking him questions about God. Gandhi had answered in the form of a prayer. This letter was found in 1968 by Madhukar Rao Chaudhari—a minister in the Maharashtra Government and President of Gandhi Centenary Committee. Chaudhari requested Vasant Desai to compose a tune on the said letter and make a record for the Centenary celebrations. It was sung by Manna Dey.

The other was *'Namrata Ke Sagar'*. The bhajan was said to have been written by Gandhi during his stay with the Birlas. No one knew such a bhajan existed until the Birlas stumbled upon it accidentally. This song was sung by Pt. Ajoy Chakraborty with music by Ilayaraja. The final words were by Pt. Bhimsen Joshi, where after Amitabh Bachchan recited some lines.

In the late 1930s, Gandhi was used for promoting films. Large size photographs of Gandhi adorned the film advertisements along with smaller photographs of the hero and heroine. Films were advertised as "helper to the cause of Mahatma Gandhi", or portraying "the ideals of Mahatma Gandhi", or claiming that "Mahatma Gandhi's immortal words inspire a picture".

Gandhi didn't think highly of the film medium. There are only two films he saw: *Mission to Moscow*, and the mythological movie, *Ram Rajya* at a special screening in 1944. He didn't sit through the film but did pat the maker Vijay Bhatt on his way out.

"The light that has illumined this country for these many years will illumine this country for many more years," cried Nehru when Gandhi died. The songs on Gandhi have made a humble contribution in keeping the light alive. Whenever the light dims, lyrics such as *"Bhoole hum raahein humein raah dikha de, aa ja re ab raah dikha de"* from *'Bande Mein Tha Dum, Vande Mataram'* (*Lage Raho Munna Bhai*, 2006) are a timely clarion call to the nation to re-dedicate itself "to carry out the mandate that our great teacher and our great leader had given us".

41

The Once in a Century Voice

KL Saigal

'*Ek Raje Ka Beta Lekar, Udane Wala Ghoda/Desh Desh Ki Sair Ki Khatir, Apne Ghar Se Nikla'* (*President*, 1937). This was my introduction to Kundan Lal Sehgal, at age five, courtesy my late father. He would sing this light-hearted children's song (Saigal didn't do too many light-hearted songs, and this was probably the only children's song he sang) to me and my siblings every night, with gestures and expressions, waving his hands about as if he was a flying horse. It was a fascinating song to sleep to—an enchanting mixture of song and speech. I would hear Saigal's record much later in life and see the video even later.

When we grew up, my father would tell us about his and his family's utter devotion to Saigal. About how he as a ten-year-old, with his father, travelled from Hoshiarpur to Lahore in 1937 to attend Saigal's concert at the Variety Theatre. He would vividly describe the packed hall, the scramble for spare tickets outside, the magic spell cast on the audience, the cries of "Saigal Zindabad" and the thunderous applause when Saigal came on stage. He remembered the opening song—*'Lag Gayi Chot Karejwa Main'* (*Yahudi Ki Ladki*, 1933). There was a standing ovation after every rendition. My father, my grandfather and everyone else were held in thrall, captivated by the most magical evening of their lives. God was on stage and the evening was soul-stirring and divine!

That's the effect Saigal had on his listeners.

Another incident that my father never tired of telling us was about his brother-in-law writing a letter to the editor of a popular film magazine in Punjab which got published in it. The letter stated—*"Jab bhi main Saigal ko sunta hun, toh jhoom uthta hun, jaise saanp 'been' sun kar"* (whenever I listen to Saigal's songs, I start swaying like a snake under the spell of a snake charmer). The editor replied: *"Aapko saanp ban na mubarak ho, par dekhiye dank na maariye ga"* (you are welcome to become a snake, but don't bite anyone). This became a family joke, and my uncle was always ribbed about it.

That's the effect Saigal had on his listeners.

With a voice dunked in a barrelful of rich baritone, soaked in innocence and earnestness, layered with pathos and yearning, and coated with honey, it could not have been a product of the assembly line in God's factory. It had to be crafted bespoke by God. And it's obvious that God fell in love with the voice he so lovingly created because he called it back too soon—at the age of 43.

Saigal adorned words with music in a manner which transported the listener to another world. He touched the innermost heartstrings. He totally submerged himself in his melodies that entranced his listeners and cast a spell on them. The tonal quality of Saigal's songs with his complete command over the three octaves and maintaining unvarying pitch gave his voice an unmatched quality. There was something other-worldly about his singing. Every song was a huge hit (film and non-film).

One incident that highlighted Saigal's talent both as a singer and actor was the recording of *'Babul Mora'* (*Street Singer*, 1938). The playback system was already in vogue, but Saigal wanted to retain the authenticity of the scene. He requested the director to let him sing the song, live, on the streets, which he did with outstanding result.

Saigal accomplished all this in a short span of 15 years (1932–47) singing just 185 songs (including 142 film songs in 39 films in six languages). But the modest oeuvre was enough for him to be acclaimed as the greatest performing artist of the 20th century.

He inspired a generation of singers like Surendra, Rafi, Mukesh, Kishore Kumar and CH Atma. During the 1930s and 1940s, it was believed that a singer had to sound like Saigal to be effective. Mukesh began his career with *'Dil Jalta Hai Toh Jalne De'* (*Pehli Nazar*, 1947), a song so Saigalesque that Saigal reportedly remarked that he did not remember singing it. CH Atma adopted the Saigal style for *'Preetam Aan Milo'* (sung for a private album in 1945); so did Surendra in the duet with Noor Jehan *'Awaaz De Kahan Hai'* (*Anmol Ghadi*, 1946).

Saigal did not belong to any *gharana*, nor was he a *shagird* of any *ustad*. He received no formal training in music. He was self-taught, by listening to other singers. His mastery over film songs, ghazals, thumris and bhajans could only be explained as a gift of God, honed to perfection by *riyaaz* as instructed by the Sufi Pir Salman Yusuf of Jammu.

He held the whole nation in thrall. Classical maestros like Ustad Faiyaz Khan were stunned by the force of his music. Kanan Devi remarked that Saigal had perfect pitch sense. He didn't need the help of a veena or tanpura to set the right pitch. At recording sessions, he would sing out a note and musicians would set their instruments accordingly.

Lata Mangeshkar as a child was so besotted with Saigal, she said she wanted to marry him. Talat Mehmood marvelled at Saigal's pronunciation, throw of voice, depth of feeling, and voice control. Suraiya was so overawed at the idea of singing a duet with him in *Parwana* (1947) that the duet had to be dropped.

Saigal was the first non-Bengali to be permitted and blessed by Rabindra Tagore to sing *Rabindra Sangeet*. Saigal put a new life into Bengali songs as no Bengali singer ever could or did. He became a darling of the Bengalis more than any other Bengali artist—the greatest compliment for anyone's art.

A little-known fact is that Saigal was a poet and recited his verses at private gatherings. No recordings are available except one devotional song written and composed by him—*'Main Baithi Thi Phulwari Main'* (1945).

Saigal was spiritually inclined and involved in mysticism; he was attached to devotional music. His very first recording *'Jhulana Jhulao Ri'* and a *hori* on the reverse side *'Hori Ho Brajraj Dulare'* (1932–33) created a sensation. The record sold half a million records, in an era when few people owned record-players. The people who had no gramophones would stand outside music shops listening to this record. In *Puran Bhagat* (1933), Saigal sang four devotional songs like *'Bhaju Main to Bhaav Se Shiri Giridhari'* and *'Radhe Rani De Daro Na Bansi Mori'*. In *Dhoop Chhaon* (1935), he sang *'Andhe Ki Lathi'*. In 1937, he recorded the ever popular *'Suno Suno Hey Krishan Kala'*. In *Dharti Mata* (1938), he sang *'Kisne Yeh Sab Khel Rachaya'*. He played the leading role in *Bhakta Surdas* (1942) whose bhajans like *'Kadam Chale Aage'* and *'Nainheen Ko Raah Dikha Prabhu'* became massive hits. Listeners could gather from Saigal's musical articulation his supreme devotion to God.

Few months before his death, he used to sit in his balcony with his harmonium early in the morning and sing his favourite bhajans. There as a devotional song which Saigal composed in the last days of his life which he got privately recorded—*'Hari Bina Koi Kaam Na Aayo'*.

Though film music brought him colossal fame, it was in his ghazal singing (both film and non-film) that Saigal reached the pinnacle of achievement as a singer. He would vary the pitch and volume of his voice according to the mood of the ghazal, inspiring the listeners to enjoy the beauty of the poet's creation. Saigal was particularly fond of Ghalib and identified himself with his spirit—his addiction to the bottle and a certain air of detachment from his own life and environment could be attributed to Ghalib's influence over him. Saigal deserved full credit for popularizing a difficult and philosophic poet like Ghalib by highlighting the depth and beauty of his verses. Saigal employed his musical genius to emphasize not only the literal meaning but its deeper interpretation as well. The musical genius and the poetic wizard were a formidable combination!

The first Ghalib ghazal was *'Nukta Cheen Hai Gham-e-Dil'* (*Yahudi ki Ladki,* 1933). Other ghazals popularized were *'Main Unhe Chhedun Aur Kuchh Na Kahen'*; *'Har Ek Baat Pe Kehte Ho Tum Ki Tu Kya Hai'*; *'Ishq Mujhko Nahin Wahshat Hi Sahi'*; *'Woh Aake Khwab Main'*. The most outstanding masterpiece which he sang most poignantly was *'Aah Ko Chahiye Ek Umr Asar Hone Tak'*.

Saigal sang ghazals of other poets too—*'Matwalepane Se Jo Ghataa Jhoom Padi Hai'* by Arzoo; *'Kabhi Ai Haqeeqat-e-Muntzir Nazar Aa Libaas-e-Majaz Main'* by Iqbal.

Saigal sang only about 30 ghazals. That he managed to render them with such charm and intensity in 3½ minutes on the 78-RPM record amply demonstrates the reason why the public placed him on a pedestal.

As a human being Naushad had remarked that Saigal was the *badshah* of singers who had the voice of an angel and a heart of gold.

Saigal was born on 11th April 1904, in Jammu, to the tehsildar of a small town. He showed a keen interest in singing and would pick up music from folk singers and wandering minstrels and even from dancing girls of Jammu. His father regarded him a wastrel. The young boy was distraught when his voice cracked at twelve, and he was unable to sing. His mother took him to a mystic Sufi Pir Salman Yusuf who asked young Kundan to stop singing for two years and start rehearsing and cultivating his voice by *zikr* and *riyaaz*.

When his father retired, the family moved to Jalandhar. Passionate about music and stifled by life in that city, Saigal left home. He took up sundry jobs and listened to music and sang whenever possible. He wandered about in several cities working various jobs such as a timekeeper in the Railways, selling Remington typewriters and saris, managing a hotel in Shimla, and others.

In Calcutta, Saigal got introduced to BN Sircar, who had just started New Theatres. Saigal's first three movies with New Theatres flopped. However, fortunes turned with *Chandidas* (1934)—its song *'Prem Nagar Main'* was a hit. The 1935 *Devdas* was a national sensation—*'Balam Aye Baso Morey Man Mein'* was a romantic gem; *'Dukh Ke Ab Din Bitat Nahin'* was the desperate cry of a person and the nation wept along with Saigal.

Success followed success with films like *President* (1937), *Street Singer* (1938), *Dushman* (1939), and others.

He got married in 1934 to Asha Rani, a girl chosen by his mother. They had three children.

In 1941, an exodus occurred of film personalities from Calcutta to Bombay, and Saigal too made the switch. Chandulal Shah of Ranjit Movietone signed a three-movie contract with him. Saigal sang memorable songs in *Bhakta Surdas* (1942) and *Tansen* (1943). In 1944, he went back to Calcutta for *My Sister* with New Theatres. His last famous film was *Shah Jahan* (1946), in which he sang *'Jab Dil Hi Toot Gaya'*.

All songs of Sehgal were classics. Some of them were—*'Ek Bangla Bane Nyara'* (*President*, 1937); *'Babul Mora'* (*Street Singer*, 1937); *'Karoon Kya Aas Niras Bhaee'* (*Dushman*, 1939); *'Main Kya Janoon Kya Jadoo Hai'* and *'So Ja Rajkumari So Ja'* (*Zindagi*, 1940); *'Aye Katib-e-Taqdeer Mujhe Itna Bata De'* and *'Do Naina Matware Tihare'* (*My Sister*, 1943).

For lack of any accounts written contemporaneously, Hindi film cinema is replete with folklore. One such is that Saigal wanted *'Jab Dil Hi Toot Gaya'* (*Shah Jahan*, 1946), played at his funeral. This has no basis. No music is played in Punjab at the funeral of a young person. This was confirmed by Saigal's sister-in-law (his wife Asharani's sister) who attended the funeral at Jalandhar.

The other myth is about Saigal singing better with or without liquor. It is claimed that out of two recordings of a song sung by him, the one sung in sobriety was much better. GN Joshi, a distinguished musician and HMV senior executive, who personally handled Saigal's recordings, has debunked this narrative. There would be about half a dozen rehearsals. Saigal would have half a peg between each rehearsal. His voice would become mellower after every rehearsal and then would come the time when the voice would become the last word in beauty. At this stage, the recording would be done, each word and note bearing the stamp of rare and rich artistry.

In an interview Saigal had said, "I have no clear understanding of the grammar of music. I manage to sing because of a strong feeling about how certain sounds should feel in a given raga. I do not use ten notes if I can manage to do the same with one. That's because I know very little."

The singer who knew 'very little' gave a lot and then some to his legion of adoring devotees. We raise a toast to the voice of the century. God doesn't make Saigal every day.

42

The Songs that Helped the Freedom Movement

'*Kahin Pey Nigahen, Kahin Pey Nishana*', the popular song from *Aar Paar* (1954), though sung in another context, could have described another song that came out 11 years earlier—a song that is considered a gold standard amongst songs that inspired the freedom movement.

'Door Hato Ai Duniyawalo, Hindustan Hamara Hai' from Bombay Talkies' *Kismet* (1943), released during World War II, was ostensibly addressed to the Germans and the Japanese with whom Britain was at war—"*Shuru hua hai jang tumhara, jaag utho Hindustani, tum na kisi ke aage jhukna, Jarman ho ya Jaapaani, aaj sabhi ke liye hamara yahi qaumi naara hai*".

By resorting to such a stratagem, the song passed the censors. But the public knew better. Coming as it did less than six months after Mahatma Gandhi called for the Quit India Movement, the actual target of the song—composed as a martial tune by Anil Biswas—was obvious. The patriotic overtones against British rule became at once evident to the people. At screenings of *Kismet*, the reels would be rewound, and the song played multiple times on public demand. The audience sitting in the cinema halls were no different from the charged-up audience shown in the song—such was the song's impact.

The unprecedented popularity of the song forced lyricist Kavi Pradeep and music composer Anil Biswas to go underground to avoid being arrested by the British authorities for sedition.

They could re-surface only when it was pointed out to the government that the song was directed against the Axis members—Germany and Japan—and was in fact, pro-British (which of course it was not). Interestingly, the map of India shown in the song included Burma, which had been separated from the Indian Empire six years earlier in 1937.

Kismet was not a patriotic film. It was an out-and-out thriller. It included the song to pack a patriotic punch while dishing out entertainment.

There were many such films which used metaphor, innuendo, symbolism, oblique reference to slip under the radar of the ever-vigilant censors to convey the true message to a public that was discerning enough to be aware of the film's or the song's real message.

As early as 1938, *Watan*, a costume drama film directed by Mehboob Khan, was released. The story, set in Central Asia, was based on the Decossackization policy, involving the Bolsheviks and the Cossacks.

The Cossack's fight for independence was a symbolic reference to the fight for independence from British rule in India at that time. It had a song—*'Jahan Tu Hai Wahin Mera Watan Hai'*, composed by Anil Biswas.

In 1941, Sohrab Modi's Sikandar hit the screens. It had a song *'Jeete Desh Humara, Bharat Hai Ghar Baar Humara, Bharat Hai Sansar Humara'*. Even though in the movie this was a prayer for victory against the forces of the Greek ruler Alexander, the song fuelled the nationalist sentiment in the Indians.

Under colonial rule, when the National Movement was at its peak, the masses understood who the 'victory' was to be wrested from.

Sometimes, it didn't work. In 1931, 'Swaraj' in the title of Shantaram's film *Swarajyache Toran (Thunder of the Hills)*, and the poster of the film depicting Chhatrapati Shivaji hoisting a flag, led to the threat of a ban, because using 'Swaraj' was considered seditious. The film was a historical film based on the military expeditions of Maratha Emperor Shivaji. The film was renamed *Udaykal*. The censors had the producers make several other changes, one of them being the climactic hoisting of the saffron flag at Sinhagad Fort.

Earlier, in the silent era in 1921, *Bhakta Vidur* became the first film to be banned in India. The film came just after Rowlatt Act was passed in India. The character of Vidur, the Hindu mythological character, was portrayed on the personality of Mahatma Gandhi. There were scenes in the film where Vidur appeared like Gandhi, wearing a Gandhi cap and *khaddar*. Many contemporary political events of India were shown in the film. As a result, the film was banned as the censors held that the character was not Vidur, but Mahatma Gandhi. The censors also held that the film was likely to excite dissatisfaction against the government and incite people to non-cooperation.

The songs and films of the pre-Independence era inspired the freedom movement, added fuel to the nationalist fire, invoked feelings of love for the country, roused patriotic fervour. But they are neither well-known, nor their contribution adequately acknowledged.

We all know the patriotic songs post-Independence, but their counterparts before 1947, not so much. But their role needs to be known and appreciated.

Their reach extended to every household, much more than any other platform, even political mobilization. The pen, the song, the composer, the singer was no less powerful in inspiring the people's fight for freedom as the non-violent political movement, or the sword (whenever rarely used).

Many films and even more songs were released during the period which, either obviously or obliquely, depicted the British as the villain. The censors made every possible attempt to throttle such messages, but most films and songs slipped through. From the mid-1940s, with freedom in the air, the British censors' grip slackened, and films and songs became more direct, and bolder.

So, which were these films? Which were these *'Azaadi ke Taraane'*?

One song that probably many would know is *'Chal Chal Re Naujawan, Kehna Mera Maan'* from *Bandhan* (1940). Kavi Pradeep was the lyricist (who else?), and the music director was Ramchandra Pal. Ashok Kumar and Leela Chitnis starred in the film. The song was parodied in *Ek Phool Do Mali* (1969) and that's probably when most people heard it for the first time.

This song became very popular. So much so that when the film opened in Delhi, the audience wanted the song to be shown again. So, it was played again after the film was over. It is an inspirational and marching song for children. For this reason, it was included in the Hindi school books of those times. The song had many versions—the most famous sung by the child star Suresh.

Ashok Kumar also sang a version.

The impact of the song was so significant that when S Mukherjee, Ashok Kumar, Kavi Pradeep, and others, left Bombay Talkies and established Filmistan Studios, their first film in 1944 was titled *'Chal Chal Re Naujawan'*! This film too had an inspirational song *'Jai Bharat Desh, Teri Jai, Bharat Ke Naujawanon Chalo Ek Raah Par, Ai Hindu Musalmanon Chalo Ek Raah Par'* sung by Ashok Kumar to the music of Ghulam Haider (who migrated to Pakistan after independence) and lyrics of Kavi Pradeep.

This song, like many others, advocated Hindu-Muslim unity.

Ghulam Haider composed another song in the film *Bhai* (1944)—*'Hindu Muslim Sikh Issai, Aapas Mein Hain Bhai Bhai'* sung by Shyam Sunder. A year earlier, in *Poonji* (1943), he composed *'Hey Mata Ab Jaag Uthe Hain Hum'* sung by Shamshad Begum.

Pehle Aap (1944) had a song *'Hindustan Ke Hum Hain, Hindustan Hamara, Hindu Muslim Dono Ki, Aankhon Ka Tara'* sung by Mohammed Rafi to the music of Naushad.

Even Noor Jehan sang a patriotic song in *Hamjoli* (1946)— *'Yeh Desh Hamara Pyara, Hindustan Jahaan Se Pyaara'* composed by Hafiz Khan. A year later, she would move to Pakistan and would star in her first Pakistani film, *Chan Wey* (1951), opposite Santosh Kumar, a famous actor of the 1950s and 1960s (he had a brother Darpan, another renowned actor of that era).

In fact, Noor Jehan acted in *Badi Maa* (1945) too, set against the backdrop of World War II, which had two patriotic songs sung by Lata Mangeshkar. Lata acted in the film too—*'Mata, Tere Charnon Mein Guzar Jaaye Umariya'* (with Ishwarlal) and *'Janani Janambhoomi… Tum Ho Maa, Badi Maa'* (with Meenakshi Shirodkar) to the music of K Dutta. The film also had Asha Bhosle in a minor role. This is the only film which had the three singing goddesses acting together.

Lata sang other such songs too. In *Sona Chandi* (1946)—the other name *Bhai Bhai*—she sang *'Pyare Bapu ke Charnon Ki Le Lo Kasam, Pyaare Pyaare Tirange Ki Le Lo Kasam'* under the baton of DC Dutta.

A brief pause here. The above film had two titles. Those days it was not uncommon to have films with two titles with *'urf'* in between such as *Satya Ki Raksha 'urf' Harishchandra Taramati; Ehd-e-Inteqam 'urf' Diler Ladki.*

Dev Anand's very first film *Hum Ek Hain* (1946) had a song *'Hum Jaag Uthe Hain So Kar'* composed by Husnlal-Bhagatram.

Even 'Fearless Nadia', famous for her stunt films, pitched in. Her *Lutaroo Lalna* (1938) directed by Homi Wadia, had *'Jug Jug Chamke Hind Ka Tara, Jhanda Ooncha Rahe Hamara'* sung by Master Mohammed (music director) and Sarita Devi which became very popular. The refrain, *'Jhanda Ooncha Rahe Hamara'*, would be sung by freedom fighters. It had one more song—*'Jug Jug Chamke Hind Ka Tara'* sung by Sarita Devi. Master Mohammed had earlier composed patriotic songs for *Veer Bharat* (1934) and *Jai Bharat* (1936).

Bombay Talkies' *Janmabhoomi* (1936) starring Ashok Kumar and Devika Rani had *'Mata Ne Hai Janam Diya, Jeene Ke Liye'* sung by Devika Rani. It had another song *'Jai Jai Janani Janmabhoomi'* sung by Ashok Kumar. The music was composed by Saraswati Devi.

Bombay Talkies made one more film—*Anjaan* (1941) starring Ashok Kumar and Devika Rani which had the song *'Kheecho Kamaan Kheecho, O Bharat Ma Ke Naujawan'* sung by Ashok Kumar. The music director was Pannalal Ghosh (the flute maestro), and lyricist was Kavi Pradeep.

New Theatres' *Hamrahi* (1945), directed by Bimal Roy, included Rabindranath Tagore's *'Jana Gana Mana'*, even before it became the national anthem of India. The song has more verses than the national anthem. There was another song in the film—*'Badhe Chalo, Chalo, Badhe Chalo Jawaano'* composed by Rai Chand Boral.

Ek Kadam (1947) went so far ahead as to show Netaji Subhash Chandra Bose on its poster.

And the list continues:

- *Amar Prem* (1936) – *'Hamara Pyara Hindustan, Pyara Hindustan'*
- *Jay Bharat* (1936) – *'Hum Watan Ke Watan Hamara, Bharat Mata Jay Jay Jay'*
- *Bharat Ki Beti* (1936), another name: *Sneh Lata – 'Hey Dhanya Tu Bharat Nari, Mahima Hai Teri Nyaari'*
- *Samaj Patan* (1937), another name: *Zaalim Zamana – 'Jaago Bharatwasi, Ek Din Tum The Jagat Guru'*
- *His Highness* (1937) – *'Bharat Hai Sukh Chain Hamara, Apna Watan Hai Subko Pyara'*
- *Toofan Express* (1938) – *'Dharti Mata Baalak Tere Charnon Mein Sheesh Nawaein'*
- *Brahmachari* (1938) – *'Chalo Sipahi, Karo Safai, Haath Dharo Jhaadoo'*
- *Karma Veer* (1938), another name: *Mard Bano – 'Saare Deshon Se Nyaari, Pyaari Bharat Mata Hamari'*
- *Wasiyat* (1940) – *'Hind Mata Ki Tum Santaan Ho, Naujawanon Tum Watan Ki Shaan Ho'*
- *Aaj Ka Hindustan* (1940) – *'Charkha Chalaao Behnon, Kaato Yeh Kachhe Dhaage'*
- *Amrit* (1941) – *'Jaago Jawano, Jaago Jawano, Navjug Aaya Re'*
- *Koshish* (1943) – *'Ai Hind Ke Sapooton, Jaago, Hua Savera, Hindu Hon Ya Musalman, Hum Sab Hain Bhai Bhai'* and *'Hindustan Walon, Hindustan Walon'* – both songs sung by GM Durrani
- Mehboob Khan's *Taqdeer* (1943) – *'Mata Mata, Meri Mata, Bharat Mata'* sung by Shamshad Begum. The music director was Rafiq Ghazanvi who later migrated to Pakistan
- *Muskarahat* (1943) – *'Bharat Desh Hamara, Hara Bhara Hariyara'* composed by C Ramchandra
- *Chand* (1944) – *'Watan Se Chala Hai Watan Ka Sipahi'* composed by Husnlal-Bhagatram, their first film

- *Parinde* (1945) – *'Doobte Bharat Ko Bachao, Mere Kartaar'* sung by Zohrabai Ambalewali
- *Naseeb* (1945) – *'Hum Panchhi Hai Aazaad, Humme Koi Pinjare Main Kyun Daale'*
- *Ghulami* (1945) – *'Ai Watan Mere Watan, Tum Pey Meri Jaan Nisar'*
- *Swayam Se Sunder Desh Hamara* (1945) – English Name: *Call of the Motherland – 'Desh Hamara, Desh Hamara, Desh Hamara, Desh Hamara Swarg Se Sunder, Desh Hamara'*
- *Pannabai* (1945) – *'Chale Musafir, Khaak Watan Ki Lekar, Desh Parai'*
- *Mansarovar* (1946) – *'Jai Hind Jai Hind, Hind Ki Kahaniyan, Yeh Hind Ki Kahaniyan'* composed by SN Tripathi
- *Zanjeer* (1947) – *'Naach Rahi Thi Bharat Mata, Azadi ke Aangan Mein'*
- *Ahinsa* (1947) – *'Sadiyon Se Hai Ghulam, Janmabhumi Hamari'*; *'Azaad Hai Hum Aaj Se, Jailon Ke Taaley Tod Do, Angrezon Bharat Chhod Do'* (sung by Chitalkar). The music director was C Ramchandra

The films not only inspired the countrymen to fight for freedom with zeal and fervour but also spoke against the social ills plaguing Indian society. Freedom meant not only throwing off the yoke of British subjugation but also the yoke of regressive facets of Indian society that Mahatma Gandhi and other leaders were fighting against. The films and songs also promoted *charkha, khadi, swadeshi* goods. One such song was *'Charkha Chalao Behno'* in *Aaj Ka Hindustan* (1940).

Duniya Na Mane (1937)—a social classic of V Shantaram, raised its voice against the treatment of women in society, specifically child marriage and dowry menace. It had a song *'Aha, Bharat Pyaara Hai, Hai Woh Jag Se Nyaara'*. Actress

Shanta Apte sang the full-fledged English song/poem—*'A Psalm of Life'*—by HW Longfellow.

Brandy Ki Botal (1939) criticized liquor consumption and exhorted Gandhian morality and self-discipline. *Ghar Ki Rani* (1940) showed the adverse consequences of aping western traditions. *Achhut* (1940) sought to promote Gandhi's movement against untouchability.

V Shantaram's *Dharmatma* (1935), on the caste system, based on the legendary Marathi religious poet and scholar Sant Eknath, was originally titled *Mahatma*. There are conflicting accounts as to why it had to be renamed. One account has it that Kanhaiyalal Maneklal Munshi, the then Home Minister of Bombay State, charged Shantaram with exploiting the name of Mahatma Gandhi for selfish purposes. The other account is that it was done due to the censors' objection.

But the British were not sitting silent. As a counter to patriotic Hindi films, the British released English language films showing Indians in poor light.

The Drum (1938) showed all Indians as untrustworthy and scheming against their British masters. Bombay city rose in revolt against the screening of the film with the 'Frontier Gandhi' Khan Abdul Gaffar Khan demanding its ban. *The Lives of A Bengal Lancer* (1935) met with stiff objections in Lahore by the Muslim community for its disrespectful portrayal of the Muslims.

'Chal Chal Re Naujawan', post 1947, led to *'Nanha Munha Rahi Hoon' (Son of India,* 1962*)*. One inspired the freedom movement, and after its attainment, the other instilled love for the nation.

Both are two sides of the same coin, and both need their rightful place in history. But 'freedom' from ignorance, from poverty, from disease, from an unequal society is still work in progress. The line from *'Chal Chal Re Naujawan'*—*"Tu aage badhe ja, aafat se lade ja, aandhi ho ya toofan, phat'ta ho aasmaan, rukna tera kaam nahin, chalna teri shaan, chal chal re naujawan"*—is still relevant.

43

When Singers Sing for Other Singers

Indian films have had their share of actor-singers: KL Saigal, Ashok Kumar, Noor Jehan, Suraiya, Kishore Kumar, Sulakshana Pandit. Talat Mehmood acted in over a dozen films in the 1940s and '50s. Even Mukesh acted in some films in the 1940s and '50s.

I haven't included other actors like Amitabh Bachchan, Dilip Kumar, Nutan, Ayushmann Khurrana, Farhan Akhtar, Diljit Dosanjh, and some others. By profession, they are actors, not singers. Their singing adds a novelty value, showcases their talent beyond acting. But they do not have to sing for their supper. They are basically actors.

It is therefore strange when other singers have sung for these actor-singers. Why did that happen?

Let's begin with Ashok Kumar. In the 1930s and '40s, simultaneous song recordings required the practice of using singing actors. However, not all singing actors were selected for their vocal prowess.

Ashok Kumar was a leading actor in that era (and, of course, way beyond) and sang many songs in his acting career, even though he was not a trained singer. About 50 odd songs were sung by him, including *'Khet Ki Mooli Baag Ko Aam'* and *'Main Ban Ki Chidiya Banke'*, both with Devika Rani (*Achhut Kanya*, 1936); *'Aaj Mausam Salona Salona Re'* with Rehmat Bano and *'Ek Chatur Naar Kar Kar Singaar'* (*Jhoola*, 1941); *'Dhire Dhire Aa Re Badal'* (*Kismet*, 1943).

Despite his enormous box-office appeal, he was not known for his singing talent. In 1940, in a letter to the editor of a film magazine, a reader requested Ashok Kumar to stop singing in movies.

The shift happened gradually. The song *'Dhire Dhire Aa Re Badal'* (*Kismet*, 1943) mentioned above, was sung by Ashok Kumar in the film but music director Anil Biswas used the voice of another actor called Arun Kumar for the record. Those days, very often, it would happen that the record version was not the same as the film version.

Once playback came in, it was not necessary for actors to sing. However, this did not apply to actors such as KL Saigal, Noor Jehan and Suraiya, who were known more for their singing than acting.

One of the songs sung by Ashok Kumar, *'Koi Humdum Na Raha'* (*Jeevan Naiyya*, 1936) and composed by Saraswati Devi, was sung many years later by his brother Kishore Kumar in his debut film as music director (*Jhumroo*, 1961). And, of course, his *'Ek Chatur Naar'* (*Jhoola*, 1941) became a cult-classic 27 years later in *Padosan* (1968), sung yet again by Kishore Kumar, and Manna Dey.

Some of the memorable songs sung onscreen in the latter part of Ashok Kumar's career when other singers did the playback for him included *'Sab Kuchh Luta Ke Hosh'* (*Ek Saal*, 1957) by Talat Mehmood; *'Poochho Na Kaise Maine Rain Bitai'* (*Meri Surat Teri Aankhen*, 1963) by Manna Dey; *'Naache Man Mora'* and *'Tere Bin Soone Nain Hamare'*, both sung by Rafi (*Meri Surat Teri Aankhen*, 1963); *'Beqaraar Dil Tu Gaye Ja'* (*Door Ka Rahi*, 1971) sung by Kishore Kumar.

Not that Ashok Kumar did not sing at all in this period. He sang *'Babu Samjho Ishare'*, along with Kishore Kumar and Manna Dey (*Chalti Ka Naam Gadi*, 1958); *'Jhingapore Taqur Taqur'* and *'Naav Chali'* (*Aashirwad*, 1968); and *'Chalo Haseen Geet Ek Banayein'* along with Chirasree Bhattacharya (*Shaukeen*, 1982).

Let's take the case of Surendra. He acted and sang in several films as main lead in the 1930s and '40s. He then switched to character roles. Who can forget his duet with Noor Jehan *'Awaaz De Kahan Hai'* (*Anmol Ghadi*, 1946)?

When she visited Mumbai in 1982, Noor Jehan sang this song, and when she came to Surendra's part (he was still alive, died five years later in 1987), she sought his permission to sing it. However, when he played Tansen in *Baiju Bawra* (1952), his playback was done by Ustad Amir Khan for all his songs—*'Raag Darbari Sargam', 'Aaj Gawat Maan Mero Jhumke'* (Pandit DV Paluskar for Bharat Bhushan), *'Langar Kankariya Ji Na Maro'* (Pandit DV Paluskar for Bharat Bhushan), *'Ghanan Ghanan Ghan Garjo Re'* (deleted from the movie) and *'Tori Jai Jai Kartaar'*.

Surendra again played the role of Tansen in *Mughal-e-Azam* (1960). This time Ustad Bade Ghulam Ali Khan did the playback (reportedly for Rs 25,000—an astronomical sum those days) for two songs—*'Prem Jogan Ban Ke'*, and *'Shubh Din Aayo Raj Dulara'* (played in the background). Obviously, Tansen required a modern-day equivalent, and Surendra had to yield to the two *ustads* who did an outstanding job. Tansen would have approved.

Some singers have played a cameo role on screen. Rafi appeared on the screen for the songs, *'Tera Jalwa Jis Ne Dekha'* (*Laila Majnu*, 1945), and *'Woh Apni Yaad Dilane Ko'* (*Jugnu*, 1947). He sang his own songs. However, in an ironic twist of fate, GM Durrani, the famous playback singer of the 1940s, who was Rafi's idol, and whose singing style inspired Rafi, had Rafi doing the playback for him in the song *'Unke Khayal Aaye Toh'* (*Lal Patthar*, 1971).

Sulakshana Pandit's career spanned the 1970s and '80s. Though she usually sang her own songs, yet there are some instances of other singers doing her playback. For instance, Lata in Sulakshana's first film *Uljhan* (1975)—*'Subah Aur Shaam Kaam Hi Kaam'* and the background title song *'Apne Jeevan Ki Uljhan Ko'*, and *'Is Duniya Mein Jeena Hai'* (*Apnapan*, 1977).

We now come to Kishore Kumar. Singers like him are born but rarely. But he too had other singers do the playback for him in the movies he was acting in, in some cases. How did this even happen?

In the film *Ragini* (1958), whose music director was OP Nayyar, the semi-classical song *'Man Mora Bawra'* picturized on Kishore, was sung by Rafi, who was a trained singer unlike Kishore. I had quizzed OP Nayyar about it.

Kishore had sung some delightful songs for OP Nayyar, including many from the same film. So why Rafi?

OP Nayyar stated that this semi-classical song could only have been done by Rafi. For the pure classical songs, OP Nayyar went beyond Rafi and used Ustad Amir Khan for *'Jogiya Mere Ghar Aaye'* during the introductory film credits, and Ustad Amanat Ali Khan and Fateh Ali Khan for *'Chhed Diye Mere Dil Ke Taar'*, picturized on Kishore.

Similarly, *'Preetam Daras Dikhao'* (*Chacha Zindabad*, 1959) was a classical song which Manna Dey and Lata rendered under the baton of Madan Mohan.

In the film *Naukri* (1954), Salil Choudhury preferred Hemant Kumar to do the playback for Kishore for *'Chhota Sa Ghar Hoga'*. It took a lot of effort on the part of the filmmakers to convince Salil to take Kishore for the song. However, for the sad version, Salil didn't budge and took Hemant who sang in the background with Kishore on the screen.

Kishore Kumar acknowledged Hemant's talent for certain kind of songs and used him as a singer in his own film *Door Ka Rahi* (1971) in *'Chalti Chale Jaaye Zindagi'*. Such objectivity by a singer/actor/director/music director that Kishore was in this film, to enrol another singer to do playback for him (albeit as a background song), is truly remarkable. He had done this earlier too—in *Door Gagan Ki Chhaon Mein* (1964), where Hemant sang all the three parts of *'Rahi Tu Mat Ruk Jana'*, once during the film credits, and twice in the background with Kishore on the screen.

In *Shararat* (1959), the song *'Ajab Hai Dastaan Teri Aei Zindagi'* was sung by Rafi. It is reported that Kishore was not the original choice for the lead actor and some songs had already been recorded when he came on board. In any case, this song too required a singer having the range and classical background that Rafi could provide. Rafi provided the perfect high pitch during the crescendo. He was the man for the job, and that is why Shankar-Jaikishan used him.

This film had another song sung by Rafi on Kishore—*'Tu Mera Copyright, Main Teri Copyright'*. Even though Shankar-Jaikishan hardly used Kishore, the few numbers that he sang for them were delightful—case in point—*'Chhoti Si Yeh Duniya'* (*Rangoli*, 1962) and *'Nakhrewali'* (*New Delhi*, 1956).

Bhagam Bhag (1956), with OP Nayyar as music director, had Rafi in *'Humein Koi Gham Hai'*, as well as *'Chale Ho Kahaan'*. Why it happened remains in the realm of mystery.

However, it perhaps made sense in the song *'Le Lo Sone Ka Laddoo'* (*Paisa Hi Paisa*, 1956) where Kishore had a double role, in which one character had Rafi do the playback, the other, Kishore; though Kishore could have done it for both—if both looked the same, they could sound the same too. But music director Anil Biswas wanted authenticity.

Krorepati (1961) had songs sung by Manna Dey—*'Aap Hue Mere'* and *'Pehle Murgi Hui Thi Ki Anda'*. It is reported that payment issues were the reason why Kishore didn't sing himself. *'O Meri Maina'* from the same film bizarrely had both Kishore and Rafi do the playback on Kishore in the same song.

Rafi sang *'Apni Aadat Hai'* (*Pyar Diwana*, 1972). It was strange to see Kishore not do his own playback in 1972 when he was *numero uno* in the film industry and ruling the charts at that stage. The reason is that this black and white film had begun production many years earlier and took several years to make.

Some more songs include *'Main Is Masoom Chehre Ko'* (*Baghi Shahzada,* 1964) by Rafi; *'Apne Haath Ko Pehchan'* (*Apna Haath Jagannath,* 1960) by Rafi; even Mahendra Kapoor has done playback for Kishore—*'Humne to Dil'* (*Albela Mastana,* 1967). The list is not exhaustive.

The days of the actor-singer are over now. Both the disciplines are rigorous and require a specialized skill set which needs to be honed to perfection to achieve success. Even earlier, the actor-singers were not equally adept at both.

KL Saigal, for instance, was a far better singer than actor. Ashok Kumar was the opposite. Kishore was an exception. Many people may not have liked his style of acting, but he couldn't have acted in 88 films just like that.

The place of the actor-singer is now part of the glorious Hindi film history, and all forays by actors these days into the recording studio, and vice versa, is just a casual occurrence adding flavour to the role—inviting sometimes awe like in the case of, say, Ayushmann, Amitabh or Diljit, or an indulgent smile, in case of others.

44

The Song that Introduces

Songs you hear while growing up stay loyal to you forever. One such song, which I heard when I was nine years old, was '*Love in Tokyo*' from the film of the same name (1966). The song was a feel-good, bubbly, and energetic song. But the icing on the cake was Mohammad Rafi belting out '*Jaaapaaaan, Love in Tokyo*'. The accent was Indian, Japan pronounced as it is in Hindi, but it did not matter. The song went on to describe Tokyo and its denizens—"*Dekho woh gori gori raahen, humko ishaaron se bulaayen, kitni rangeen hai fizayen, Jaapani pariyan muskaraayen...*"

As a title song, it was doing its job: that of giving a preview of what could be expected in the next three hours. The song encapsulated the essence of the film and introduced its theme—a sort of a preamble to the storyline. The viewer would have no doubt, after listening to the song, that the film dealt with love, with Tokyo as a setting, with all its attendant formulaic accoutrements.

The title song is amongst the many genres that exist in the delightful world of Hindi film music—especially till the mid-70s. Not that they are extinct now, but it is a breed that is on its way out like the other genres such as the Club Song, Break-up Song, Tandem (or Twin) Song.

Till the mid-70s, its fecundity was remarkable—many Hindi films had it. It was *de rigueur*. How was a film possible without it? How else would the name of the film, embedded in the title song, live endlessly? The film could remain forever in national consciousness if its title song remained so. And most did and do!

Remember *An Evening in Paris* (1967) with its title song '*An Evening in Paris*'? Shammi Kapoor introduced the audience to Paris in his inimitable style—"*Aji aisa mauka phir kahan milega, hamare jaisa dil kahan milega. Aao tumko dikhlata hoon Paris ki ek rangeen sham, dekho dekho dekho dekho dekho, an evening in Paris*".

While talking about this song and others, Sharmila Tagore told me that Shammi Kapoor had an innate sense of rhythm and music, and would dance with abandon and energy, which the viewers loved.

Shankar-Jaikishan specialized in the genre. Raj Kapoor gave them the green signal to go for it from the very first film the duo did for him—*Barsaat* (1949)—'*Barsaat Mein Humse Mile Tum Sajan, Tumse Mile Hum, Barsaat Mein*'. Then came others: *Awara* (1951)—'*Awara Hoon*'; *Jis Desh Mein Ganga Behti Hai* (1960)—'*Hoton Pe Sachai Rehti Hai*'; *Sangam* (1964)—'*Bol Radha Bol*'; *Mera Naam Joker* (1970)—'*Kehta Hai Joker Saara Zamaana*'. And it was not just in films made by Raj Kapoor. Other films of his too had title songs: *Anari* (1959)—'*Sub Kuchh Seekha Humne Na Seekhi Hoshiyari*'; *Main Nashe Mein Hoon* (1959)—'*Mujhko Yaaron Muaff Karna, Main Nashe Mein Hoon*'; *Deewana* (1967)—'*Deewana Mujhko Log Kahein*'; *Around the World* (1967)—'*Duniya Ki Sair Kar Lo*' and many others.

Shankar-Jaikishan did title songs for other actors too. Consider this: For Shammi Kapoor in *Junglee* (1961), *Dil Tera Deewana* (1962), *Rajkumar* (1964), *Tumse Acchha Kaun Hai* (1969), *Pagla Kahin Ka* (1970), *Jaane Anjaane* (1971). For Biswajeet in *April Fool* (1964); Manoj Kumar in *Hariyali aur Raasta* (1962); Shashi Kapoor in *Jahan Pyar Mile* (1969); Rajendra Kumar in *Aas Ka Panchhi* (1961), *Dil Ek Mandir* (1963), *Aayi Milan Ki Bela* (1964), *Aman* (1967), *Jhuk Gaya Aasmaan* (1968); and Dharmendra in *Yakeen* (1969) and *Pyar Hi Pyar* (1969).

The other music directors, though not as prolific as Shankar-Jaikishan, also composed title songs. For instance, Kalyanji Anandji for *Chhalia* (1960), *Don* (1978), *Muqaddar Ka Sikandar* (1978); Naushad for *Mere Mehboob* (1963), *Dil Diya Dard Liya* (1966), *Palki* (1967); OP Nayyar for *Tumsa Nahin Dekha* (1957), *Phir Wohi Dil Laya Hoon* (1963); SD Burman for *Tere Ghar Ke Saamne* (1963), *Talash* (1969), *Ishq Par Zor Nahin* (1970), *Naya Zamana* (1971); Roshan for *Barsaat Ki Raat* (1960), *Dil Hi To Hai* (1963); Madan Mohan for *Ek Kali Muskai* (1968), *Hindustan Ki Kasam* (1973); Laxmikant-Pyarelal for *Dosti* (1964), *Anjaana* (1969), *Aaya Saawan Jhoom Ke* (1969), *Aan Milo Sajana* (1970), *Satyam Shivam Sunderam* (1978); Ravi for *Chirag Kahaan Roshni Kahaan* (1959), *Waqt* (1965), *Dus Lakh* (1966), *Dhund* (1973); and many others.

I had mentioned earlier that the title song carries out the role of previewer. Not entirely correct. In most cases, it does that by being embedded in the opening credits. Say '*Shatranj Ki Chaal Hai Hamari*' from *Shatranj* (1969) and '*Jo Bhi Kiya Humne Kiya Shaan Se*' from *Shaan* (1980), are in the initial part of the film. But in some instances, it can make an appearance in the middle of the film too, like '*Dil Apna Aur Preet Parai*' from *Dil Apna Aur Preet Parai* (1960) as if to reiterate the theme of the film already discerned by the audience by then. Or at the very end like '*Ek Jagah Jab Jama Hon Teenon, Amar Akbar Anthony*' from *Amar Akbar Anthony* (1977), or '*Aman Ka Farishta*' from *Aman* (1967). In these instances, it plays the role of the summarizer and encapsulator.

The film need not have one title song. *Haryali Aur Raasta* (1962) had two—'*Yeh Haryali Aur Yeh Raasta*' and '*Jeevan Ke Do Pehlu Hain, Haryali Aur Raasta*'. The film *Shaan* (1980) had, other than the title song, the word '*Shaan*' appearing in other songs in the film too. This was perhaps to ensure that there was no doubt whatsoever about the film's thematic offering. Sometimes, besides the title song appearing more than once in a different avatar, its instrumental music also appears in the film repeatedly. Case in point—*Kal Ho Na Ho* (2003). The film's title song is not only rehashed in a sad version later, but its central melody is played out over several scenes to evoke a distinct set of emotions.

One interesting incident involves the title song of *Jhanak Jhanak Payal Baje* (1955). Vasant Desai composed the tune in Raag *Darbari* to suit the singer Ustad Amir Khan's voice and temperament. But V Shantaram, the filmmaker, was not satisfied. Desai could not believe that Shantaram would be unhappy with such a beautiful composition. He changed the raag to *Adana*. The two raags have the same scale but *Adana* accentuates the upper half of the octave whereas *Darbari*, the lower half. The shift to the new raag did the trick; the song sounded more sparkling and more appropriate for the credit titles.

Many of Shantaram's films had title songs such as *Geet Gaya Patharon Ne* (1964), *Jal Bin Machhli Nritya Bin Bijli* (1971). The music for *Boond Jo Ban Gayee Moti* (1967), which had a title song, was composed by my uncle, Satish Bhatia. It featured Manna De and Asha Bhosle.

Sometimes, the title song is a twin, or a tandem song sung by two singers, such '*Zindagi Bhar Nahi Bhoolegi Woh Barsaat Ki Raat*'. In this song, Roshan, while using the sarangi and sitar for the Rafi version, kept the stanza almost bare of instrumentation, only focusing on Rafi's singing genius and not filling in instrumental ornamentation.

Sometimes the title song faces a challenge. If the song is solely situational and does not convey the theme in the audio, then it does not convey the sense of the film effectively, like '*Dil Toh Paagal Hai*'. On the airwaves, it appears to be a duet because it involves only two singers. But the song involves four characters in a situation fraught with emotion and taking place simultaneously. Would the song have been better if four singers were singing it? Perhaps not. However, the song, with two singers, makes it more acceptable, never mind that it may not completely and appropriately convey the film's motif.

The style in which the title song is composed needs to follow the script and characters. Khayyam composed the title song of *Kabhi Kabhie* (1976) in the traditional style because it involved the love story of an older generation, whereas another love song from the film—'*Pyar Kar Liya Toh Kya*' was more modern in its approach because it involved the younger generation.

Title songs may sometimes be altered for the audio. The '*Kabhie Kabhie*' song ends abruptly in the film to convey the ending of Amitabh-Rakhee romance when Rakhee is getting married to Shashi Kapoor. However, in the audio, such a thing would have spoilt a perfectly good song. So, the entire song is retained.

Sometimes the title song goes beyond the film to do things its makers could not have possibly imagined. '*Kal Ho Na Ho*' was used in 2015 by the German Embassy in India, which produced an eight-minute video *Lebe Jetzt* ('*Kal Ho Naa Ho*' in German). The video features the German Ambassador to India, his wife and Salman Khurshid in the roles played by Shah Rukh Khan, Preity Zinta and Saif Ali Khan respectively.

From the late '70s, the concept of the title song began waning. There were much fewer instances in the next decades, some of them being *Shaan* (1980), *Hero* (1983), *Mard* (1985), *Saagar* (1985), *Ram Teri Ganga Maili* (1985), *Roja* (1992), *Baazigar* (1993), *Dil To Pagal Hai* (1997), *Kuchh Kuchh Hota Hai* (1998), *Dil Se* (1998), *Taal* (1999), *Baadshah* (1999) and others.

The numbers came down in the new century—*Kabhi Khushi Kabhi Gham* (2001), *Salaam Namaste* (2005), *Bunty Aur Babli* (2005), *Wake Up Sid* (2009), *Prem Ratan Dhan Payo* (2015), and *Kesari* (2019).

These days an odd film here and there may have a title song. The reason is probably that the film titles these days do not lend themselves to a title song. Earlier the film titles were rather straightforward. Now with films such as *Once Upon A Time in Mumbai* (2010), *Tanu Weds Manu* (2011), *Welcome Back* (2015), *Black* (2005), *Shamitabh* (2015), *Ab Tak Chhappan* (2004), *Kapoor & Sons* (2016), *Raman Raghav 2.0* (2016) and many such, the title song makes a rare appearance.

Now, the trend has reversed. Instead of the movie's title spawning the title song, the song inspires the movie title—*Pal Pal Dil Ke Paas* (2019), *Yeh Jawaani Hai Deewani* (2013), *Ae Dil Hai Mushkil* (2016), *Bachna Ae Haseeno* (2008), *Rab Ne Bana Di Jodi* (2008), *Mere Yaar Ki Shaadi Hai* (2002), *Mumbai Se Aaya Mera Dost* (2003), *Jab Tak Hai Jaan* (2012) and others. The role has reversed, and popularity of songs released earlier is being harnessed by filmmakers to name their films after these songs. The son has become the father of the man!

45

When Songs Do Not Make the Cut

Remember *'Aati Kya Khandala'* from *Ghulam* (1998), sung by Aamir Khan himself? The song, penned by Nitin Gaikwad, drew the ire of lyricist Majrooh Sultanpuri. At a function to honour Talat Mehmood, he flogged the lyrics as the "prostitution of the pen". The comments kicked up a massive storm with Mukesh Bhatt, the film producer, leading the charge. He cited Majrooh's own song: *'C.A.T. Cat, Cat Mane Billi, R.A.T. Rat, Rat Mane Chooha'* from *Dilli Ka Thug* (1958) for setting off the rot. In Guru Dutt's *Aar-Paar* (1954), he had introduced *Bambaiya* into the song—*'Sun, Sun, Sun, Sun Zaalima, Humko Tum Se Pyaar Ho Gaya'*—*'humko'* not being a word.

Though nobody pointed it out, Majrooh had introduced another non-word, a four-letter 'F' word in another Guru Dutt film *CID* (1956), that lead to penal consequences. The song was banned and removed from the film. No film footage exists of the song. The offending non-word was *'Fifi'*. As OP Nayyar told me, it was just a random word that Majrooh had thrown in because they could not find anything to fit the meter. The Censor Board, for reasons unfathomable, took objection to the word and guillotined the song, otherwise a fantastic Geeta Dutt ditty, still very popular today. In fact, it was re-created, and renamed as *'Fifi'* in *Bombay Velvet* (2015).

Apparently, the song was deleted from the film *CID* within a week of its release. Why would they not excise the song at the time of certifying the film? In the process, we not only lost out on a great song but one that helped the flow of the narrative. When you see the film, the cut is obvious.

Waheeda Rehman, however, had a different take. She said the censors had a problem not with "*Fifi*" but with the suggestiveness of "*Jaata kahaan hai deewane, sab kuch yahan hai sanam*". "The Censor Board had dirty minds," were her words that I quote.

Another twist was added by Nasreen Munni Kabir's book *Guru Dutt: A Life in Cinema*, which suggests the song was edited out because it showed the CID officer "in a bad light".

The Censor Board was doing something which was subsequently done in the US. In 1963, a band called *The Kingsmen* covered a Richard Berry number called '*Louie Louie*' who had recorded it in 1955. *The Kingsmen's* recording was the subject of an FBI investigation about the supposed, but nonexistent, obscenity of the lyrics, an investigation that ended without prosecution. The nearly unintelligible (and innocuous) lyrics were widely misinterpreted, and the song was banned by radio stations.

The case of '*Balma Khuli Hawa*' from *Kashmir Ki Kali* (1964) was even weirder. The audience of the first week saw the song. However, the Censor Board belatedly discovered that in the song Sharmila Tagore's *dupatta* flew off in the breeze exposing her breasts (covered by her *kameez*) which were heaving a bit too much for the Censor Board's liking. The *dupatta* eventually descended and settled on her head without fluttering down to cover her modesty. This 'immoral' behaviour of the *dupatta* led to the whole song being axed.

Some other songs too faced the Censor Board's ire, like '*Mose Chanchal Jawani Sambhali Nahin Jaaye*' from *Bahu Beti* (1952), composed by SD Batish and written by Kaifi Azmi, and '*Jab Jab Tujhko Chhua*' from *Jaal Saaz* (1959), composed by N Dutta and written by Majrooh Sultanpuri, and on the same tune '*Hip Hip Hurray*' was recorded.

To cut the long story short, these songs belong to the category of 'Deleted Songs' of Hindi films. The above-mentioned songs were deleted on the orders of the Censor Board. There is no footage, only the audio.

But there is a long list of other songs which were deleted for other reasons.

The government body is not always the cause; sometimes public opinion is. Guru Dutt's film *Sahib, Bibi Aur Ghulam* (1962) had a song '*Sahil Ki Taraf Kashti Le Chal*' sung by Hemant Kumar (who was also the music director) and written by Shakeel Badayuni. The song had a shot which showed Meena Kumari (playing Chhoti Bahu) resting her head on Guru Dutt's (playing Bhoothnath) lap in the carriage. Audiences resented the filmmaker showing a married woman behaving intimately with a man, who was not her husband. Guru Dutt removed the song and the offending shot. Hemant Kumar reused the tune for the song '*Ya Dil Ki Suno*' from *Anupama* (1966) four years later, this time penned by Kaifi Azmi. That is the advantage of being the music director; the tune never goes waste. But we will never know what the original song sounded like. Incidentally, in *Sahib, Biwi Aur Ghulam*, the haunting Geeta Dutt solo '*Koi Door Se Awaaz De Chale Aao*' was used in a shortened form with the entire second stanza edited out. Thankfully, the audio of the entire song exists.

Sometimes the public's behaviour also plays a role.

The popular '*Aaj Dil Pe Koi Jor Chalta Nahin*', composed by Laxmikant-Pyarelal, figured initially in *Milan* (1967), placed just after the interval. Producer LV Prasad learnt that many of those taking a break outside did not return to their seats in time to catch the song. So, it was axed. Ten years earlier, something similar had happened. Guru Dutt learnt that many in the audience extended their break during Geeta Dutt's boat song '*Rut Phire Par Din Hamare*' from *Pyaasa* (1957). The song was removed from the prints almost immediately.

Then there are cases where the entire film gets banned and prints destroyed. Kishore Kumar's film *Begunah* (1957) was accused by Paramount Pictures of being a copy of their 1954-movie *Knock on Wood*. It won the matter, and the Mumbai High Court ordered all prints of the film to be destroyed. All the prints were thought to have been destroyed but miraculously some segments have survived. The film had a song '*Ae Pyase Dil Bezubaan*', featuring Jaikishan (of Shankar-Jaikishan) on the piano and actor Shakila dancing. The song was sung by Mukesh. Hopefully, the song footage would be available soon. Till then, we will have to make do with the audio.

Let us see if the footage of the other songs from the film such as Kishore Kumar's comic number '*Aaj Na Jane Pagal Manwa Kahe Ghabraye*', and Manna Dey-Lata Mangeshkar duet '*Dil Albela Pyar Ka Mausam*' is also retrieved.

Most of the songs do not get to see the light of day because the films either do not get released or are shelved or remain incomplete.

Madan Mohan had songs composed and recorded for his films, which were either shelved or remained incomplete. The total number was staggering. Some of these were released in the form of the album *Tere Bagair* (2009) which was a huge hit.

Anand-Milind, sons of composer Chitragupt, brought out an album titled *The Last Songs* recorded by Mohammed Rafi in December 1979, under the baton of their father for Dilip Bose's film *Sorry Madam*. The film was never released.

Guru Dutt had some aborted projects. One was the Bengali film *Gouri,* launched in 1957, starring his wife, Geeta Dutt. Two scenes were filmed, and music director SD Burman had recorded two songs when Guru Dutt stopped production on account of his personal life being in turmoil. The two songs were recorded by Geeta Dutt. One was '*Jani Bhromora Keno*', a song that SD Burman also sang and whose tune he would later use in *Dr Vidya* (1962) as '*Jaani Tum Toh Dole*', this time rendered by Lata Mangeshkar. The other song was '*Banshi Shune Aar Kaaj Naai*', also sung by SD Burman and again used by him later in a Hindi film *Anuraag* (1972) as a Lata Mangeshkar solo—'*Neend Churaye Chain Churaye Daka Dale Teri Bansi*'.

Guru Dutt started another project—*Raaz* around 1959 which was adapted from the Wilkie Collins classic tale *The Woman in White*. Some scenes were shot, and two songs were recorded by RD Burman, who was making his debut. But after shooting and editing five or six reels, Guru Dutt shelved the film since he was unhappy with the way it was shaping up. The tunes lay in the cans for three years before one of them '*Ghar Aaja Ghir Aaye*' was used for Mehmood's *Chhote Nawab* (1961), which was officially RD Burman's first film as music director. Another tune based on the theme of Charlie Chaplin's *Limelight* (1952) was used in the Lata-Kishore duet '*Tum Meri Zindagi Mein*' for *Bombay to Goa* (1971). But that song did not see the light of day.

Another aborted film was *Picnic* (1964) starring Guru Dutt and Sadhna with music by N Dutta. Fortunately, snippets of two songs have survived. One is a lovely duet sung by Mohammed Rafi and Asha Bhosle—'*Kitni Rangeen Hai Yeh*'.

Mughal-e-Azam (1960) took a heavy physical toll on Madhubala's health. Sometime around 1964, once she felt a little better, Madhubala decided to make a comeback and finish her work on yet another film that was stalled for quite some time called *Chalaak*, where she was cast opposite Raj Kapoor with the music by Shankar-Jaikishan. Some ten reels were in the can by then. Some more filming took place before Madhubala's ailment again brought the film to a halt.

She collapsed on the sets and was advised strict bed rest thereafter. Still determined to finish it, sometime around 1966, Madhubala again made a valiant attempt to complete the film. However, the physical effort to complete the film proved too much for the actress. The film was shelved. It was even more tragic as the film had just a few more days of filming left. While no records of the film's music came out, Mukesh did sing a song '*Bata De Meri Jaan*' from the film at some of his concerts. At one such function in the 1960s, he declared the film had not been released but would soon be seen in the theatres. But that never happened.

Then there are unreleased films, whose songs remained unseen. One was '*Kabhi Kabhi Mere Dil Mein Khayal Aata Hai*' sung by Sudha Malhotra and Geeta Dutt from Chetan Anand's *Kafir* (1950) with music by Khayyam. This song was later used in the film *Kabhi Kabhie* (1976) and became a superhit reviving Khayyam's career.

Some other songs from unreleased films, many of them being low budget, starting from the late 1940s, include '*Tum Tana Tum Tana*' and '*Ek Jahan Aur Bhi Hai*' from *Jwalamukhi*, '*Tore Bina Raja Mohe Chain Kahan*' from *Poojya Gandhiji*, '*In Kaali Kaali Ankhon Mein*' from *Black Prince*, '*Gul Khile Ya Na Khile*' from *Raat Ki Uljhan* (in this song, there is a debate on whether it was sung by Geeta Dutt or Sabita Chaudhuri—the wife of composer Salil Chaudhari), '*Tujhe Doon Mein Kya*', '*Hey Baabu Hey Bandhu*' and '*Ja Chhup Nazron Se Kya*' from *Insaaf Kahan Hai*, '*Chunnilal Tera Bura Haal*' from *Shahzadi*, '*Angaare Hain Mat Chhoo* and *Aa Dil Ki Baazi Laga*' from *Jasoos*, '*Tumhari Mohabbat*' from *Bahadur Shah Zafar*, '*Mere Humnasheen Mere Humnawaa*' from *Bhool Na Jana*, '*Chale Aa Rahe Hain*' from *Ladaki*, '*Tere Bin Sajna Dil Mera*' and '*Zindagi Naam Hai Thokar Ka*' from *Naagan*, '*Matrubhumi Ka Aaya Bulawaa*' and '*Sona Sona Kya Karte Ho*' from *Veer Balak*, and '*Hum Khoob Janate Hain*' from *Saajan Ki Galiyan*.

It is not only the unreleased films. Even completed films have had songs deleted for various reasons.

One reason is the length of the film. *Sholay* (1975) had a qawwali—*'Ke Chand Sa Koi Chehra'*—but it was dropped owing to the length of the movie. One of the singers of the song was the lyricist Anand Bakshi while the others were Manna Dey, Kishore Kumar and Bhupendra.

Similarly, *Mera Naam Joker* (1970) was shot as a six-hour movie, but later it was realized that such a long movie would never work, so it was cut to four hours. In the process, some songs were also cut including the song *'Gaao Gaao Gaao, Jhoom Ke Gaao'* sung by Mukesh and Sharada.

For *Pakeezah* (1972), Ghulam Mohammed had recorded nine songs that had remained unused. These songs, including a faster-paced version of *'Chalo Dildar Chalo'*, were released separately in 1977 in an album titled *Pakeezah Rang Barang*.

One reason is personal. OP Nayyar's muse, Asha Bhosle, had *'Chain Se Humko Kabhi'* deleted from the movie *Pran Jaye Par Vachan Na Jaye* (1973) because she had parted from her mentor on bitter terms. It was a song for which, ironically, she would receive the Filmfare Award for Best Playback Female Singer. She did not attend the Filmfare Awards that year. OP Nayyar received it on her behalf and on the way back from the function, he flung the award out of the moving car and heard it break. OP Nayyar told me he was initially very bitter about Asha's behaviour and her refusal to acknowledge his significant contribution to her career, but later he turned philosophical about it.

In fact, OP Nayyar would scratch his head and would have no definite answer as to why so many of his other songs were deleted like *'Hothhon Pe Hansi Aankhon Mein Nasha'* from *Saawan Ki Ghataa* (1966), *'Tumhaare Ye Nakhre'* from *Kahin Din Kahin Raat* (1968), *'Main Pyar Ka Raahi Hoon'* from *Ek Musafir Ek Hasina* (1962), *'Darshan Kab Doge Bolo Na'* from *Bhagam Bhaag* (1956), *'Humne Toh Dil Ko Aapke'* from *Mere Sanam* (1965).

Composer Madan Mohan was one of those who had the unfortunate experience of seeing some of his best tunes being left out, too many to enumerate here. The Rafi solo *'Chirag Dil Ka Jalao'* from *Chiraag* (1968) was deleted, as was the Rafi-Asha duet *'Jis Din Se Tumko Dekha Hai'* from *Parwana* (1971). The poignant Lata solo *'Khelo Na Mere Dil Se'* from *Haqeeqat* (1964) had to be dropped because the film was too long, and the pace was getting bogged down. In fact, the song was one of Lata's favourites and she sang it in concert with the Wren Orchestra in Royal Albert Hall in 1979.

Music director Naushad had composed 20 songs for *Mughal-e-Azam* (1960), but only a dozen was finally used. The rest were discarded. One never knows whether Naushad recycled them for use later. Or whether, since they were composed exclusively for this film, they became the property of K Asif, to be used at his discretion. *'Husn Ki Baraat Chali'*, however, was shot but deleted owing to the length of the movie. It is a rare triad—Lata, Mubarak Begum and Shamshad Begum.

Some other songs that were deleted from released films were *'Chaand Hain Wohi'* from *Parineeta* (1953), *'Gaaye Ghabra Ke'* from *Paying Guest* (1957), *'Theharo Zara Si Der Toh'* from *Savera* (1958), *'Nazron Mein Hain Sau Afsaane'* from *Kya Yeh Bambai Hai* (1959), *'Yunhi Dil Ne Chaha Tha'* from *Dil Hi To Hai* (1963) sung by Suman Kalyanpur, *'Le Chal Wahan Piya'* and *'Dard Bhari Kisi Ki Yaad'* from *Sangdil* (1952), *'Jamuna Kinare Aaja'* from *Mehbooba* (1976), *'Sun Lo Dil Ka Afsana'* and *'Kyun Pheri Nazar'* from *Andaz* (1949) (the film already had 10 songs! It is no wonder that these two songs were excluded), *'Anari Re'* from *Munimji* (1955)—the tune was already composed by SD Burman earlier for the Bombay

Talkies Bengali film *Samar* (1950); however, he did not use the tune.

An opposite phenomenon was also occurring—songs in films but not on the record.

Guru Dutt's film *Pyaasa* (1957) had songs in the film which were not released on record. One was *'Ho Lakh Museebat Raste Mein'*—a short song sung by Rafi. The other was the verse *'Phir Na Kije Meri Gustakh Nigahi Ka Gila'* which was the prelude to *'Jaane Kya Tune Kahi'*. Later this verse became part of the Mukesh-Asha Bhosle duet in the film *Phir Subah Hogi* (1958) composed by Khayyam.

In the case of *'Aye Hai Dilruba'* from *Dr Vidya* (1962), the song was sung by Geeta Dutt for Helen with Asha Bhosle singing for Vyjayanthimala. Since it was more than eight minutes long (being a competition between the two dancing sensations), its length could have played a role in it not getting released on the record.

Some other songs that were in the films, but not on the record were *'Teena Tan Taa Teena'* from *Tangewali* (1955), *'Jiya Hai Udaas'* from *Ek Do Teen* (1953), *'Jee Bhar Ke Pyar Kar Lo'* (Sad version) from *Farar* (1955), *'Tu Mera Chaand Main Teri Chandni'* from *Dillagi* (1949)—Geeta Dutt sang this duet with Shyam (this song is the tandem version of the famous song *'Tu Mera Chand Main Teri Chandni'* sung by Suraiya and Shyam for the same film), *'Aa Jane Wafa Aa'* from *Anarkali* (1953) (this song was composed by Basant Prakash before C Ramchandra took over the baton).

There existed another category: the songs that were recorded in the voice of one singer but released in the voice of another.

For instance, *'Tum Jiyo Hazaaron Saal'* from *Sujata* (1959). The birthday song was supposedly first recorded in Geeta Dutt's voice. It was said to be released on the record as well. Later, the same song was recorded in Asha Bhosle's voice.

This was the version which was used in the movie. All these years, the song sung by Asha Bhosle was credited to Geeta Dutt. It continued to be wrongly credited to Geeta Dutt till Asha Bhosle and R D Burman had to convince HMV and get the credits corrected.

The song *'Us Chand Se Pyare Chand Ho Tum'* from *Raat Ki Rani* (1949) was originally recorded in the voice of Geeta Dutt and Mukesh. However, this was deleted from the film and the same then was re-recorded as a Lata-Rafi duet.

'Na Kajre Ki Dhaar' was a song that was originally sung by Mukesh and was composed by Kalyanji-Anandji with Indeevar as the lyricist. But the song went unreleased and was later used in movie *Mohra* (1994) with singer Pankaj Udhas and music by Viju Shah.

'Kaisi Haseen Aaj' from *Aadmi* (1968) was recorded first with Talat Mahmood. However, Manoj Kumar requested a change, so it was recorded again with Mahendra Kapoor. The film features this latter recording, but the album features the Talat version. Mahendra Kapoor also sang *'Na Aadmi Ka Koi Bharosa'*, but the song sung by Rafi (with a different tune) was eventually used and Mahendra Kapoor's version axed.

This phenomenon of deleted songs still exists. *Ae Dil Hai Mushkil* (2016) originally had *An Evening in Paris*—Rafi's hit number which was recreated by Ranbir and Anushka. The duo is seen listening to it on their headphones while exploring the streets of Paris. The song was deleted given the film's length.

Heard melodies are sweet, those unheard are sweeter. But those that are unseen are a matter of regret. Ask any music lover!

46

Judging Me Softly With a Song

Who would have known that a song dealing with isolation and emotional detachment would be relied upon by a judge in pronouncing his order? '*I Am A Rock*' by Paul Simon (1965) begins:

> *"A winter's day/In a deep and dark December*
> *I am alone/Gazing from my window*
> *To the streets below/On a freshly fallen, silent shroud of snow*
> *I am a rock/I am an island."*

Judge Stanley Marcus of the Eleventh Circuit in the USA used the song to decide an issue of maritime jurisdiction where the question was whether an interdiction occurred at sea near a rock or an island. According to the song, as the Judge pointed out, it can be both. He even went on to quote the entire song in his order.

One judge quoted Johnny Cash in an order to help determine the meaning of the word 'whenever' as used in a state constitutional provision. It helped corroborate the judge's ruling in terms of his interpretation of the word.

Take the case of this line from Bob Dylan's '*Subterranean Homesick Blues*' (1965)—*"You don't need a weatherman/To know which way the wind blows."* This line has been used so frequently that it has become a legal maxim in and of itself, to express the concept that there are some evidentiary issues that are so extensively known and commonly accepted that an expert opinion on that topic is unwarranted.

There are several other verses that have become legal maxims as well.

Reference to song lyrics in court judgments in the West is widely prevalent.

In India too, the phenomenon exists, though in modest number. Song lyrics—from films in Hindi and regional languages, lyrics of English songs, Urdu couplets, Shakespeare, English poets, have been quoted in court judgments.

When Sahir Ludhianvi penned the song '*Chalo Ek Bar Phir Se, Ajnabi Ban Jaayen Hum Dono*' for the film *Gumrah* in 1963, he could scarcely have imagined that 48 years later the lines of the song would mark the end of a controversial case. While discharging Ottavio Quattrocchi from the Bofors case on 4th March 2011, Chief Metropolitan Magistrate Vinod Yadav concurred with the CBI's contention that continuing proceedings against Quattrocchi would be a waste of money. He recited the iconic line from the song—"*Woh afsaana jise anjaam tak laana na ho mumkin, Use ek khoobsoorat mod dekar chhodna achha.*" The couplet was quoted in relation to the situation the case found itself in: It's better to put an end to a story on a good note if it cannot be taken to a logical conclusion.

The Magistrate also cited a passage written by an author regarding the prevailing condition in a village in Amravati district in Maharashtra to say that the common man was not concerned at all about the high-profile cases.

If Bob Dylan is among the most quoted artists abroad, Sahir Ludhianvi is in India. That is perhaps because Sahir Ludhianvi was sensitive to the plight of the downtrodden. He wrote about both romance and revolution with a rare sensibility.

In the case of *Budhadev Karmaskar vs State of West Bengal*, on 14th February 2011, the Supreme Court bench of Justices Markandey Katju and Gyan Sudha Misra dismissed the appeal of a man, accused of murdering a sex worker. The Supreme Court *suo moto* converted the appeal into a public interest litigation on the rehabilitation of sex workers.

The Court stated that sex workers were also human beings, and no one had a right to assault or murder them. A person became a prostitute not because she enjoyed it but because of poverty. Society must have sympathy towards the sex workers and must not look down upon them. They were also entitled to a life of dignity in view of Article 21 of the Constitution.

The Court observed that the plight of prostitutes had been depicted by Sahir Ludhianvi in his poem *Chakle* which had been sung in the Hindi film *Pyaasa* (1957)—*'Jineh Naaz Hai Hind Par Wo Kahan Hain'* (simplified version of the verse *'Sanaa Khvaan-e-Taqdiis-e-Mashriq Kahan Hain'*).

The Supreme Court also made references to the novels and stories of Bengali writer Sarat Chandra Chattopadhyay and mentioned that many prostitutes had been shown to be women of very high character, such as Rajyalakshmi in *Shrikant*, and Chandramukhi in *Devdas*.

The Court also referred to the character Sonya Marmeladova in Dostoevsky's novel *Crime and Punishment*. Sonya is depicted as a girl who sacrifices her body to earn bread for her impoverished family. Reference was also be made to Amrapali, who was a contemporary of Lord Buddha.

The Supreme Court order on 2nd August 2011, in the same matter, dramatically began with Ghalib's:

"Pinha Tha Daam-e-Sakht Qareeb Aashiyaan Ke
Udhne Hi Na Paaye The Ki Giraftaar Hum Hue"

Explaining the use of the couplet, Justice Katju, years later, said: "There are millions of sex workers in India, and these girls become prostitutes not because they enjoy the profession but due to abject poverty. So, I compared them to the young chick referred to by Ghalib which is caught in the hunter's net even before it could make its first flight. Surely Ghalib could never have imagined that his *sher* could be given such a meaning."

The Supreme Court also made a reference to Charles Dicken's novel *Oliver Twist*, in which the sex worker Nancy is shown to be a girl of high character who sacrifices her life to save Oliver. The Court also stated that in Victor Hugo's novel *Les Misérables*, Fantine sacrificed her hair and teeth to provide for her daughter Cosette. Martha in *David Copperfield* was also depicted as a woman of noble heart.

In the same case, the Supreme Court order dated 24th August 2011, began with some stanzas of Sahir Ludhianvi's *Chakle*, which were also mentioned in the earlier order.

In the case of *Radha and Ors. vs State of U.P. and Ors.* on 28th November 2002, Justice Katju made a similar observation and made the same references.

Wait, we are not over with Sahir Ludhianvi just yet.

Additional Sessions Judge Kamini Lau dismissed an appeal on 8th October 2011, against an order acquitting a Delhi resident and three members of his family on a dowry harassment complaint filed by his wife in 1999 on the ground that her allegations did not find any independent corroboration. In the verdict, the court also gave a piece of advice to the wife, quoting Sahir Ludhianvi, that she should dissociate herself from sour relations rather than being revengeful. The court said: *"Taarruf rog ho jaaye to usko bhoolna behtar, Taalluk bojh ban jaaye to usko todna achha, Woh afsaana jise anjaam tak laana na ho mumkin, Use ek khoobsoorat mod dekar chhodna achha."*

"Not all relationships are successful. In fact, most relationships which appear to succeed are only based upon compromises. Let go the past which is painful since attaching yourself to it will only give pain and miseries and help none," the court advised.

Which begs the question as to why the judges make references to songs, poets, and books in their judgments?

Judges do that to illustrate their reasoning, bridging the gap between laypersons and the judiciary and making the court's work more accessible to the public. They refer to the musical and literary works to bridge an understanding gap. Of course, quotes are never used to decide cases, but they are used to help provide a degree of understanding of the analysis. When judges write a judgment, they not just writing it for the lawyers, but also writing it for the parties and for the public at large.

A song becomes quotable if the lyricist can take a concept and distil it into a short phrase that conveys the facts in a memorable and concise way. Sahir Ludhianvi is one example.

However, this referral needs to be very carefully used. Great care needs to be taken that the quoting is done in a way that fleshes out the legal analysis. The parties shouldn't think that, by quoting a song, the judge is minimizing their case or making light of them.

The public perceives the law to be a dry subject and that judges lack emotion. Referencing allows judges to show that they are not disconnected from society. They try to convey to litigants that they don't just issue rulings from some ivory tower, but that indeed they watch TV, read books, and listen to music as anyone else does. So, when judges make rulings, they are ruling from the same world that the litigants live in. To bring them closer to humanity, to create that sense of compassion, judges find it a good idea to quote a relevant couplet or a song to drive home the legal point.

However, care needs to be taken that lyrics are only used if it is appropriate to the situation, otherwise it might create unnecessary confusions in the mind of people. Philosophical couplets especially in Urdu can be interpreted differently by different people. Writing Urdu couplets in a judgment raises responsibility for the judges.

Why Urdu?

Many judges have a fascination for the Urdu language. Even today, terms like *Vakalatnama* (authority given by a litigant to his lawyer in writing), *Dafa* (Section), *Halafnama* (Affidavit) and *Banam* (versus) are still in use in courts.

It is interesting to note that Urdu is not solely found in judgments, but in courtroom proceedings as well between judges and lawyers.

There was an instance of an exchange in the courtroom of Justice TS Thakur, the then judge of the Delhi High Court, and Najmi Waziri, then a lawyer, who later became a judge of Delhi High Court. After the conclusion of the matter, Justice Thakur gave a long date and was rising for lunch. However, Waziri needed a shorter date in the matter. Justice Thakur had almost left the courtroom when Waziri recited a line of Ghalib: *"Kaun jeeta hai teri zulf ke sar hone tak."* The Justice came back to his seat and said, *"Pehla misra padhiye zara."* Waziri recited: *"Aah ko chaahiye ik umr asar hone tak."* Justice Thakur was so impressed that he gave him a date in the next week.

Among the judges, Justice Katju was famous for making it a point to either open a judgment with an Urdu couplet or state one in his judgments. In the case of *Gopal Das thru Anand Vir vs. Union of India,* delivering a judgment on 14th March 2011, on a petition filed by a brother of one Gopal Das, who was illegally detained by Pakistan in the Lahore Central Jail, Justice Katju started the ruling with a couplet by Faiz Ahmed Faiz: *"Qafas udaas hai yaaron, sabaa se kuchh toh kaho, Kaheen toh beher-e-khuda aaj zikr-e-yaar chale"* from his famous ghazal *'Gulon Mein Rang Bhare, Baad-e-Naubahaar Chale'*. He also quoted Portia's speech on mercy in Shakespeare's *Merchant of Venice*.

In the case of *Aruna Ramchandra Shanbaug vs Union of India & Ors* on 7th March 2011, Justice Katju quoted Ghalib while delivering judgment in the Aruna Shanbaug mercy killing case: *"Marte Hain Aarzoo Mein Marne Ki, Maut Aati Hai Par Nahin Aati."* Shanbaug, a nurse at Mumbai's King Edward Memorial Hospital who was sexually assaulted in 1973 by a hospital staff, had been in a vegetative state for 37 years. To convey a sense of pain and agony Shanbaug went through all these years, Justice Katju quoted Ghalib in his judgment.

On 10th March 2018, when the Supreme Court recognized the right to passive euthanasia for the terminally ill, the judgement included lines from the Amitabh Bachchan film and song *'Muqaddar Ka Sikandar'* (1978): *"Rote hue aate hain sab, hasta hua jo jayega/Woh muqaddar ka Sikandar jaaneman kehlayega."* Shakespeare and Plato were also referred to.

On 7th February 2018, a judgment was passed by the Kerala High Court in the case of a divorced woman and a mother of a five-year-old child who had filed a petition after her child was taken away by her in-laws in her absence. Justice Chitambaresh opened the judgment with the lyrics of a song from a Tamil movie *Mannan*: *"Amma endrazhaikatha uyir illaiye Ammavai vanangatha uyir illaiye"* (There is no life form which does not call for its mother, there is no life form which does not respect its mother).

Apart from Urdu couplets, judges incorporate, as noted earlier, works of writers in their judgments. In 2003, hearing an appeal of a lawyer over alleged professional misconduct with his client, the judges added humour in the ruling, citing a line from Shakespeare's *Henry VI: "The first thing we should do is let us kill all the lawyers."*

Similarly, lyrics from a Bob Dylan song featured during the Kerala High Court proceedings when Justice Dama Seshadri Naidu quoted *"The times they are a-changing."*

The Special Court at Delhi, on 12th May 2022, while denying bail to Chitra Ramkrishna, the former CEO and MD of the NSE said, "It appears that accused Chitra Ramkrishna prima facie seems to have been running the affairs of NSE akin to that of a private club; singer writer, Nobel Laureate Bob Dylan once said *'While money doesn't talk, it swears'*, which is a line of the song *'It's Alright Ma (I'm Only Bleeding)'* released on his 1965 album *Bringing It All Back Home*. It means that money not only has influence, but it has great influence, even a perverse influence on people."

In a historic judgment on 6th September 2018, the five-judge Constitution Bench of the Supreme Court announced the strike down of the 158-year-old Section 377 of the Indian Penal Code that criminalized homosexuality. The verdict, which ran into 493 pages, borrowed heavily from English literature.

"I am what I am, so take me as I am", is how CJI Dipak Misra began pronouncing the judgment, quoting Goethe. This was immediately followed by a statement from another German philosopher Arthur Schopenhauer: *"No one can escape from their individuality."*

To emphasize on the significance of individuality, CJI Misra borrowed John Stuart Mill's statement: *"But society has now fairly got the better of individuality; and the danger which threatens human nature is not the excess, but the deficiency of personal impulses and preferences."*

Further, the Supreme Court, at different instances, quoted lavishly from Shakespeare. Stressing on the importance of identity, the judgment sought the help from the play *Romeo and Juliet*: *"What's in a name? That which we call a rose by any other name would smell as sweet."*

Stating that Indian Constitution is built on the Fundamental Rights, the Supreme Court said: "The Fundamental Rights Chapter is like the north star in the universe of constitutionalism in India." The 'north star' was in reference to Shakespeare's *Julius Caesar*.

Later in the order, the Supreme Court narrated an incident from Oscar Wilde's life, when the latter was prosecuted for homosexuality.

While reading out the judgment, Justice Dr Dhananjaya Y Chandrachud (now CJI of India) quoted Leonard Cohen's '*Democracy*' from the album *The Future* (1992):

> *"It's coming through a hole in the air,*
> ...
> *It's coming from the feel*
> *that this ain't exactly real,*
> *or it's real, but it ain't exactly there.*
> *From the wars against disorder,*
> *from the sirens night and day,*
> *from the fires of the homeless,*
> *from the ashes of the gay:*
> *Democracy is coming..."*

The judgement didn't go unappreciated in the music world. YouTuber Poojan Sahil came up with a parody video of the song '*Pyaar Kar*' from the 1997 movie *Dil Toh Pagal Hai*. The song titled '*Pyaar Kar: The 377 Song*' is a melodious ode to the landmark judgement.

The short parody video altered the lyrics of the original song with words like *"Ancient jo tark tha, ek number ka jerk tha, Kehta Teen-Sau-Satatar—Pyaar kar."*

Poojan also paid tribute to the Supreme Court judges in the song with the lyrics: *"SC ne bhi kahaa, Dillagi ki na denge sazaa, Befikr, thukraa ke darr—Pyaar kar."*

In the case of *Kanhaiya Kumar vs State of NCT of Delhi*, the Delhi High Court while granting bail to him, made critical observations on the people who indulged in the alleged sloganeering. The order dated 2nd March 2016 began by quoting the song '*Mere Desh Ki Dharti*' from Manoj Kumar's *Upkar* (1967) to describe the love for motherland. It read: "This patriotic song from *Upkaar* by Lyricist Indeevar symbolizes individual characteristics represented by different colours and love for motherland."

On 11th September 2014, the Delhi High Court dismissed a petition seeking a ban on the theatre release of *Finding Fanny*. The ban on the film was sought on the ground that the word *'Fanny'* would hurt the feelings of citizens of India especially immature brain of minor children. The court disagreed with the petitioners and cited other examples where the word 'Fanny' had been used, such as *Fanny Price* (in Jane Austen's novel *Mansfield Park*), and *Aunt Fanny* (in Enid Blyton's *The Famous Five*). It went on to mention the film *King Uncle* (1993) in which Anu Agarwal's character was named *Fenni*. The order said, "In the Hindi movie, *King Uncle*, released in the year 1993, the name of the lead female character was *Fenni Fernando* pronounced as *Fanny* only and the said movie also had a song with the lines of *'Fenni Ne Mujhe Bulaya'*. It is, thus, not as if the Indian movie viewers would be exposed to the name *Fanny* for the first time."

Sometimes, film songs get sung during court proceedings. On 2nd June 2021, the Delhi High Court's virtual hearing of a plea filed by actor Juhi Chawla against the rollout of 5G technology was disrupted when an unidentified person kept singing songs from her movies during the proceedings.

Soon after Juhi joined the virtual hearing, the individual started humming *'Ghoonghat Ki Aad Se Dilbar Ka'* from the actor's 1993 movie *Hum Hain Rahi Pyar Ke*. Despite the uproar, Juhi's fan remained undeterred and proceeded to sing other songs from her films like *'Laal Laal Hoton Pe Gori Kiska Naam Hai'* and *'Meri Banno Ki Ayegi Baraat'*. Justice JR Midha got agitated, asked to mute the audio feed, and issued a contempt notice.

A reference to the *Game of Thrones* was made by the Special Judge (PC) (CBI), Delhi District Court, Tis Hazari. In the judgement dated 9th July 2018, regarding the infamous Urea Scam Case, the Judge observed:

"'Winter Is Coming' happened to be the motto of House Stark of Westeros in Game of Thrones; *such phrase has been used by both the Turkish accused incessantly after inking the contract. It actually meant, in the serial, that the difficult times were coming ahead and thereby alerted everyone to be constantly vigilant. Such meaning is in conformity in the present context as well."*

For good measure, the Judge alluded to the Turkish proverb, *'Ruzgar eken firtina bicer,'* which meant that one who sows wind will reap whirlwind. He stated that it fitted aptly for both the accused.

Not only do judges quote film songs in their judgments, but some of them also shed their traditional reserve and reveal their musical sides. On 27th August 2018, two Supreme Court judges—Justice Kurian Joseph and Justice KM Joseph—both Malayalis, sang at cultural programs conducted by journalists covering the apex court in Delhi to raise money for Kerala for relief and rehabilitation following the floods. The audience included the Chief Justice of India.

While Justice KM Joseph sang a song from the classic Malayalam movie *Amaram*, chronicling the tale of fishermen, and a Hindi song, Justice Kurian Joseph performed *'We Shall Overcome'* alongside singer Mohit Chauhan.

"Fishermen were the first to react when the state was reeling under severe floods. This song is a tribute to them," said Justice KM Joseph.

If the judges can quote film songs, its par for the course that film songs also feature the theme of law and justice.

The song *'Insaaf Ki Kursi'* is one such from the 1983 movie *Justice Chaudhury.*

"Insaaf ki kursi pe pehale/Tum khud ko bithaao
Maine galat kya kiya hai/Mujhe phir bataao
Aansu bahaake mujhe/Tum na doshi banaao
Yeh mera nahi, insaaf ka faisala hai

Insaaf ka faisala, bhagwaan ka faisala."

Another 1983 film *Andhaa Kanoon* had a song *'Yeh Andhaa Kanoon Hai'*:

> *"Yeh andha kanoon hai*
> *Jaane kahan daga de de/Jaane kise saza de de*
> *Saath na de kamzoron ka/Yeh sathi hai choron ka*
> *Baaton aur daleelon ka/Yeh hai khel wakeelon ka*
> *Yeh insaf nahi karta/Kisi ko maaf nahi karta*
> *Maaf ise har khoon hai"*

Hard hitting words. But if film songs can bridge the perception gap between the judge and the common man, then it's a worthwhile endeavour to quote and be quoted in film songs.

47

The Funmeister

Johnny Walker—One of the Best Loved Comedians

In BR Chopra's 'man versus machine' classic, *Naya Daur* (1957), Dilip Kumar and Vyjayanthimala play the lead roles. A journalist, played by Badruddin Jamaluddin Kazi, comes from Bombay to their village to cover the race between a tonga and a bus—the film's highlight. He sings a song in the film, while Dilip, Vyjayanthimala and other villagers frolic around—*'Main Bambai Ka Babu, Naam Mera Anjaana, English Dhun Mein Gaoon, Main Hindustani Gaana.'*

Badruddin Jamaluddin Kazi was the actor's name on his passport. But the world knew him as Johnny Walker.

The *'English Dhun Mein.... Hindustani Gaana'* not just described that song, but two other songs as well that he will forever be known for.

'Ae Dil Hai Mushkil Jeena Yahaan' from *C.I.D.* (1956) was based on *'Oh My Darling, Clementine'*—the American western folk ballad. The music of OP Nayyar and the lyrics of Majrooh Sultanpuri took it to another level altogether.

'Sar Jo Tera Chakraye' from *Pyaasa* (1957) was the other. It was based on a song in Hugo Fregonese's British film *Harry Black and the Tiger*. SD Burman's composition and Sahir Ludhianvi's writing transformed the song into a timeless classic.

It's very interesting how Johnny Walker entered the film industry. He was working as a BEST bus conductor in Bombay, regaling passengers with funny tales and cracking jokes while he issued them tickets. He had an inimitable way of calling out the names of the stops.

That was when he caught the eye of actor Balraj Sahni, who was travelling in a BEST bus. An amused Balraj, who was scripting the screenplay for Guru Dutt's *Baazi* (1951), recommended him to Guru Dutt. Following a successful audition with Guru Dutt as a drunkard, Kazi was immediately taken on board for *Baazi* though it was nearing completion. Expectedly, the role was that of a drunkard, and Kazi was rechristened by a delighted Guru Dutt as Johnny Walker, after Guru Dutt's favourite whisky.

Ironically, Kazi was an avowed teetotaller.

Johnny Walker never looked back after that. He acted in around 300 films till his last role in Kamal Haasan's *Chachi 420* (1997). Interestingly, more than 40 years earlier, he had acted in *Shrimati 420* (1956). His busiest period was that of the 1950s and 1960s. There was even a film named after him—*Johnny Walker* (1957)—in which he acted opposite Shyama. What's more, two songs carried his name—*'Sach Kehta Hai Johnny Walker'* from *Aji Bas Shukri* (1958) sung on screen by Geeta Bali (playback Asha Bhosle); and *'Main Hoon Mr Johnny'* from *Mai Baap* (1957) sung on screen by Johnny Walker to Minoo Mumtaz (playback Mohammed Rafi).

The meaty roles that he got in the films made him a supporting actor or a 'second hero' rather than, strictly speaking, a comedian. He always managed to corner attention in the roles he played, in many instances overshadowing the main actor. Comedy was well-integrated into the story and Johnny Walker played a part that blended into the main story. He enjoyed a pride of place in the film's screenplay and influenced the box-office figures. In many films, he shouldered more responsibility than the main hero in making them great hits.

In three films, he played the lead role—*Chhoo Mantar* (1956), *Johnny Walker* (1957) and *Mr. Qartoon M.A.* (1958).

The reasons behind his popularity were many—his unrestrained cheeriness; his unconventional face; his unique dialogue delivery; his style of flirting and teetering during his song and dance routine; his twitch of the eyebrows; his well-timed smirk; his witty remarks; his funny gestures; his thin face, pointed nose and skinny body; his peevish voice; his slurring and exaggerated diction; his goofy demeanour. I could go on and on. He had charisma written all over him. The audience loved him.

Johnny Walker had the inborn ability to come up with one-liners. He was perhaps the only comedian who had stories written keeping him in mind. And all he had to do was to appear before the camera for the chuckles to begin. But his comic act had undertones of social commentary. Playing the simpleton, he dissipated the grave overtones in many a film, albeit driving home some profound truths.

He became so popular that a bus-stop near his house, Noor Villa, at Parry Cross Road in Bandra was called 'Johnny Walker Stop'. Johnny Walker would stand at the intersection of the road and wave out to his fans.

His act in Bimal Roy's *Madhumati* (1958) won him the Filmfare Best Supporting Actor Award. He got his second Filmfare for Best Comedian in *Shikaar* (1968).

Johnny Walker became an indispensable part of Guru Dutt films and got important roles in his films. Except for *Sahib, Bibi Aur Ghulam* (1962), he acted in every Guru Dutt film. He even featured in songs in all these films—in *Chaudhvin Ka Chand,* he sang two—*'Mera Yaar Bana Hai Dulha'* and *'Yeh Duniya Gol Hai'*. Guru Dutt had complete faith in him. He used to give Johnny Walker his scene and dialogue and if he could do better, he would accept it. In every rehearsal, Johnny Walker would come up with something new and Guru Dutt would love it. He used to look at everyone on the sets and see if the light boys, the cameraman, the assistants were laughing at his dialogues. Guru Dutt then had an assistant write down whatever Walker had said in the rehearsal.

With each successive film of Guru Dutt, Walker's role became more substantial—from being just a sidekick to being the hero's confidante; from being just a drunkard in Guru Dutt's first film to a rich person who is friends with the hero (*Kaagaz Ke Phool*, 1959).

He enlivened quite a few films of tragedy king Dilip Kumar (*Naya Daur*, *Madhumati* and *Paigham* in the 1950s, *Dil Diya Dard Liya* in the 1960s and *Gopi* in the 1970s). He played some non-comic roles as well—*Railway Platform* (1955) and *Mai Baap* (1957).

He left an indelible impression even in small roles like in Hrishikesh Mukherjee's *Anand* (1971), where he played a bearded stage director who humours the dying cancer patient Rajesh Khanna with pithy philosophies of life.

In his last film, *Chachi 420,* Johnny Walker played a drunkard makeup artist transforming Kamal Haasan into Lakshmi Godbole.

Mohammad Rafi had a huge contribution in making Walker's career successful. Most of the songs sung by Rafi for Johnny Walker were huge hits. Rafi was the only singer who could modulate his voice to match the voice of the actor. By listening to the way Rafi sang, one could make out who was singing on the screen. Rafi imitated the dialogue delivery style of Johnny Walker perfectly and their combination yielded memorable songs. Filmmakers not only gave Johnny Walker a big slot in their films, but also gave him a song because they knew that with Rafi providing the playback the song would be a success.

How many comedians can boast of such a status?

Let's talk about a few such songs.

1. ***'Ae Dil Hai Mushkil Jeena Yahaan, Yeh Hai Bombay Meri Jaan',*** *C.I.D.* (1956): The song was a pessimistic commentary on the inhumanity of a large city and dealt with the vagaries of urban life. Walker played

a pickpocket in the film but his philosophy about the city was profound. The viewer was taken on a tonga ride through Bombay's streets, along with Kumkum and Johnny Walker. The upbeat composition, Johnny Walker's jaunty walk and inimitable grin mitigated the poignancy and brought cheer to the viewer. The sunny song belied the dirty underbelly of the city and that's where the genius of OP Nayyar lay—delivering a bitter pill with sugar coating.

2. ***'Sar Jo Tera Chakraye,'*** *Pyaasa* (1957): Quintessential Johnny Walker—completely loony, irreverent, but with a heart of gold. Johnny Walker was perfect as he went about drumming up business, massaging heads, dispensing advice. He also went philosophical—*"Naukar ho ya maalik, leader ho ya public, iske aage sabhi jhuke hain, kya raaja kya sainik."* This song had a very interesting history. Guru Dutt chanced to see a *maalishwala* wearing a checkered lungi, a jaunty cap, banian, and carrying bottles of oil. A role was conceived. The role required a song. Guru Dutt had picked up some records during his visit to England. There was one tune he liked a lot from the film, *Harry Black and the Tiger,* which he decided to use.

   SD Burman, who was composing the music for the film, was asked to copy the song note-for-note. SD Burman was very upset. But Guru Dutt was adamant—the tune would have to be copied in the *mukhda* at least; SD Burman could do whatever he wanted in the *antara*. SD Burman's genius ensured that the 'inspiration' was not noticed, and the song acquired a different form (even the sounds of the *champi* were incorporated into the music). So much so that when the producer visited India, he heard the song and not only failed to recognize the tune, but commended SD Burman. The song went a long way in breaking the tedium of an otherwise intense film on the hypocrisy of society. In the ocean of gloom and doom, this song stood out for its *joie de vivre*.

3. ***'Jungle Mein Mor Naacha Kisi Ne Na Dekha,'*** *Madhumati* (1958): This was a delightful song. The lyrics could only have been written by Shailendra and there was a story behind it. Shailendra came home one day drunk. Hemant Kumar, his neighbour, saw his condition and smirked contemptuously. That incident triggered this song. His complaint? No one had seen a peacock dance in the jungle, but when he drank 'a little', the whole world came to know about it!

   Johnny Walker sang to an interested audience of inebriated villagers. Salil Choudhary's music was bubbly and complemented Johnny Walker's antics which were hilarious.

4. ***'Arrey Na Na Na Taube Tauba,'*** *Aar Paar* (1954): Again, a frothy number with Johnny Walker doggedly romancing his lady in, of all the places, a zoo. She demured, he cajoled, mixing English with Hindi to come up with lines such as *"Dard-e-jigar se main weak hun, bahut karo aaisa na julam, arey ho jaayenga fail abhi heart hamara, tere sarr ki kasam"*.

   This was a real-life romance being played out: Johnny Walker and Noor (who was actress Shakila's sister) fell in love on the sets of *Aar Paar* and got married. This was the song which reportedly started it all.

5. ***'Jaaney Kahan Mera Jigar Gaya Ji,'*** *Mr and Mrs '55* (1955): Another delightful peppy song. Here Johnny Walker was indulging in office flirting, watched by a bemused chowkidar. Yasmin, all dimpled and cute, was wooed by Johnny Walker who insisted he'd lost his heart somewhere. He looked under the table, amongst the files while Yasmin was not very

> sympathetic. Johnny Walker wondered: *"Kahin maare dar ke chuhaa toh nahin ho gayaa, kone kone dekhaa, na jaane kahaan kho gayaa,"* and so it went on, back and forth.

The list goes on and on. OP Nayyar, who had done 15 films with Johnny Walker—the maximum among all music directors—told me that Johnny Walker, for whom he had high regard as an actor and human being, owed a lot of his success to his music.

An immodest statement but a true one!

Johnny Walker quit films when comedy turned vulgar. His career slowed down and he retired with grace. But there was never any sense of frustration. He died a contented man on 29th July 2003.

The greatest tribute we can pay him is to forever cherish his work. In the song *'Main Bambai Ka Babu'* mentioned in the opening paragraph, Johnny Walker sang: *"Kaam ki baat bataa di maine comedy gaana gaakey, sun lo aji sun lo yeh jaaduu ka taraanaa."*

Yes, indeed, Johnny Walker was a cult Funmeister, a good human being, whose plummy voice and infectious grin, whose zest for life touched every film viewer.

He gave us good cinema, good songs, and lots of laughter.

48

The Trailblazer

I vividly remember berating my late father, an Air Force officer, about not letting me stand next to the taxiway and wave him off as his plane taxied towards the runway. In fact, I also demanded that I be allowed to run alongside. If the lady in white could do it to the taxiing Canberra, why couldn't I? I protested, only to bring forth an indulgent chuckle.

I was referring to the scene in Raj Kapoor's famous love triangle *Sangam*. It was released in 1964 and is still etched in the national consciousness for its novel theme, extraordinary performances, spectacular locales, and outstanding music (by Shankar-Jaikishan). The film was a massive hit and fetched Raj the Filmfare Award for Best Direction and Best Editing, and Vyjayanthimala the Best Actress award.

Interestingly, Rajendra Kumar, who played the third angle, performed a reverse role in *Aas Ka Panchhi* that was released three years prior to *Sangam*. He joined the military (as Raj did in *Sangam*) and went out of the scene for a while. Later, when he returned, he found his love interest getting married to his childhood friend, a doctor. That lady was Vyjayanthimala as well. Raj was originally to make this film in the late 1940s under the title *Gharonda* with Dilip Kumar, Nargis and himself but the project got postponed till 1962. Nargis had by then, quit films following her marriage to Sunil Dutt. When Raj approached Dilip Kumar, the latter wanted the right to edit the final copy of the film. Raj, rejecting such a condition, then approached Dev Anand who too declined the role. The role ultimately went to Rajendra Kumar.

This beautiful cinematic tale of love, misunderstanding, separation, and sacrifice was a trailblazer in several respects. It was Raj's first colour film and, distinguished by its epic length of 238 minutes, it had two intermissions. This was also the first Hindi film in colour that was shot abroad. Radhu Karmakar's masterful cinematography of the foreign locales under Raj's visionary stewardship mesmerized the audience and started a vogue for foreign shoots with *Love in Tokyo* (1966), *Evening in Paris* (1967), *Around the World* (1967) and several others. This movie was the first of its kind whose central theme was male bonding which went well beyond an ordinary friendship. The woman was incidental: to be used as a gift by the men, as a proof of their mutual friendship. She resented it but no one was interested in her feelings.

It was a brave Raj who brought this unsettling issue for the first time on the big screen. The film's songs have since then become classics. The popular '*Bol Radha Bol*' stood out for Vyjayanthimala's appearance in a swimsuit. She later confessed that "she swims like a dead fish" and all the close-up shots were taken in a swimming pool, while the long shots were done by her body double. This song also had Vyjayanthimala uttering a few dialogues, a trend which caught on with Saira Banu in *Aman* (1967), Sharmila Tagore in *An Evening in Paris* (1967), and many others.

Then there was the evergreen '*Prem Patra,*' which was gentle and romantic. There was a story behind this song. Hasrat Jaipuri (the lyricist) fell in love with a neighbourhood girl called Radha and wrote this poem for her. The poem may never have been delivered, but Raj was to later deliver it to the world as the perennial mantra for lovers. Not many are aware that in this melodious Rafi rendition, Lata joined in at the end. '*Buddha Mil Gaya*' was a trend-setter. Vyjayanthimala later stated that it was not a dance but a parody. Picking up the lampshade, dancing on the stool, it was all very impromptu. Incidentally, Lata was tricked into singing this song. Several years later, Lata said in an interview that in her entire career she had felt embarrassed only while recording this number! So miffed was she that she decided neither to see the film nor sing a note for Raj's next, *Mera Naam Joker* (1970). They made up again for *Bobby* (1973).

In *'Har Dil Jo Pyar Karega'*, Raj was at his best, handling the departments of accordion, singing and dancing and emoting with consummate skill. Rajendra, who was mostly play backed by Rafi, had Mahendra Kapoor to back him. Mahendra's son, in an interview, stated that Raj had grown very fond of Mahendra during a tour of Russia and promised him a chance to sing for the second lead in his films. Mahendra remarked that Raj would forget his promise once he reached India, but Raj took the cigarette he was smoking and burnt his hand and said the mark would remind him.

'Dost Dost Na Raha' became a legend. The way its picturization brought out the characters' inner feelings, illustrated Raj's total mastery of the medium of the Hindi film. The piano riffs were played by Shankar himself. *Sangam* brought out differences between Shankar and Jaikishan. When Ameen Sayani's *Binaca Geetmala*—then a litmus test for popularity—selected *'Prem Patra'* for the top spot over *'Dost Dost Na Raha'*, the seeds of dissent were sown. Rafi's song was the creation of Jaikishan-Hasrat team, whereas the Mukesh song was conceived by Shankar-Shailendra combination.

Shankar accused Jaikishan of having revealed this in an interview in violation of an understanding between them that the tunes, despite being composed separately by them, would always be identified as Shankar-Jaikishan's. For him, *'Dost Dost Na Raha'* was his life's best composition, but it had been bested by his colleague's tune which was lightweight.

The bitterness of the controversy took its toll on subsequent assignments. Their friendship began to crumble.

In the climax scene where Rajendra was about to die after having shot at himself, he uttered, *"Sangam Ganga aur Jamuna ka hi hota hai aur sangam ke liye Saraswati ko lupt hona hi padta hai,"* as his face disappeared from the screen. The audience was left to wonder whether Raj's attaining his *'manzil-e-maqsood'* (being Vyjayanthimala's affections which he articulated in *'O Mehbooba'* song) didn't come without a usurious penalty!

49

The Man in Khaki

Jagdish Raaj—The Forever Policeman

The Ministry of Aviation has exempted VVIPs from the pre-embarkation security check at the civilian airports in the country. Such exemption is granted based on protocol, reciprocity/bilateral agreement in respect of foreign dignitaries, and on security grounds. Dignitaries ranging from the President, Prime Minister, Ambassadors, Chief Ministers, Judges, the Dalai Lama, SPG Protectees, and others are covered.

The list did not cover one name. But informally, that person never had to go through the metal detectors—there was no frisking, no pat-downs. The airport security officials would escort him right to the aircraft. Such was the love and respect they had for him. He was their man, albeit in reel life. But that didn't matter. He was their hero.

That person would be Jagdish Raaj.

Why only the airport security? Even the traffic policemen would salute him when they saw him in the car; he was never issued a challan. If he broke a traffic rule (which would be rare and unintentional), his fine would be an autograph and a picture with the policeman. The housing society guards, the mall guards and other security personnel, would stand up and acknowledge him with affection. And he would reciprocate with genuine warmth and patience. He did that for five decades.

Why? Because during these decades, he mainly played the role of a police inspector—an astonishing 144 times (you read that right: 144 times!) in over 250 films. Enough number of times to make it to the *Guinness Book of World Records* as the most typecast actor. So entrenched did he become in this pigeonhole, that the producers were loath to experiment with other roles—though he did play an odd negative role, like in *Ek Mahal Ho Sapnon Ka* (1975), or as a judge in *Dhool Ka Phool* (1959) and *Insaniyat Ke Devta* (1993), or a doctor in *Pyaar Ka Sager* (1961) and *Do Anjaane* (1976), or other characters. But his bread-and-butter came from khaki.

Interestingly, it was a Hollywood casting director behind the entry of Jagdish Raaj in the Guinness Book. He called the Guinness Book team to Mumbai for verification after seeing his unending list of films as a policeman. When his name finally achieved official recognition, Jagdish Raaj got the role of Police Commissioner in films like *Loha* (1987) and *Na-Insaafi* (1989), prompting him to quip that the powers that be had at last thought it fit to give him a promotion! In his last film *Meri Biwi Ka Jawaab Nahin* (2004), he played the role of Deputy Inspector General of Police. But essentially, he started as an Inspector and remained one, exceptions apart.

If the police were ever to have a national mascot, it would be him. It is a wonder why he wasn't made an honorary police inspector, or better still, after 50 years of diligent service, an honorary Director General of Police.

It needn't have been like that. Jagdish Raaj started as a child actor in *Ek Hi Raasta* in 1939. However, his first actual role was in *Seema* (1955), in which he played the role of a doctor. He could have been typecast as one. But fate had other plans for him. He played the role of a policeman for the first time in Raj Khosla's *CID* (1956) with Dev Anand and Waheeda Rehman where, coincidentally, he played a character named Inspector Jagdish. And that was the launching pad of a career in the police.

Jagdish Raaj was born in Sargodha (now in Pakistan) in 1928. Before joining films, he had donned khaki in real life.

He was in the Royal Indian Air Force during World War II but had to leave due to medical reasons. In 1992, in the film *Deedar*, he would play the role of an Air Force officer.

Though I had seen him in many films earlier, his presence in the song *'O Mere Raja'* from *Johny Mera Naam* (1970) made me sit up and take notice. The song, featuring Dev Anand and Hema Malini, was shot in the ruins of Nalanda University and on the ropeway in Rajgir. Jagdish Raaj and his police team followed them, at a close distance. The actors were aware but went about their business nonchalantly—Hema seeking forgiveness for *der se aana* and Dev Anand admonishing her for *wohi purana tera bahana*. While keeping a hawk-eye on the goings-on, Jagdish Raaj would look away at certain parts of the song as if embarrassed or maybe to avoid eye contact. At one point he even smiled. When the couple boarded the chairlift of the Rajgir ropeway and left the police behind, he looked askance, but in an innocent way. I found his conduct endearing and atypical.

A genteel, but firm, approach is what Jagdish Raaj came to epitomize. Iron fist in velvet gloves. Never compromising the integrity of the office yet maintaining decency in official conduct—never a foul word, no intimidation, nor threats, and certainly no third-degree, no extortion, no encounters, no planting of evidence, no malice. Honesty in official dealings. Living on the frugal salary, no protection money, no *hafta*—playing by the book, in a decent, civilized manner. Your friendly neighbourhood policeman, who knew his IPC and CrPC. This conduct harked back to an era of cultured behaviour.

Some of his memorable films include *Kala Bazaar* (1960), *Hum Dono* (1961), *Ilzam* (1970), *Deewar* (1975), *Aaina* (1977), *Don* (1978), *Silsila* (1981), *Naseeb* (1981), *Shakti* (1982) and *Mazdoor* (1983).

When you play a police officer on screen day-in-day-out, it's inevitable that some of the office work finds its way back to the house. Jagdish Raaj got a police uniform stitched, which would be kept crisply ironed in his cupboard. He would reach the shooting wearing the uniform. God knows how many times he must have been mistaken for a real police inspector by people who didn't know any better!

In the documentary, *The Immortals*, filmmaker, and archivist Shivendra Singh Dungarpur assembled key moments and memorabilia from India's rich film past. He was commissioned by the Busan International Film Festival to direct a commemorative documentary on Indian cinema. The documentary weaved together a history of Indian cinema through objects and fragmented memories. The documentary revealed that Jagdish Raaj's daughter had retained the uniform that her father had donned in numerous Hindi movies.

Policemen, lawyers, doctors, army officers, priests do not have many songs in Hindi films. Their role requires gravitas, and they can't be shown running around trees. Jagdish Raaj was no exception. He may have been present during a song picturization, in the line of duty, as in *'O Mere Raja'* referred to earlier, but never got to sing on screen (as attested to by his son Bobby Raaj). Even when he played a role other than a policeman, he didn't get any opportunity though he may have been present during a song, like playing a drunk at the bar in *'Aao Huzoor Tumko Sitaron Mein Le Chalun'* (*Kismat*, 1968). Maybe his police persona was too overwhelming to merit a song, even in civilian roles. However, Iftekhar, who played a policeman in many films (not as many as Jagdish Raaj, though), did get to sing a line in Kishore Kumar's *'Ek Chhoti Si Naukri Ka Talabgaar Hoon Main'* (*Naukri*, 1954).

I first met Jagdish Raaj in 1974 at the shooting of BR Ishara's *Rahu Ketu* (1978) in a scene with Prem Nath. I had just finished school and was in Mumbai for an interview. Twenty years later, when I was posted in Mumbai, I would meet him and his family socially and become friends. He was one of the most charming and warm-hearted people I had ever met. The age difference notwithstanding, he treated me as a close friend and regaled me with *filmi* anecdotes. He had acted with the entire industry and was on excellent terms with each and every one. This was evident when the entire industry turned up at the prayer meeting when his wife passed away. Such was the high regard in which he was held.

Jagdish Raaj died on 28th July 2013, at the age of 85.

His legacy continues through his son, daughter, and grandchildren.

His son Bobby Raaj is a producer, director, and writer. He has also acted in a film. In 1994, Bobby invited us for the premiere of *Zamane Se Kya Darna*, starring Sanjay Dutt and Raveena Tandon, which he had directed. Except for *Mera Haque* (1986)—Bobby Raaj's first film as producer/writer—none of the subsequent films that he produced and directed, had Jagdish Raaj. In other films, the scripts would be written to incorporate Jagdish Raaj's role but in his in-house productions, it was decided that if the script didn't demand it, Jagdish Raaj would have no role to play. How many actor-producers would have done this?

Jagdish Raaj's daughter, Anita Raaj, made her Bollywood debut in the 1981 film *Prem Geet*, garnering critical acclaim for her performance. She went on to make a name for herself in the 1980s, starring in a series of successful thrillers opposite Sanjay Dutt, Dharmendra, Vinod Khanna, Shashi Kapoor, Rishi Kapoor, Shatrughan Sinha, Rajinikanth and other stalwarts. She also acted in many TV serials.

Bobby Raaj's daughter Sonakshi is a much sought-after costume and fashion designer in Bollywood. His other daughter Malvika is a model and acts in Hindi and Telegu films.

"Tumhen police ne chaaron taraf se gher liya hai. Bachne ka koi raasta nahin hai. Apne aap ko kanoon ke hawaale kar do." How many times Jagdish Raaj must have shouted this warning through the megaphone to the bad guys! The same could be said about how his uniform did the same thing to him. I salute this quintessential policeman who brought dignity and flair to the role.

50

Oh Doctor, I'm in Trouble

The image of Hanuman flying with a mountain atop his palm is etched in the mind of every Indian. A doctor, that too of an enemy state, was responsible for this flight. According to the *Ramayana,* in the fierce battle between Lakshman and Meghnad (Ravan's son), a deadly arrow downed Lakshman. He lost consciousness, much to the anguish of Ram. In that critical hour, Hanuman approached the Lankan Royal Physician, Sushena, for help. The good doctor asked Hanuman to rush to Dronagiri Mountain to fetch four herbs including the *Sanjeevani Booti*. Hanuman, not being able to identify the herbs from the multitudinous numbers growing on the mountain, uprooted the entire mountain and brought it back.

The doctor exhibited the highest level of medical ethics which transcended considerations of the patient being a friend or foe.

Humanitarianism, in its purest form, was at display here, never mind the consequences. The Hippocrates Oath in its formal manifestation did not exist then; this treatment was its forerunner.

From the very ancient times in India, doctors (*vaidyas*) have contributed to the development of medicine. Charaka, the father of Indian medicine, wrote *Charaka Samhita*. Dridhbala, Sushruta, Nagarjuna, Vagbhata, Jivaka, and Rusa (female) are some of the doctors whose contribution was significant. Doctors have been held in high esteem throughout the ages. The respect remains intact, and during the days of the coronavirus pandemic, it reached stratospheric levels—and rightly so.

It is therefore no surprise that Hindi films, whose themes reflect Indian society, has a large repertoire of films with the doctor as the central character.

The film that leads the pack is *Dr Kotnis Ki Amar Kahani* (1946)—an iconic film, a brave film made and acted by the legendary V Shantaram. It is a true account of Dr Dwarkanath Kotnis, one of the five volunteer physicians, who was sent to China during the Second Sino-Japanese War in 1938, to provide medical assistance to the troops fighting the Japanese invasion.

The film showed that four months after having arrived, the doctors felt homesick, and rummaging through the boxes they were carrying, found a record player and a record of the song—*'Pardesi Re Kahe Chhoda Mora Desh'*.

Their ecstatic reaction was a sight to behold. They sat around and listened with complete attention. When the song ended, one doctor remarked—*"Maloom hota hai hum Hindustan mein hain."* What a way to capture the human side of the profession!

Dr Kotnis' job as a battlefront doctor was very stressful. There was always an acute shortage of medicines. During one battle, he performed operations for up to 72 hours, without getting any sleep.

In 1940, Dr Kotnis met Guo Qinglan, a nurse (played by Jayashree, Shantaram's wife) and they got married in December 1941. They had a daughter who was named Yinhua, derived from India (Yin) and China (Hua).

The stress as a frontline doctor finally started to take its toll on him and epileptic seizures killed him on 9th December 1942.

Mao Zedong (later Chairman Mao) mourned his death: *"The army has lost a helping hand; the nation has lost a friend. Let us always bear in mind his internationalist spirit."*

His tomb is located at the Martyr's Memorial Park in Shijiazhuang in the Northern Chinese province of Hebei. Both China and India have honoured him with stamps. The Chinese government continues to honour his relatives in India during every high-level official trip.

Another film, where an Indian doctor, also exhibiting the 'internationalist spirit' but in favour of Japan, was *Aman* (1967). Rajendra Kumar was a UK-trained doctor who volunteered to go to Japan in the aftermath of the Hiroshima and Nagasaki nuclear bombings at the end of World War II, to help find a cure for atomic-bomb survivors—and to spread the message of world peace. *"Kal jo kuchh bhi Japan mein hua, woh aaj yahaan bhi toh ho sakta hai,"* he told his father.

Lord Bertrand Russell, philosopher, pacifist, nuclear disarmament advocate and Nobel Laureate appeared in a cameo role, giving the doctor his blessing.

The devastation caused by the nuclear bombing was starkly exhibited in the song *'Barbad Hiroshima Ki Tasweer Dekh Lo'*.

The untold suffering of the radiation victims was a reminder of the long-term damage caused by atomic weapons. The doctor undertook a mission to rescue fishermen who had been exposed to nuclear radiation. He eventually died.

The story, presenting the whole world as one family, which needed to look out for each other—the theme of unity will never lose its relevance.

A reverse brain drain took place in the film *Dard ka Rishta* (1982). Sunil Dutt was a doctor in New York. His wife Smita Patil, also a doctor, was doing research on leukaemia. The doctor yearned to return to India and join as the head of surgery at Tata Memorial Hospital. His wife wanted to continue her research in the US, which lead to their divorce.

However, Sunil Dutt was forced to go back to the US for the treatment of his daughter (by his second marriage) who was suffering with leukaemia. By a twist of fate, his former wife treated her with bone marrow donated by Smita's son, who, unbeknownst to Sunil Dutt, was his son too. Not a very happy commentary on the state of cancer care and treatment in India then. Have things changed now? Not sure since the well-heeled and the political fat cats still make a beeline for the US.

The opening credits featured the song *'Pain Is A Many Splendoured Thing'* sung by Usha Uthup.

Then there have been some films where doctors have kept aside their personal feelings of hurt, jealousy and anger and behaved in a professional manner as behoves their profession.

In *Dil Ek Mandir* (1963), Rajendra Kumar, a doctor, was treating the cancer-stricken Raj Kumar, who was married to his former love interest Meena Kumari. Meena Kumari justifiably thought that her ex-lover would not be able to give her husband proper medical treatment. But the doctor assured her that he would extend the best care possible and went out of his way to prepare himself for the operation. Raj Kumar, predictably, was saved, but the doctor succumbed to his death brought about by long hours and stress.

But in *Aarti* (1962), Meena Kumari, herself a doctor, had no such qualms about Ashok Kumar—a brain surgeon (who lost her to Pradeep Kumar) when Pradeep Kumar underwent a brain operation. Pradeep Kumar did have his doubts, which he screamingly articulated, as did her relatives, but Meena Kumari was dead sure that Ashok Kumar, the Doctor, would prevail upon Ashok Kumar, the Spurned Lover. And that's what happened.

Wait, we haven't finished with Meena Kumari just yet. In *Dil Apna Aur Preet Parai* (1960), she played a nurse to Raj

Kumar's surgeon. They fell in love, he was forced to marry Nadira, but eventually everything turned out fine.

While on nurses, who can forget Waheeda Rehman's role as a nurse in *Khamoshi* (1970)? Working in the psychiatric ward, she forgot the cardinal principle of keeping her professional and personal lives apart. Don't get too attached to your patients, they are told. Though she cured both Dharmendra and Rajesh Khanna, by pouring love and affection into the care, she resultantly became emotionally deranged and got admitted into that very room in the ward.

They train you to keep professional and personal apart for a very good reason.

While compassion and empathy are essential in order to provide good quality of care, objectivity is also needed. Her role of a nurse underlined the humane side of the profession and how sometimes the divide got breached.

There have been films where the doctors have learnt a thing or two from the patients. *Anand* (1971) was one such film. Oncologist Amitabh Bachchan—straightforward, no-nonsense, humourless—met a patient suffering from lymphosarcoma (Rajesh Khanna), who, despite his condition, had a cheerful, helpful, and vibrant disposition. He lived his limited life to the fullest, spreading warmth and positivity. "*Zindagi badi honi chahiye, lambi nahin*" was the timeless message which the patient delivered to the dour doctor and the audience. The doctor learnt to look at the world differently—with empathy—looking for good in everyone and not worrying about matters not in his control.

In *Munna Bhai MBBS* (2003), the message delivered by Sanjay Dutt was that the mechanical, impersonal relationship between doctors and patients needed to include compassion and a more empathetic regimen. The '*Jadoo ki*

Jhappi'—encapsulating this very concept—became a national phenomenon.

And finally, *Ek Doctor Ki Maut* (1990) depicted the ostracism, bureaucratic apathy, and reprehensible insult of a doctor and his research, instead of recognition. It also told us why brilliant doctors migrated to greener pastures. The film was based on the life of Dr Subhash Mukhopadhyay, an Indian physician who pioneered the In-vitro fertilization treatment. This film underlined the many trials and tribulations doctors faced in India who wished to work within the system.

And now on to some Hindi film songs dealing with medical conditions. There aren't too many, unlike in the West, where every possible disease/condition is fair game.

> *'Seene Mein Jalan, Aankhon Mein Toofan Sa Kyun Hai,*
> *Is Sheher Mein Har Shaqs Pareshaan Sa Kyun Hai.'*

This Suresh Wadkar song from *'Gaman'* (1978) best described the human condition in the time of Coronavirus.

Hindi film songs have delved into every aspect of life, but strangely, by and large, have stayed away from disease and sickness. *'Dard-e-Dil,' 'Dard-e-Jigar,' 'Prem Rog'* do not count. This 'affliction' has stayed with the human race from the very beginning and is not going away. *'Sardi Na Khansi Na Malaria Hua'* (*Raju Ban Gaya Gentleman*, 1992) misled the listener into believing that a medical song was underway, before it showed its true colours—*"Main gaya yaaron, mujhko loveriya hua"*.

'Sar Jo Tera Chakraye, Ya Dil Dooba Jaaye' (*Pyaasa*, 1957) was almost there but not quite.

But one song, completely unacceptable today, stood out.

Tum Haseen Main Jawaan (1970) had a song *'Chheenk, Meri Jaan Chheenk'*, a cabaret song by the 'Cabaret Queen' Helen. She appeared as a *jalpari*, happily moving around, sneezing into the faces of the audience. By the time she finished, the entire restaurant was sneezing. Though to be fair to Helen, she did do the right thing in the title song (a cabaret) of *Jaane Anjaane* (1971) where she cautioned, "*Milenge phir kabhi jhoom ke hazoor se, aaj toh dekhiye dur hi dur se*". Sound advice on social distancing.

Rajesh Khanna in *Safar* (1970) sang in despair: "*Hai pareshan nazar, thak gaye charah gar* (doctor), *koi samjha nahin koi jaana nahin.*"

But there is no need for such despair in these troubled times.

As the song in *Boot Polish* (1954) teaches us—"*Mutthi main hai taqdeer hamari, humne kismet ko bas mein kiya hai*". It is up to us to combat the pandemic menace with fortitude, discipline, and faith. If we do that there is no reason why wouldn't, as the song further declares: "*Badley ga zamana yeh sitaron pey likha hai.*"

Our doctors, nurses and medical staff did, and are doing, a yeoman service, much beyond the call of duty, during the pandemic.

Jai Jawan, Jai Kisan, coined in 1965, has over the years expanded to *Jai Jawan, Jai Kisan, Jai Vigvaan, Jai Anusandhan.* The time has come to expand it even further.

51

Repackaging One's Own Song

Remember *'Maine Poochha Chand Se'*, the romance-imbued, tribute-to-beauty song from *Abdullah* (1980)? This was one of Rafi's bright and dazzling luminescent displays before he bade a final goodbye to his countless fans. RD Burman, who had more Kishore Kumar than Rafi in his repertoire, did a stellar job with Rafi in this song. The tune was bewitching, innovative in its conversational approach, penned very evocatively by Anand Bakshi. The song was nominated for Filmfare Best Male Playback Singer.

But the tune was not unique. It was a re-hash of RD Burman's tune, note for note, from another song in an earlier film *Pyar Ki Kahani* (1971)—*'Koi Aur Duniya Mein Tumsa Haseen'*. The song was again a paean of praise to beauty and written by Anand Bakshi. The only minor difference was the faster beat.

As if one song being lifted lock, stock and barrel was not enough, RD Burman used the melody of *'Jaane Jaana, Jao Kal Phir Aana'* from *Samadhi* (1972) in *'Lalla, Allah Tera Nigehbaan'*, in a slower beat, in the same film—*Abdullah*. Great way of reducing workload!

But RD Burman was not the only composer who used his old tune, dusted, and polished it, and used it again.

The film *Cha Cha Cha* (1964) had outstanding songs by Iqbal Qureshi. One was a Rafi-Asha Bhosle duet *'Ek Chameli Ke Mandve Tale,'* written by Makhdoom Mohiuddin, which became very popular. However, this was based on the melody of an earlier song of his *'Aaj Mausam Ki Masti Mein Gaaye Pawan'* from *Banarasi Thug* (1962), sung by Rafi-Lata, and written by Hasrat Romani.

SN Tripathi did that with *'Janam Janam Ka Swath Hamara'* from *Been Ka Jadoo* (1963) sung by Mahendra Kapoor and Suman Kalyanpur, written by BD Mishra. It was a copy of his *'Phul Bagiya Mein Bulbul Bole'* by Rafi-Lata, written by Bharat Vyas, from *Rani Roopmati* (1957).

Ravi used the tune of *'Woh Dil Kahan Se Laaoon'* from *Bharosa* (1963) in *'Dil Mein Kisi Ke Pyaar Ka'* in *Ek Mahal Ho Sapnon Ka* (1975).

Roshan did that with *'Rahein Na Rahein Hum'* (*Mamta*, 1966). It was an exact replica of the earlier *'Tera Dil Kahan Hai'* from *Chandni Chowk* (1954)—both songs written by Majrooh Sultanpuri.

Laxmikant-Pyarelal used the same melody in *'Ki Gal Hai Koi Nahin'* (*Jaaneman*, 1976) and *'Bhoot Raja Bahar Aaja'* (*Chacha Bhatija*, 1977). Since both the films were released within a year, it's difficult to establish which was the original, and which the copied song. They were probably recorded not far apart in time when the tune was still fresh. Hema Malini, who figured in both songs, must have wondered why the tune appeared familiar.

Jaidev repeated the tune of his evergreen *'Kabhi Khud Pe Kabhi Haalaat Pe'* (*Hum Dono*, 1961) in *'Ajeeb Saneha Mujh Par Guzar Gaya Yaaron'* (*Gaman*, 1972). It is rather strange he did that; he didn't do too many films and couldn't have run out of tunes, making him re-use this iconic song eleven years later. Probably, the filmmaker had his way.

Film composers copying/getting 'inspired' by foreign songs, including Pakistani songs, is a known fact. No one has been immune from it. Some did/do it once in a while; some more often.

But why on earth should they use their own tunes again? Is it because the first-time round, the tune didn't succeed, and the composer felt it deserved a second chance? Maybe, in some instances. Or they thought they had a good product and why not use it again; perhaps the public wouldn't notice (which is what has happened in most of the above examples cited)? Could be. Or did the filmmaker force them to do it? Your guess is as good as mine.

In some cases, it was understandable. A composer composed a song, which for some reason was not included in the film; he then refurbished it, and used it later in another film. Why waste a perfectly good melody!

Guru Dutt's film *Sahib, Bibi Aur Ghulam* (1962) had a song *'Sahil Ki Taraf Kashti Le Chal'* sung by Hemant Kumar (who was also the music director) and written by Shakeel Badayuni. The song had a shot which showed Meena Kumari (playing Chhoti Bahu) resting her head on Guru Dutt's (playing Bhoothnath) lap in the carriage. Audiences resented the filmmaker showing a married woman behaving intimately with a man, who was not her husband. Guru Dutt removed the song and the offending shot. Hemant Kumar re-used the tune for the song *'Ya Dil Ki Suno'* in *Anupama* (1966) four years later, this time penned by Kaifi Azmi. That was the advantage of being the music director; the tune never goes waste. But we will never know what the original song sounded like.

But we do know what the original song sounded like in another instance. Guru Dutt approached SD Burman to compose the music for *Baharein Phir Bhi Aayengi* (1966). According to journalist Raju Bharatan, Guru Dutt did not like the title tune composed by SD Burman and sung by Rafi and opted for OP Nayyar instead. SD Burman later used this tune for *'Yeh Dil Na Hota Bechara'* (*Jewel Thief*, 1967), sung by Kishore Kumar. It was alternatively reported that Guru Dutt opted for OP Nayyar due to SD Burman's prolonged illness. SD Burman requested that RD Burman be made the music director, with SD Burman supporting him. But Guru Dutt was in a hurry.

The original song, *'Koi Na Tera Saathi Ho'* has recently been released in public domain after almost 60 years in cold storage. Hearing a familiar tune sung by a different singer, with different lyrics, can be disconcerting for some, fascinating for others. Comparisons will certainly be made, as also conjecturing whether the original song would have attained the same level of popularity as its successor.

It's not only the whole tune being re-used in another song by the same music director in another film. There have been many instances of composers using excerpts of their songs as interludes in other songs, and vice versa.

Consider for example Salil Chowdhury's *'Aaja Re Pardesi'* (*Madhumati*, 1958). The first interlude would sound immediately familiar—it would since it's a copy of the *mukhra* of *'Ghadi Ghadi Mora Dil Dhadke'* from the same film. This could be explained by two songs in a film being linked to each other through musical unity. But the songs didn't need to be necessarily in the same film. In Salil Chowdhury's *'Saathi Re, Tujh Bin Jiya Udaas Re'* (*Poonam Ki Raat*, 1965), the interlude was Salil's *'Baagh Mein Kali Khili' (Chanda Aur Suraj*, 1965). Here perhaps, the music director, besides using a tune which, used as an interlude, thematically enhanced the song's appeal, also left his imprint to show both proprietorship and continuity.

It happened the other way round too—interludes turning into songs.

Anu Malik used the prelude and the first interlude of *'Aa Zara Mere Humnashin'* from *Poonam* (1981) as the melody of *'Chori Chori Jab Nazrein Milin'* in *Kareeb* (1998). Not content, he used another interlude from the same song as main melody of *'Tu Hawa Hai Fiza Hia'* in *Fiza* (2000).

Rajesh Roshan used the prelude of *'Frenny O Frenny'* in *Khatta Meetha* (1981) as the melody for *'Tanhai Tanhai Tanhai'* in *Koyla* (1997).

Then there were songs made from the background music of earlier films, usually of the same music director. This was particularly true of Raj Kapoor films.

The background score of *Awara* (1951) spawned at least three songs—*'O Basanti Pawan Paawan'* in *Jis Desh Main Ganga Behti Hai* (1960); *'Duniya Banane Waley Kya Tere Man Mein Samayi'* in *Teesri Kasam* (1967); and *'Na Maangu Sona Chandi'* in *Bobby* (1973). The musical notes played in the backdrop of *Shri 420* (1955) were adapted to make *'Jeena Isi Ka Naam Hai'* in *Anari* (1959).

Except for *Bobby* (Laxmikant-Pyarelal), all the above films had music by Shankar-Jaikishan, with Raj Kapoor being the common factor.

'Mora Nadaan Balma' from *Ujaala* (1959) was derived from the opening titles music of *Mayurpankh* (1954)—both composed by Shankar-Jaikishan.

The song *'Koi Hota Jisko Apna'* from *Mere Apne* (1971) could be heard in the background score of *Anand* (1971) in the final scene of the film, both composed by Salil Chowdhury. Which song inspired which is difficult to determine, the year being the same.

The list of songs is not exhaustive. It's indicative of the fascinating fact that not only did/do composers find 'inspiration' from outside sources but were/are also not averse to regurgitating their own creation, adding a fresh coat of paint, and presenting a new package to the world.

About the Author

Ajay Mankotia pursued BA in Economics (Honours) from St. Stephen's College, Delhi University followed by a Master's Degree in Economics from the Delhi School of Economics, Delhi University. He also has a Diplôme D'études Superiéures Spécialisées in International Economic Relations from the University of Paris-XI, Paris, and Bachelor's Degree in Law (LLB) from Law Centre, Delhi University.

Ajay, who joined the Indian Revenue Service in 1982, has worked at a wide variety of posts in the Indian Government and, during the course of his career, he was also deputed as Chief Vigilance Officer of some public sector fertiliser companies. When he was Commissioner of Income Tax, he decided to opt for Voluntary Retirement in 2008 after having spent twenty-six years as a taxman and joined a media company as President (Corporate Planning and Operations). He presently runs his own Tax and Legal Advisory.

He released a book titled *There's Seven For You, Three For Me* in 2019, offering a glimpse into the working of the officers of the Income Tax Department. He writes regularly on music, amongst other matters, in various publications and, along with his wife, runs a music theatre company—producing, directing, scripting, anchoring and singing in plays on music directors, actors and film-makers.

He likes to sing old Hindi songs of Mohammed Rafi and ghazals of Mehdi Hassan. A passionate follower of several classic rock bands such as Jethro Tull, Yes, The Who, Deep Purple, The Rolling Stones, Pink Floyd and Uriah Heep, and solo artists such as Neil Young, Steve Winwood, and Eric Clapton, he has been attending their live concerts for several decades.

He has written three articles in Jethro Tull's *Lend Me Your Ears: A Fan History* published in September 2022. The book is a history of Jethro Tull, mixing hundreds of fan anecdotes with memories from the band, their collaborators, other musicians and celebrity admirers.

In his leisure time, he likes to swim, play golf and snooker, and tries to solve the daily cryptic crossword.

He is married to author and academician Atima Mankotia and has a daughter and a son.

Ajay can be contacted at:

Email: ajaymankotia@hotmail.com
Twitter: @ajaymankotia
Website: amataxandlegal.com

Readomania

Readomania exists to nurture, curate, and bring to you content you love. We are a publishing house that takes pride in encouraging talent, new or old, and provides a wonderful platform for awesome stories.

We make this possible in multiple ways.

The first as an independent publishing house. Readomania boasts of multiple imprints across various categories—fiction, nonfiction, children, to name a few. An eclectic mix of content for its readers, when you read a Readomania title, you enter a world that's yours, supported by unique and quality narratives.

The second, as an online publishing platform for writers—a place to share stories, poems, opinions, travelogues, a way to explore your creative talent. Available as premium, as well as free-to-read content across multiple genres, the reader is spoilt for choice.

Join us in this journey, as we explore, develop, and present stories to our readers and audiences. Welcome to the world of Readomania, get ready to craft stories that enrich lives.

You can visit us at: www.readomania.com